DESTRUCTIVENESS, INTERSUBJECTIVITY, AND TRAUMA

Developments in Psychoanalysis Series

Peter Fonagy, Mary Target, and Liz Allison (Series Editors)
Published and distributed by Karnac Books

Other titles in the Series

Developmental Science and Psychoanalysis: Integration and Innovation.
Celebrating the Renewal of the Collaboration of the Yale Child Study Center
and the Anna Freud Centre in Promoting Psychoanalytic Developmental
Research
   Edited by Linda Mayes, Peter Fonagy, and Mary Target

Mentalizing in Child Therapy: Guidelines for Clinical Practitioners
   *Edited by Annelies J. E. Verheugt-Pleiter, Jolien Zevalkink,
   and Marcel G. J. Schmeets*

Taboo or Not Taboo? Forbidden Thoughts, Forbidden Acts in
Psychoanalysis and Psychotherapy
   Edited by Brent Willock, Lori C. Bohm, and Rebecca Curtis

Orders

Tel: +44 (0)20 7431 1075; Fax: +44 (0)20 7435 9076

E-mail: shop@karnacbooks.com

www.karnac books.com

DESTRUCTIVENESS, INTERSUBJECTIVITY, AND TRAUMA

The Identity Crisis of
Modern Psychoanalysis

Werner Bohleber

KARNAC

First published in 2010 by
Karnac Books Ltd
118 Finchley Road, London NW3 5HT

British Library Cataloguing in Publication Data

A C.I.P. for this book is available from the British Library

ISBN: 978 1 85575 672 4

Edited, designed and produced by The Studio Publishing Services Ltd
www.publishingservicesuk.co.uk
e-mail: studio@publishingservicesuk.co.uk

www.karnacbooks.com

CONTENTS

ACKNOWLEDGEMENTS

The present work includes a selection of papers on conceptual issues surrounding questions of intersubjectivity and identity, trauma, and ideological destructiveness. My heartfelt gratitude goes to Peter Fonagy for his encouragement to collect some of my papers for book publication in English. He generously accepted it as a part of the series "Developments in Psychoanalysis", which he edits with Mary Target and Liz Allison. The initial impetus and encouragement for this project came from my wife, Marianne Leuzinger-Bohleber, whom I thank for her constant support throughout. I am grateful to my translators: Eric Jarosinski, Andrew Jenkins, Doris Linda Jones, and Sophie Leighton. They did an excellent job translating the texts and suggesting solutions for specific German terms and idioms. I also want to thank Liz Allison, Alexandra Bateman, Alex Bleiberg, and Jeremy Vooght from the editorial team of the UCL Psychoanalysis Unit for their very skilful help in editing my manuscript.

Most of the following chapters were first published elsewhere, as noted and reprinted with permission. I have largely reworked and revised most of them.

Introduction: translated by Andrew Jenkins.

Chapter One: this is a slightly abbreviated version of "Inter-subjektivitismus ohne Subjekt? Der Andere in der psychoanalytis-chen Tradition" in *Die vernetzte Seele. Die intersubjektive Wende in der Psychoanalyse*, edited by M. Altmeyer and H. Thomä. Stuttgart: Klett-Cotta, 2006, pp. 203–226. Published with permission of Klett-Cotta. Translated by Eric Jarosinski.

Chapter Two: originally published here. Translated by Eric Jarosinski.

Chapter Three: some material from this chapter originally appeared in the paper "Psychoanalyse, Adoleszenz und das Problem der Identität" in *Psyche, Zeitschrift für Psychoanalyse und ihre Anwend-ungen, 53*: 1999, pp. 507–529. Translated by Eric Jarosinski.

Chapter Four: a somewhat longer version was originally published under the title "Die Entwicklung der Traumatheorie in der Psycho-analyse" in *Psyche, Zeitschrift für Psychoanalyse und ihre Anwend-ungen, 54*: 2000, pp. 797–839. A shortened version was published in *Upheaval: Psychoanalytic Perspectives on Trauma*, edited by S. Varvin and T. Stajner-Popovic. Belgrade: International Aid Network, 2002, pp. 207–234. Translated by Doris Linda Jones.

Chapter Five: originally delivered as a keynote address at the 45th Conference of the International Psychoanalytic Association, 2007 in Berlin, and published in *International Journal of Psychoanalysis, 88*: 2007, pp. 329–352. Translated by Sophie Leighton.

Chapter Six: originally published here. Translated by Eric Jarosinski.

Chapter Seven: a revised version of a paper first published under the title "Die Konstruktion imaginärer Gemeinschaften und das Bild von den Juden—unbewusste Determinanten des Antisemitismus in Deutschland" in *Psyche, Zeitschrift für Psychoanalyse und ihre Anwendungen, 51*: 1997, pp. 570–605. Translated by Andrew Jenkins.

Chapter Eight: an extended version of a paper published under the title "Idealität und Destruktivität—Zur Psychodynamik terroristis-cher Gewalt" in *Terrorismus und Rechtsstaatlichkeit. Analysen, Hand-lungsoptionen, Perspektiven*, edited by K.Graulich and D. Simon. Berlin: Akademie Verlag, 2007, pp. 15–28. Published with the per-mission of the Berlin-Brandenburgische Akademie der Wissen-schaften. Translated by Eric Jarosinski.

ABOUT THE AUTHOR

Werner Bohleber, PhD, is psychoanalyst in private practice in Frankfurt am Main, Germany. He is a training and supervising analyst, and a former President of the German Psychoanalytical Association (DPV). He is the editor of the German psychoanalytical journal *PSYCHE*. He was a member of the Board of Representatives of the International Psychoanalytical Association (IPA) (2003–2007). He was Co-chair for Europe of the IPA Research Advisory Board (2000–2008). He is a member of the Working Party on Theoretical Issues of the European Psychoanalytical Federation (EPF). In 2007, he was the winner of the Mary S. Sigourney Award for Psychoanalysis. He is the author of several books and numerous articles. His research subjects and main publication themes are: adolescence, especially late adolescence and young adulthood; identity and theory of the self; psychoanalytic theory; history of psychoanalysis in Germany; transgenerational consequences of the Nazi period and the war on the second and third generation; nationalism, xenophobia, racism, and anti-Semitism; trauma and violence; terror and terrorism. His most recent book as editor, with H. Radbold and J. Zinnecker, is: *Transgenerationelle Weitergabe kriegsbelasteter Kindheiten -Interdisziplinäre Studien zur Nachhaltigkeit historischer*

Erfahrungen über vier Generationen (Childhood in the war—transgenerational transmission. Interdisciplinary studies of lasting historical experiences over four generations), Weinheim (Juventa) (2008; 2nd edn 2009).

FOREWORD

Peter Fonagy

Werner Bohleber is one of a handful of major intellectual figures in psychoanalysis. His intellectual, clinical, and organizational leadership has played a very significant part not only in the development of German psychoanalysis over the last quarter of a century, but also in bringing to the international psychoanalytic scene a sense of balance and open-mindedness that is vital if psychoanalysis is to survive and flourish in its pluralistic form. As one of the major editors of psychoanalytic journals, Bohleber has been in a position to review, absorb, and distil that which stands out as most significant in modern psychoanalytic achievements. With the benefit of rigorous training in continental philosophy as well as psychology behind him, he has arrived at a sophisticated, integrated view of some of the most complex and controversial topics within the psychoanalytic field.

We owe a debt of gratitude to Werner Bohleber for this volume. It contextualizes modern psychoanalysis better than any other monograph. Rooted in the author's total comfort with almost the entire spectrum of the plurality of psychoanalytic ideas and modern philosophical and sociological thought, he enables the reader to quickly acquire a grasp of the tectonic shifts within psychoanalytic theorization over the last quarter of a century. It is, to say the least, unusual to find an author who is completely at ease with the major European philosophical traditions and able to see and convey with crystal clarity how these have had an impact on the concept of subject and object in psychoanalytic discourse in Europe, and North and South America. In this book, he addresses the impact of the intersubjective field on clinical theory development as well as clinical practice. In tackling the concept of identity in its social, cultural, developmental, and psychoanalytic clinical setting, he is able to represent this most profound recent change in our psychoanalytic approach against the background of key developments in the philosophy of mind. The scope of Bohleber's thinking is awe-inspiring.

But this is only the first part of this outstanding volume. Bohleber's special expertise is trauma. He is, without doubt, one of the great trauma theorists of psychoanalysis working today. His comments on the history of this construct in psychoanalysis show the same mastery of historical movements within trauma theory as the first part of the book showed in relation to intersubjectivity. The integration offered by the book, in my view, represents one of the most mature psychoanalytic formulations of what is traumatic. While retaining the plurality of ideas that define modern psychoanalysis, the model advanced is coherent, crystal clear, and utterly compelling. Bohleber brings controversies concerning personal memories of trauma into the frame of this discussion and addresses the recent controversy in relation to recovered memories with even-handedness and sophistication. He brings the same crystal clarity to the somewhat shadowy concept of dissociation, which, as Bohleber points out, has not been well addressed by psychoanalytic writers unfamiliar with the devastation that genuine trauma can leave behind. The three chapters on trauma, memory, and dissociation constitute an outstanding introduction to the psychoanalytic study of trauma, arguably a better introduction than the reader is likely to find anywhere in the literature. The integration he advocates brings with it creative insight in addition to scholarship. For example, seeing dissociation as a form of self-regulation is a substantial theoretical advance and it is also an essential clinical contribution.

The third part of the book is perhaps the most ambitious, and brings together beautifully the ideas of identity and trauma explored in the earlier chapters. These chapters speak to the most destructive forces within European culture. The notion of collective phantasms, embodied and intergenerational, is revealed in Bohleber's exploration of the systems of unconscious fantasy that underpin nationalistic and anti-Semitic ideas in Germany over the past two hundred years. The unconscious fantasies that fuel anti-Semitism, Bohleber is able to link to early attachment relationships. The idealization of purity, free from otherness, and an unconscious fantasy of fusion with a maternal primary object, drives nationalism and racist ideology that is, tragically, as much part of our current cultural concerns as it was in the 1930s and 1940s. Of course, these ideas are as helpful in addressing present terror as they are in understanding the past. The unconscious fantasies underpinning fundamentalism and terrorism Bohleber sees as similarly linked to religious certainty, the fantasy of an ideal state, and he draws persuasive parallels between nationalism, anti-Semitism, and Islamic extremists.

Bohleber's thoroughly theoretically grounded psychoanalytic approach gives one hope for the future of the discipline. The book is highly intelligent, makes psychoanalysis relevant to some of the deepest intellectual quandaries of our generation, including the nature of the bipersonal field, the impact of interpersonal violence on human development, the ideologies that permit and possibly fuel such violence, and the cultural forces that are unconsciously at work, making all of us potential perpetrators as well as victims. Bohleber's book is a gem. It is the product of one of the most creative psychoanalytic minds of our generation. It purposefully avoids the extreme, is rooted in a balanced portrayal that eschews rhetoric or other attempts at short-circuiting serious balanced enquiry. It stands as a testament to the values within psychoanalysis that it celebrates, to resist idealization and the destructiveness which it skirts.

Introduction

The chapters in this volume revolve around a variety of issues and problems unified by one overriding concern: the way in which the changing present and the individual situated within it are conceptually mirrored in psychoanalytic reflection. Although, for Freud, the clinical realm was the matrix from which psychoanalysis evolved, he always regarded psychoanalysis as more than a therapeutic method. In his understanding, its purview extended to the analytic investigation of cultural phenomena and the consequences of social disasters. Freud's psychoanalytic disciples espoused this view in different ways and to varying degrees, as did subsequent psychoanalysts. The historical context and the historical perspective have invariably been involved in defining which topics will be particularly rewarding subjects for psychoanalytic reflection. My own concerns focus on three specific areas:

Psychoanalysis is now over 100 years old and has gone through a number of crucial developments, both in theory and clinical practice. It has also extended the range of its inquiries, both in regard to the disorders it investigates and the methods it considers for treating those disorders. While it is possible to describe and understand these developments purely in analytic terms, closer inspection reveals that they also reflect societal, cultural, and intellectual changes. In western societies, processes of individualization and democratization have had repercussions on the status and identity of the individual. Although it is primarily the task of the social sciences and philosophy to engage with this phenomenon, the impulses deriving from it have also had an impact on analytic theory formation.

The most significant response of psychoanalytic theory and clinical practice to the disasters of the twentieth century is the engagement with trauma, for many the phenomenon that most trenchantly epitomizes the character of that century. It has achieved this prominence not only in connection with its consequences for the individual, but also in regard to its collective impact on societies and ongoing generations.

The ideologies of the twentieth century have provided an interpretative challenge for psychoanalysis because of their patently unconscious motivations, as reflected in their irrational and destructive nature. This applies in the first place to anti-Semitism, but also to nationalism in general and Nazism in particular. In the twenty-first century, we are now faced with a new ideological offshoot, that is, the ideology derived from religious fundamentalism and incarnated by terrorism.

These three focalizations map out the terrain covered by the chapters in this book. The following is a brief summary of the issues they address.

Part I

For the unprejudiced observer, psychoanalysis today is synonymous with a vast array of theoretical and therapeutic approaches. Its pluralism has achieved almost proverbial status. Depending on one's viewpoint and scientific persuasion, such pluralism can be seen either as a danger or as an opportunity. Accordingly, critics and commentators tend either to stress irreconcilable divergences or to foreground conceptual commonalities. Independently of this, it is fair to say that, in the past few decades, all psychoanalytic schools of thought (although to differing degrees within the field) have been receptive to interactive and relational concepts (to an extent, that has prompted some commentators to speak of an "intersubjective turn" in psychoanalysis) as reflected and propelled by the following developments: the incorporation of the analyst's subjectivity as an instrument of investigation through the concept of countertransference; the extension of transference to encompass the entire analytic situation; and the elevation of terms like "projective identification" and "enactment" to the status of key concepts in psychoanalytic treatment theory. This inclusion of the intersubjective aspect has transformed the role of the analyst from that of a clinical authority / objective observer of the analytic process. Today, the enhancement of analytic knowledge takes place largely on the basis of the intersubjective reality of analyst and analysand in the analytic situation, with radically intersubjective approaches not only emphasizing the inevitability of mutual and reciprocal influence, but also denying the very possibility of objective recognition of a patient's psychic reality.

A look at neighbouring fields of inquiry will quickly identify the impulses for these developments. They stem from attachment theory, research on infant development, and—more recently—from the neurosciences. Infant research has indicated how, from the outset, the infant self emerges from reciprocal regulation and recognition processes in the primary relationship. Modern research on early mentalization processes postulates a self that can only materialize by being mirrored by the psyche of the primary object: we need another person in order to experience our own self. Such a conception of self-emergence has its parallels in philosophical and sociological thought, by which it has indeed, been influenced. Here we arrive at a level of reflection—the societal, cultural, intellectual, and philosophical currents of a given period—to which the changes in analytic theory and technique can be related. The scope of our understanding is extended accordingly, and it becomes clear that psychoanalysis has been responding to the altered status of the individual in societal development and receiving impulses from approaches in the social sciences and philosophy that have themselves negotiated an intersubjective and constructivist turn. Against this background, I should like to make some remarks on recent interactive–intersubjective concepts in psychoanalysis.

In one-person psychology, with its intrapsychic focus, the ego or the self was the focus of attention. Description concentrated on structural conflicts, drive conflicts, defence mechanisms, or the dynamics of self and object representations. But, in accordance with the intersubjective categories of two-person psychology, description has necessarily focused not only on two actors interacting, but also on the interaction that evolves between them—an encounter that is more than the effect that it has on both of them. The first thing that strikes us here is that the arrival of intersubjectivity marks the advent of the concepts of subject and subjectivity in psychoanalytic discussion to designate the personhood of the actors. In a largely unreflected manner, this turn of events has smuggled an old and venerable philosophical concept into the discussion of analytic theory. In the analysis of countertransference, subjectivity has advanced to the status of an epistemological instrument. The traditional concern with the subject–object relation has been replaced by the focus on a subject–subject relation with a view to emphasizing the intersubjective reciprocity of analytic processes. Another new arrival is the dialectic of self and other inherited from philosophy. The self described in these terms emerges from interaction with an Other, initially the primary object, and in the further course of life it remains dependent on the Other if it is to achieve self-knowledge. The analytic situation is also conceived of differently than in the period of the intrapsychic paradigm. It is now seen as the prototypic situation for intersubjective encounter, and a whole array of terms and concepts have been introduced to capture this intersubjective aspect, among them "the analytic third", "encounter", "mutuality", "mutual recognition", "between", "moment of meeting", "bi-personal field", etc. While such concepts can indeed exert a powerful fascination, they are often used in ways that display inadequate theoretical consideration or insufficient conceptual anchorage. In certain modern theories, the self is seen exclusively as a factor in intersubjective situations, situations from which it cannot be segregated. Other theories conceptualize only the intersubjective field as a whole. In this way, the self/subject conceived of as an autonomous entity (however limited that autonomy may be) is excluded from theoretical consideration. It is, then, only logical that this theoretical development should lead to the conception, as the general rule, of multiple selves anchored and incorporated in different interactional situations. Here, it is not difficult to identify the impact of postmodernist thinking with its deconstruction of the subject and the rejection of an essentialist concept of identity.

The first three chapters in this volume attempt to engage with this problem. My concern is to demonstrate that individuality and the intrapsychic aspect transcend the intersubjective field. Chapter One discusses the danger of losing sight of the individual and his/her independence or autonomy by giving unconditional precedence to the intersubjective mode. The intersubjective perspective conceives of the analytic relationship as a close-knit psychic system, or a jointly constructed intersubjective field or matrix. The present relationship as an encounter creating meaning is elevated to become the central element in the therapeutic situation. Transference and countertransference become special cases of a more comprehensive intersubjective relationship regarded as a basic category; the subject is reduced to the contingent effect of contexts. In the discussion of this point, it is helpful not to restrict oneself too exclusively to present-day advocacy of a relational form of psychoanalysis, but to take a broader view of the category of intersubjective theories. This would include South American bi-personal field theories, as well as link theories, deriving from couple and family therapy and continental European (notably French and German) psychoanalytic theories that draw upon the philosophical traditions of the relationship between self and other.

In the second chapter, I discuss how the development of clinical theory is reflected in the metaphors most frequently used to describe the analytic process and analytic attitudes, and trace the development of clinical theory through the metaphors it deploys. The range of metaphors extends from Freud's mirror metaphor to present-day intersubjective field metaphors and the metaphor of negotiation prominent in relational analysis. Metaphors are particularly enlightening in the way they make mental matters susceptible to conceptualization and description. They invariably carry implicit meanings with them, and it is highly interesting to study how ongoing clinical developments and their theoretical explication link up with the explication of covert meanings in such prominent metaphors. But the function of metaphors is also ambivalent. As they influence lines of thought, they may also obscure aspects of the whole phenomenon that lie outside the semantic field of the respective metaphor.

The third chapter deals with changes in conceptions of adolescence, as well as in psychoanalytic theories of personality and identity, occasioned by societal changes in the late modern age. Structural transformation in society has diluted and partially dissolved the earlier notion of a stable identity that retains its cohesion and coherence throughout a person's life. In western societies, lifestyles have become hugely pluralistic and gender roles a great deal more flexible. Identity formation no longer ends in late adolescence; it remains open and frequently assumes the character of a life-long project. Psychologically, these developments are ambivalent. They encourage the desire for self-realization, but, at the same time, the priority given to self-fulfilment may be experienced as an excessive and overtaxing demand. In the past forty years, object relations psychology, intersubjective theories, research on infant development, and attachment theory have created a situation where, in comparison to ego psychology, psychic development has been situated more and more squarely in the interpersonal matrix. This is the basis for a number of more recent psychoanalytic personality theories seeking to take due account of the role played by changing societal conditions in the formation of personality and identity. One of the central issues here is the unity of the self. Can we still proceed on the assumption of a unified self that will eventually be formed, or must we jettison this assumption in favour of an ensemble of multiple selves whose unity is an illusory, albeit necessary, notion? I attempt to answer this question with reference to a modern dialectical concept of identity that builds on and extends Erikson's identity concept.

Part II

This first cluster of chapters engages with developments in psychoanalytic theories and attempts to conceptualize them against the background of social change and with reference to approaches taken from the social sciences and philosophy. Part II focuses on problems encountered in psychoanalytic trauma theory, problems whose resolution has become especially urgent in the face of the disasters affecting humanity in the twentieth century. In Chapter Four, I trace the development of trauma theory, which was long overshadowed by psychoanalytic drive theory. Treatment for the survivors of the Holocaust made it imperative to come to grips with this extreme form of traumatization, and led to the development of new theoretical approaches, as well as to changes in treatment designs. Further impulses came from the effects of the Vietnam War in the USA, and increasing social sensitivity to sexual abuse and the maltreatment of children. Psychoanalytic trauma theories have evolved on the basis of two models, one psycho-economic, the other hermeneutic and based on object relations theory. To grasp the phenomenology and long-term consequences of trauma, we need both models. The psycho-economic model focuses on excessive arousal and on anxiety that cannot be contained by the psyche and that breaks through the shield against stimuli. The model based on object relations theory concentrates on the collapse of internal object relations and the breakdown of internal communication, which produces an experience of total abandonment, precluding the integration of trauma by narrative means.

The fifth chapter centres on problems encountered in the effort to remember traumas, and on the significance of collective memory. In the present-day clinical theory of psychoanalysis, autobiographical memory and the reconstruction of the past have forfeited the central therapeutic function they once held. The emphasis on traumas, and on trauma remembrance, squares poorly with this development. Traumatic memories are not subject to a transformation by the present in which they are recalled. They form a more or less isolated foreign body in the associative network of the mind. The psychic dynamic that is operative in the case of trauma, and the question of the accuracy of memories and of their reconstruction in the therapeutic process, are some of the focal points in this chapter. Another central issue is the vital significance that societal discourse on the historical truth of man-made disasters has for both the individuals affected and for society. Here, we frequently encounter a desire not to know, to evade confrontation with atrocities, horrors, and the suffering of the victims. The recollection of crimes develops a special dynamic of its own. I attempt to describe both this dynamic and its transgenerational effects on post-war German society.

Chapter Six is devoted to a concept long marginalized in psychoanalysis: dissociation. Freud initially used the term, but then dropped it in favour of repression. It took renewed intensive engagement with mechanisms of traumatic experience and a revival of interest in dissociative phenomena to reinstate the concept in psychoanalytic discussion. Dissociative states of the self range from the highly subtle to severe dissociative identity disorders. According to present research, dissociative consciousness disorders are a specific consequence of severe traumatization in childhood and adulthood. Dissociation has a dual function: on the one hand, it acts as a protective mechanism against the onslaught of unbearable reality represented by the traumatic situation; on the other, it is (or may be) a pathological form of self-regulation. In the chapter, I draw upon clinical material to discuss dissociative states of consciousness, some of the research problems involved, and the difficulties encountered in therapeutic treatment. I advocate liberating dissociation as a clinical phenomenon from its marginal position and reintegrating it into the mainstream corpus of theoretical psychoanalytic inquiry.

Part III

For Freud, the evolution of culture and the development of the individual were inextricably interwoven. In human history, and in cultural phenomena like religion, Freud found reflections of the dynamic conflicts between ego, id, and superego that he had discovered in the individual. Today, we have become a great deal more circumspect about positing such parallels between the individual and society. We no longer believe that these two phenomena can be regarded as simple mirrors of one another, as we now hold it necessary to take into account the abstract control mechanisms that are operative in social processes. As they are anonymous, these mechanisms intervene in the life-world of the individual in very different ways from how persons do it. There is, however, one field where psychoanalysis can make a direct contribution to the understanding of society and social history: the study of the mass ideologies of the last century. Psychoanalysis can help us to explain how these ideologies were able to gain such a vice-like grip on people's ideas and way of thinking. Recent psychoanalytic insights on the collusion between destructiveness and narcissism have proved extremely fruitful in analysing collective phantasms such as ethnocentric nationalism, anti-Semitism, and fundamentalism. The third section of the book is devoted to a consideration of these phenomena.

Chapter Seven investigates the interdependence between nationalism and anti-Semitism. The idea of the nation is a mixture of fact and fiction, and often, particularly in Germany, it was highly charged by its definition as a homogeneous ethnic community. The idealized image of the nation was a powerful force-field and an organizing fantasy, allotting to the Jews the role of a negative counter-image. Even if one does not agree with Daniel Goldhagen's theory of eliminationist anti-Semitism, the question remains: how can we explain the increasing radicalization of anti-Semitism in nineteenth century and, above all, in twentieth century Germany? Was there a mental disposition that is fuelled by unconscious sources and provided anti-Semitic notions with a form of psychic organization that contributed to their radicalization? Collective phantasms thrive on bodily notions and familial representations. Proceeding on this insight, I have succeeded in uncovering unconscious fantasy systems based on nationalist and anti-Semitic convictions and centring on notions of purity and ideality that involve a propensity for extremism and violence. The first of these fantasies is that of being the only one entitled to maternal care and affection; all rivals are eliminated. The second is the fantasy of participating in a state of ideal purity not disrupted by any form of otherness. The third is the fantasy of being part of an imagined organic whole, envisioned as the restoration of union with the maternal primary object, a fantasy whose purpose is to overcome a form of existence that is cut off and alienated.

Today, religion has reasserted itself with a vengeance on the political and social stage in the form of fundamentalist terrorism. The dark and destructive side of this phenomenon challenges psychoanalysis to explain how religious certainty, hatred, apocalyptic notions of paradise as a narcissistic fantasy of the ideal state, and murderous violence intermingle and mutually reinforce one another on the psychological plane. In Chapter Eight, I investigate Islamic fundamentalism and the terrorism it spawns. A comparison of the beliefs of Islamic terrorists with the convictions operating in radical German nationalism and anti-Semitism reveals astounding parallels. The unconscious fantasy systems identified as exerting an influence among the German nationalists, one finds, are also powerfully operative in the mental world of the Islamic extremist, and act as an incitement to terrorist activity. Terrorist action, however, requires more than a conglomeration of notions radicalizing thought and behaviour. Specific group practices achieve a transformation of the personality of individuals, and it is this transformation that enables the individual to perform acts of terrorism.

PART I

THE INTERSUBJECTIVE PARADIGM IN PSYCHOANALYSIS AND LATE MODERNITY

CHAPTER ONE

Intersubjectivity without a subject? Intersubjective theories and the Other

Introduction

I n the past decades, a change has been under way in the clinical theory of psychoanalysis, as an exclusively intrapsychic perspective has given way to an intersubjective understanding of the analytical situation. Indeed, nearly all schools of analysis have now come to embrace interactive concepts, and such concepts (e.g., countertransference, enactment, and projective identification) have established themselves as dominant within psychoanalytic clinical theory. Countertransference, for instance, has unfolded in a dynamic that has continually expanded the term conceptually and that has resulted in bringing the analyst's own subjectivity largely to the fore. Renik (2004) has taken a further step forward arguing that the use of the concept of countertransference has led to a naïve underestimation of the role of the analyst's own subjectivity in clinical work. Some go so far as to deem this change a paradigm shift within psychoanalysis: in the wake of the narrative turn of the 1980s, it is argued, one can now discern a "relational turn" in psychoanalysis (Mitchell, 2000). At present, concepts in keeping with this perspective continue to come to the fore, including "intersubjective encounter", "moments of meeting", "mutual recognition", "authenticity", and "spontaneity", among others.

In the original subject–object paradigm, the two sides are reciprocally related. If one side is active, then the other is considered passive. While this complimentarity can be reversible, mutuality is categorically excluded (see Benjamin, 1998). In intersubjective conceptions of the analytic process, however, the analyst and patient are thought of in methodological terms as part of a subject–subject relationship, a relationship structured more by symmetry than polar complementarity. In conceptualizing this relationship, the term "mutuality" is thought to provide a more useful term than symmetry for characterizing that which is shared in intersubjective positions (Aron, 1996). In distancing themselves from the so-called "classic" perspective of one-way influence, intersubjective analysts emphasize the inevitability of a mutual and reciprocal two-way influence between patient and analyst.

The attention to this "in-between" position in the analytic situation largely explains the appeal of intersubjective perspectives. Aron (1996) compares it to Winnicott's "potential space", in which a mutual, creative co-construction of meanings can come about:

> Meaning, in the analytic situation, is not generated by the analyst's rational (secondary) processing of the analysand's associations; rather, meaning is seen as relative, multiple, and indeterminate, with each interpretation subject to continual and unending interpretation by both analyst and analysand. Meaning is generated relationally and dialogically, which is to say that meaning is negotiated and coconstructed. Meaning is arrived at through a "meeting of minds". [*ibid.*, p. xii]

Indeed, the aim of this intersubjective position is to move beyond the conception of an isolated monadic mind (Stolorow & Atwood, 1992). At the same time, however, these models pose the danger of conceptually watering down, and ultimately dissolving, the individual subject in an intersubjective context. In order to avoid sinking into a theoretically untenable position of melding and fusion, by necessity such intersubjective theories must elaborate on the elements of difference, separation, and autonomy in the mutual relationship (as in Aron, 1996).

Analysts subscribing to this intersubjective approach have also criticized and challenged the position of the analyst as an objective, observing expert and clinical authority. Indeed, when insights are co-created by the analyst and analysand, the analyst is, strictly speaking, no longer the expert. It is the patient, however, who seeks help from the analyst; the latter is therefore vested with both the authority and responsibility of an expert in carrying out his duties, and, as a result, any partial symmetry in the analyst–patient relationship is necessarily supplemented by a relative asymmetry. The balance of therapeutic efficacy in intersubjective theories has also shifted, moving away from an emphasis on the analyst's verbal interpretation and towards the pole of interactive influence by way of experience.

The shared, the other, and the experience of the present

Intersubjective conceptions of psychoanalysis fault classic metapsychology both for an entrenchment of subject–object modes of thinking and for a positivist reductionalism. This critique is taken the farthest by Stolorow, Atwood, and Orange, who have continually built upon their intersubjective variant of psychoanalysis over the last several years (I am referring here primarily to Stolorow & Atwood, 1992 and to Orange, Atwood, & Stolorow, 1997). These writers disparage previous psychoanalytic conceptions for operating according to a theory of the mind that posits it as atomistic and isolated. Two-person psychology, they argue, has fallen into the same trap; it can only conceptualize intersubjectivity as two separate minds "bump[ing] into each other" (Orange, Atwood, & Stolorow, 1997, p. 68). Not only does our deepest sense of self emerge ontogenetically from interactions with primary objects, they argue, but it requires life-long interactive support to be maintained:

> The intrinsic embeddedness of self-experience in intersubjective fields means that our self-esteem, our sense of personal identity, even our experience of ourselves as having distinct and enduring existence are contingent on specific sustaining relations to the human surround. [Stolorow & Atwood, 1992, p. 10]

They draw on Hegel's phenomenology for support in present-
ing one's individuality as something that emerges from, and is
maintained by, the "interplay between subjectivities" (Orange,
Atwood, & Stolorow, 1997, p. 6). The fundamental components of
subjectivity are no longer the ego, id, and superego, as in classical
structural theory; instead, subjectivity consists of so-called "organizing principles". These include, for instance, the emotional
convictions that the individual has formed throughout his life as a
result of his or her experiences with the emotional environment.
Beebe and Lachmann (2002) similarly refer to "patterns of experience", which are organized as "expectancies of sequences of reciprocal exchanges" (p. 13). These consist of successive co-construc-
tions formed during pairings with an other. Such organizational
principles (or patterns of experience), it is claimed, are often unconscious, either in the pre-reflexive (in keeping with the modern
conception of the implicit unconscious) or the dynamic sense.
According to this formulation, the encounter between two subjects
in the analytic relationship is an interaction between "organizations
of experience" (Orange, Atwood, & Stolorow, 1997, p. 9), from
which a distinctive, extremely tightly woven psychic system
emerges. In this interaction, both subjectivities are, in at least one
respect, equal participants, in the sense of creating the interaction
together; at the same time, however, the interaction is organized
asymmetrically, as the analyst assumes the task of providing orientation, while the patient, as an other, attempts to reorganize his
experience. It follows that a patient's experience cannot be examined in isolation, but only as part of a jointly constructed intersubjective field. Resistance is therefore not seen as the individual
behaviour of the patient, and the task of interpretation is not to
uncover the causes of resistance in the patient him or herself; rather,
the question is "how analyst and patient have co-constructed this
logjam" (*ibid.*, p. 76).

With this, we arrive at a central problem of intersubjective conceptions of the analytic relationship. In order for something to be
examined, it has to be shared by each partner and be common to
both: "What they do together is a product of their experience in the
unique intersubjective field they create together" (*ibid.*, p. 18).
Hence, it is said of the analyst and patient that "The intersection
[allows] them to create a space where the unbelievable [can] be

explored together" (*ibid.*). The partners do, in fact, differ, however, in the way in which they have structured their experience, though these differences and contrasts appear solely as something that stands in the way of an understanding and as something to be ignored or eliminated. A subject–subject relationship is centred on the encounter between two clearly distinguishable subjects, hence, on that which the two can share with each other. The otherness or foreignness involved remains theoretically undefined, however, and does not represent further material to be examined in the relationship. Clinical theory, and its associated treatment technique, can serve as a sort of hermeneutic pre-understanding (*Vorverständnis*) to help us focus our efforts to understand the otherness of the Other; here, however, it is seen as an obstacle, which is more apt to obscure or distort the encounter than to promote comprehension. In this sense, it is argued that the rules of therapeutic technique only serve to "replicate massive structures of pathological accommodation . . . in both patient and analyst . . . The purpose of the rules is to induce compliance, not to facilitate the interplay of subjective worlds and perspectives" (*ibid.*, p. 25). Hence, it is argued that no attention is paid to those particularities of the relationship for which rules do not apply: "technically oriented thinking blinds us to the particularity of our patients, of ourselves, and of each psychoanalytic process" (*ibid.*).

Stern (2004) goes yet a step further in the direction of a clearly discernible intersubjectivity. For him, intersubjectivity is not solely an inter-mental process, but a discrete primary motivational system similar to that of attachment or sexuality. As such, it regulates the psychological feeling of belonging as well as of being alone. The human mind is, then, no longer considered independent and isolated. Likewise, we are no longer considered the sole owners, masters, and guardians of our subjectivity. Instead, we find ourselves constantly in dialogue with other subjects and their consciousnesses, and our mental life is "co-created". Stern refers to this continuous co-creative dialogue as an "intersubjective matrix", which he defines as "the overriding crucible in which interacting minds take on their current form" (*ibid.*, p. 78). The basic unit of this "intersubjective matrix", formed by an intersubjective consciousness, is the "present moment", which stages the intrapsychic event in which two subjects encounter each other. This intersubjective encounter in the here and now of the present moment is marked by a specific temporality: both subjects simultaneously assimilate an experience, creating a temporal connection that makes them part of one and the same structure. Such an experience is often only implicitly conscious.

While psychoanalysis persists in viewing the conscious as self-evident and the unconscious as unknown, Stern reverses the two, regarding the implicit intersubjective consciousness as the primary component of that which is unknown/that which is to be clinically and therapeutically examined and illuminated. Indeed, to the extent that psychoanalysis has ever been concerned with events in the "present moment", it has viewed them only as events or enactments in which patterns of the past are staged. In intersubjective approaches, however, the present relationship comes to be viewed as a central element of the therapeutic relationship in its formative power as an encounter. Likewise, transference and countertransference come to be seen as special cases in a much broader intersubjective relationship. The emphasis on experience is thereby shifted away from the comprehension of past patterns as they reappear in the here and now between the analyst and patient, and towards present experience, which becomes part of a new constellation in the intersubjective matrix at the moment of encounter between subjects.

Stern is critical of psychoanalytical treatment technique for far too hastily departing from the present moment of encounter and experience in order to search for meaning. He distinguishes between in-depth experience, which is lived, and understanding, which seeks to explain. In order for explanation to come about, lived experience must be caught up with after the fact (*après coup*) and transposed into language. "Usually psychoanalysis is more interested in the (re)construction than in the happening (if knowable)", Stern argues.

> After all, it is the (re)construction that revises and changes the happening into a psychodynamically pertinent psychic reality. In a sense, psychoanalysis is so focused on the verbally reconstructed aspect of experience that the phenomenal gets lost. [*ibid.*, p. 140]

I have tried to show in the intersubjective theories of Stolorow, Atwood, and Orange, and Stern, how the weight lies on the particularity of the jointly constructed new experience between two subjects. As we have seen, here the context, or the intersubjective matrix, becomes a fundamental category. To take this to an extreme, one could say that the subject is thereby reduced to a contingent effect of contexts.

Here, it could and should be objected that we are always more than our contexts and more than a co-created subject. The self disappears in its independent function as author and active agent and as an autonomous, self-determinant agency. In this way, the holistic thinking in terms of subjects that has become commonplace in the intersubjective paradigm obscures the psychodynamics traced in structural theory. Hence, the intrapsychic dissolves in the intersubjective, whose formative concepts consist of intersubjective "organizing principles" and "patterns of experience". Absent in this theorization is an ego, specifically an ego that is dependent on unconscious forces but has nevertheless acquired a certain degree of autonomy. Primarily, when addressing something stemming from the recognition of one's own unconscious, while also following the ego-ideal as an individual guideline, this allows the ego a certain amount of freedom from its integration into the intersubjectively structured environment.

Intersubjectivity and alterity

Many intersubjective conceptions, mainly those of North American origin, exhibit an inadequate understanding of the position of the Other in the intersubjective relationship. However, the assumption of an intersubjective dialectic of self and other, as posited in continental philosophy, has been fruitful for a number of newer psychoanalytic conceptions. Indeed, the intersubjective turn of psychoanalysis cannot be understood apart from the philosophical movements of the past century. In their attempts to overcome Freud's Cartesian dualism, for example, Stolorow, Atwood, and Orange, and Stern, all explicitly made use of Husserl's phenomenology, invoking both his positing of the ego as intersubjectively constituted and his views regarding consciousness and intentionality, according to which consciousness is *a priori* directed towards something. Hans Georg Gadamer's hermeneutics was likewise highly influential in shaping and enabling this intersubjectivist trend.

Psychoanalytic intersubjective theories flourished in Germany as early as the 1950s and 1960s, and their influence endured well into the 1980s, but they have been forgotten in Germany and were never noted in North America. (Presented in more detail in Bohleber, 2003.) "Encounter" [*Begegnung*] was a key concept in philosophical anthropology throughout the 1950s, first introduced into psychotherapeutic theory by Ludwig Binswanger and Viktor von Weizsäcker, among others. The concept was based on social–ontological models of a philosophy of dialogue, which had been articulated in the work of Martin Buber, Franz Rosenzweig, Ferdinand Ebner, and others as early as the 1920s. (In the following, I call upon the excellent study by Theunissen, 1977.) The philosophical trend towards intersubjectivism that these developments reflected ran contrary to traditional German Idealism, which was built on the assumption of an abstract subject. The place formerly occupied by the abstract subject was now occupied by the actual human self. Martin Heidegger's fundamental ontology is characterized by a similar turn from the abstract subject. In formulating a concept of origins, similarly, Buber (1954) replaced the originally philosophically isolated "I" with a "between" [*Zwischen*], describing the phenomenology that resulted from this substitution as a phenomenology of the encounter [*Begegnung*]. It is not an "I" and a "You" as already complete entities that bring about an encounter, according to Buber; instead, these entities spring purely from the action of the encounter itself. The "I" does not become a person by way of the "You"; rather, the coming into being of each one takes place in the encounter. In this way, the encounter of "You–I" is afforded the standing of the true subject. For Ludwig Binswanger (1942), a person is always located within a framework of meaning and interpretation, and this framework must first be made explicit before the position of psychoanalytic examination and the understanding of human psychology can be determined. The actual context of mental experiences is not captured within it, however, only the context of meaning. This is what creates a unity that can then be hermeneutically explicated. For Binswanger, the process of psychoanalytical interpretation becomes a special case of Wilhelm Dilthey's hermeneutics of the humanities. Binswanger then proceeds to work from an even stronger assumption of a "between" than Buber did. He speaks of a constitutive primacy of duality, which he conceptualizes as "We-hood" [*Wirheit*] and understands as an ontological unity, contra Heidegger, who thought of the "being-with" (*Mit-Sein*) of the Other only in terms of "being-there-with" (*Mit-Dasein*). For Binswanger the self is constituted in terms of the "we".

This conception of encounter was widespread in psychoanalysis in Germany in the 1950s. According to this conception, the analyst must come into communicative contact with the patient's world in order to understand his worldview [*Weltentwurf*] and mode of existence. This can only come about in a genuine encounter, one that goes beyond the dynamics of transference and countertransference. In this way, the relationship between analyst and patient constitutes a new and previously unknown communicative experience, and both transference and encounter are necessary if psychotherapy is to be successful (Schottlaender, 1952). All of these approaches emphasize the fundamental significance of intersubjectivity in the human and therapeutic relationship. Yet, despite their empirically anthropological perspective, they also hollow out the actual "You" and the actuality of the relationship. Methodologically, the immediacy of the relationship, which as a present intersubjective experience of encounter cannot be captured by the concept of transference, is inadequately conceptualized in terms of its intersubjective significance. The encounter becomes a metaphysical and transcendental fact, and ultimately seems to assume a nearly religious basis. Hence, adherents of ego psychology conceived as an objective natural science had little trouble in criticizing this concept as "too unfathomably deep, resisting any thorough exploration" (Scheunert, 1959). Their criticism had some merit, but it also resulted in some fruitful elements of this school of thought being discarded, elements that certainly could have been further developed in psychoanalysis. These elements made their reappearance later, however, both in the debate about the scientific standing of psychoanalysis and in the development of intersubjective concepts of treatment.

In the mid-1960s, new scientific methodological approaches came to the fore, fuelled primarily by Gadamer's philosophical hermeneutics. Gadamer (1960) explicated intersubjective communication phenomenologically as hermeneutic experience. In his work, the intersubjective relationship between the I and the Other unfolds according to the inherent structure of question and answer. The encounter with the Other as a You begins with something address-ing us. To directly subject oneself to this experience means, literally, to allow oneself to come into question. Every action and every expression of the patient represents an answer to a question, and the analyst must be aware of what that question is if he or she is to understand the patient's words and behaviour. As Loch (1965) observed, countertransference thereby becomes the focus of the analyst's attention, since his task is to ensure that the question, to which the patient's behaviour and emotions are the answer, can first fully unfold within himself, the analyst.

Argelander (1968, 1970) developed a model of psychoanalytical hermeneutics that he described as "scenic understanding". In the scene, within which the interaction of analyst and patient unfolds, no single infantile experience is ever manifested, but, rather, what is expressed is an infantile configuration, one that has been con-structed from multiple scenes. This is a present creation, arising out of the "scenic function of the ego", yet it is also always intersubjec-tively tied to both partners, and it cannot be isolated from them. Transference reactions derive their significance as a vehicle of meaning entirely from this configuration. The scene is an intersub-jectively created dynamic construction, built by both analyst and patient; it is not simply something from the patient's past that is then discovered in the present. Lorenzer (1983, 2002) built upon this concept of scenic understanding in developing his theory of "forms of interaction".

While in Germany, intersubjective theories of the therapeutic relationship sprang from the concept of encounter, in French psy-choanalysis intersubjective approaches centred on alterity. It was Jacques Lacan, of course, who first called upon the work of Hegel, Husserl, and Heidegger, writers who had conceived of the self as internally split. Likewise, in the mirror stage, the child identifies himself in something (the optical image) that is not himself, but through which he re-cognizes himself. The mirror stage presup-poses, by its fundamental nature, the destiny of the "I" as alienated in the imaginary dimension; it can only encounter itself in the imag-ination, as an other in an Other. This imaginary intersubjectivity is, however, more or less arrested in the moment of mirroring, and the entrance into the symbolic order of language is necessary for it to become an intersubjectivity that is based on recognition and communication.

Unlike the followers of intersubjective approaches, Green (1999, 2000), invoking the philosophy of Hegel, argued that humans incarnate an inherent heterogeneity, stemming from the alterity of the Other. This heterogeneity is not resolved by subject- philosophical conceptions, which see the Other as being the same as the I, nor is it overcome by the assumption—held in certain schools of the philosophy of language—that language shares a common foundation among different individuals. In fact, this heterogeneity is insoluble. The Other is never fully subsumed in its function as the other person's other. Moreover, he remains an other who is not determined by this role. Yet, from his position as the counterpart of the subject, an answer is expected of him – both in the sense of a satisfaction of a desire, as well as an interpretation of the situation, which presents itself to him as a question. Green discerns alterity in another sense as well: in his relatedness to the drive as something that is not tied to language, the subject is also an other to himself. The drive, which stems from the sphere of the body, constitutes a relationship that cannot be fully subsumed by language and discursivity. The drive contains the dependency on an Other as the object of the drive, who responds to it but whose answer can never completely correspond to the desire. The subject will spend a lifetime working to diminish this double, interpersonal, and intrapsychic alienation. For Green, alterity only becomes comprehensible and tangible through psychoanalysis and the creation of an analytical situation, the use of free association, and the unfolding of transference. This appears to enable the return to oneself via the detour of the other.

Laplanche (1988, 1992) works from the assumption of an anthropological basic situation in which the adult transmits both verbal and non-verbal messages to the child, messages that are pervaded by unconscious sexual meanings; since the child can only partially decipher them, they remain largely enigmatic. These messages pose a challenge for the child, the challenge of translating them using prevalent narrative cultural codes. The unconscious is formed out of the repressed, untranslatable remainder left behind by these messages, but it is not simply the embodiment of the imprint of these messages; it is the product of the subjective processing of the encounter with this adult and his enigmatic message. Laplanche, consequently, assumes a double alterity: alongside the adult other is the unconscious, which acquires the status of an alterity and a foreign body.

Both Green and Laplanche view the relationship between self and other as a dialogical–communicative situation. The Other is not only he through whom I comprehend myself as a subject; instead, the Other also will elude this communicative relationship and thereby remains the person I am encountering in an immediate way. In this conception, something originary and innovative is ascribed to the encounter, which far exceeds its meaning for the respective partners. It, thereby, contains an excess of meaning that cannot be adequately captured by the concept of transference.

Lévinas (1968, 1978) has integrated this notion of the excess of meaning into his philosophical conception of the Other, a perspective that has proved attractive for psychoanalysts, as is clearly witnessed by the number of psychoanalytic studies that have made use of it. (Primarily Berenstein, 2001; Küchenhoff, 2004; Puget, 2004; Warsitz, 2004.) Lévinas's philosophical approach can be seen to serve as a critique of theories of subject constitution, in which human individuation by mutual recognition is presented as a consensual process in a way that some might find overstated, and in which a symmetry of the subject–subject relationship is assumed in which, one could argue, the fundamental alterity of the Other is lost from sight, as is the difference this alterity gives rise to. Lévinas, like Green, assumes the inner heterogeneity of the self, "which hears itself think", and is an other to itself. The absolute Other, however, is another human being. Lévinas emphasizes the alienness of the other, which also exceeds one's own imagination of the other. The other is not the alter-ego but something different, in the strictest sense of the word. The encounter with him is not about mutual recognition; it is about the Other putting me into question and breaking me open. The shock that the Other triggers in me in the immediate encounter becomes the paradigm of intersubjectivity, not the experience of mutuality. This absolute otherness grants the ego a new experience, one not accessible to the ego alone. Lévinas conceives of this as the presence of the infinite that comes about in the social relationship to the other.

Such a one-sided conceptual emphasis of the radical alienness and difference of the Other and the immediacy of the encounter has its own problems, however; it may lead us to overlook how much we need the Other in his function as alter-ego and depend on his empathy and recognition for the constitution of our own self. (This is a criticism of Lévinas formulated most prominently by Alford, 2002.) It also has to be asked if an immediate encounter between self and other always, from the beginning on, assumes the existence of a third, something through which, alone, self and other are able to encounter each other in the first place (Bedorf, 2003).

Intersubjectivity and new experience

Encounter, mutuality, spontaneity, and authenticity are concepts that have gained a special appeal, not only for scholars, but as concepts that correspond to modern social consciousness in general. Something new can spring from encounter that is not already present in the patterns of transference and countertransference. The encounter thereby obtains a particularly creative potency. Within the field of the philosophy of dialogue, Theunissen (1977) has advanced the thesis that the ego cannot model and understand itself on the basis of the Other; rather, the encounter, as an event, always precedes those who encounter each other. In its aspect of encounter, the intersubjective relationship thereby contains a quantity of meaning that exceeds its intrapsychic significance for each partner. Green (2000) makes a similar argument, though he does not draw a conceptual distinction between the aspect of encounter and the intersubjective relationship. Psychoanalytic theory thereby faces the task of conceptualizing two interlocking aspects of the intersubjective relationship without polarizing them or dissolving them into each other.

In the work of Balint, Loewald, and others, attempts were already being made to understand how new experience becomes possible in the analytical process; these writers used such terms as "a new beginning" (Balint, 1965), or proposed such mechanisms as the analyst emerging as a new object for the patient (Loewald,

1960). According to current understandings, new experience becomes accessible in treatment only once the transference has been thoroughly analysed, but, in the course of this interpretation of the transference constellation, it is not only the patient's inner perception that is altered, but also his or her perception of the analyst, who suddenly appears as an other. The unavoidable personal involvement of the analyst gives rise to the question of the spontaneity and authenticity of self-expression, and this becomes a central problem in intersubjective theories. Hoffman (1998) conceives the actions of the analyst as constituting a dialectic between, on the one hand, self-expression/spontaneity, and, on the other, role-specific conduct. The new, which is the experience of a spontaneous interaction, can only be formed against the foil of the standardized, role-specific conduct of the analyst. Moments of a new form of encounter between analyst and patient acquire their innovative power, or their influence, only against the backdrop of the conventional ritualized asymmetry of the analytical situation: the new form of encounter occurs when the routinized role-behaviour, marked by transference and countertransference, is broken open. This argumentative position is likewise reflected in the concept of "moments of meeting", as formulated by the Boston Process of Change Study Group (PCSG), 1998.

Here the following question arises: how is new experience in the analytical situation, that is, experience in which the otherness of the analyst becomes palpable, to be described conceptually when it cannot be discussed in terms of self- and object-representations that are actualized in transference? One could perhaps make use of Winnicott's concept of "potential space", in the sense of a transformative experience in a "transitional space", which allows the true self to be reawakened. In regard to this form of experience, Bollas (1987) writes of existential knowledge, which he defines in opposition to representational knowledge. According to Bollas, existential knowledge originates in early infancy, when the mother is not yet fully identified as an other but is instead experienced mostly as a process of transformation. This peculiarity of early experience lives on later, manifesting itself in a particular sort of object-search, one that does not seek an object of desire but rather an object "identified with such powerful metamorphoses of being" (ibid., p. 17).

Likewise, the notion of an innovative encounter emerges as the concept of a "link" in the work of the Argentine psychoanalysts Berenstein (2001) and Puget (2004). Berenstein and Puget developed this concept using insights they gained in their therapeutic experience with couples and in family analysis. Their basic question is how we can acquire a perception of an other that is not subsumed by projective identifications, repetitions, or actualizations of pre-existing representations. They begin by positing an object-relationship, in which the desires of the ego are projected on the object. This object-relationship is ego-centred and articulated in the analytical relationship as transference. They then distinguish this from the link between the subjects. Here, the other appears as an Other, not as an object. This means that the encounter between the two has an innovative potential, because there exists an otherness of the other that is not represented as something that already existed in the counterpart's inner world. For the counterpart, in the encounter, the otherness of the other represents something new and alien that cannot be inscribed as his own. This realization inflicts a narcissistic wound. If the encounter and the inscription of the new into the subject is avoided, the relationship remains on the level of a represented object relationship and does not become present, that is, form a new "link" between subjects. In a subject relationship, "the subject not only pre-exists the relationship, but is also constituted by it" (Berenstein, 2001, p. 145).

Towards a critique of intersubjective
conceptions in psychoanalysis

Of the individual in his autonomy and difference to system,
interaction, and relatedness—a theoretical and clinical
shift of focus

The findings of empirical infant research have been enormously fruitful for the development of intersubjective theories, as empirical research has demonstrated that—and allowed us to describe in the smallest behavioural units how—the child's self unfolds in the reciprocal interaction processes with the mother. Such research has contributed to making the patient's legitimate developmental needs into a central focus within intersubjective analytic treatment. Psychoanalytic clinical theory has long viewed the therapeutic relationship, alongside verbal interpretation, as an important factor in mental transformations, but it has not been until recently, in the work of some theorists of intersubjectivity and using findings from infant research, that the therapeutic relationship, and, particularly, "the pure interaction process" contained within it, has been identified as the central factor (Beebe & Lachmann, 2002). Beebe and Lachmann present a model whose aim is "to reframe psychoanalysis within a systems view of interaction consistent with infant and adult research" (*ibid.*, p. xv). In this model, subject and object, self and other, are no longer conceptualized as unities, but rather as "processes of relatedness per se". According to these writers, it is not the self that interacts with the other; rather, they reconceptualize autonomy and relatedness in terms of self- and interactive processes of regulation:

> We reconceptualize autonomy as emerging from "good enough" interactive regulation. Likewise, we see interactive regulation in the optimal range as emerging from "good-enough" self-regulation of both partners. Rather than seeing autonomy and relatedness as two separate poles, we see both as simultaneously co-constructed. [*ibid.*, p. 226]

Simultaneous with the shift towards viewing "the pure interaction process" as central to mental transformation has been another shift, one likewise stemming from infant research: the shift in focus from explicit autobiographical memory to implicit procedural memory. The latter is now thought to have a much greater impact, but is not thought capable of being activated by narrative or by the interpretation of transference.

By implication, the implicit mode is far more pervasive and potentially more powerfully organizing than is the explicit mode. The idea that therapeutic action can occur at the implicit level without verbalization is an important change for a theory of therapeutic action (Beebe & Lachmann 2002, pp. 216f). (See also Fonagy, 1999; Fonagy, Target, & Allison, 2003.)

Such reconceptualizations of treatment theory, stimulated by findings from infant research, seem, in many respects, radical, in that, within these reconceptualizations, the significance of the spoken word, comprehension, and autobiographical memory is diluted. However, the individual self and its structures that arise intersubjectively and interactively in childhood development are not necessarily equally intersubjectively interwoven and dependent in adulthood. A systems-theory model of interaction that adequately and accurately describes behaviour regulations and patterns of expectations in infancy does not have to be equally valid in the description of therapeutic interactions and verbal exchange in grown-up patients. Many of these conclusions, drawn about adults from findings in childhood research, seem, therefore, somewhat tenuous. The emphasis on mutuality, the shared, and relatedness inevitably results in a theoretical and clinical neglect of difference, independence, and autonomy.

The potential disappearance of triangulating reality

On several occasions, intersubjective theories have been faced by the critical question of how the partners in a therapeutic dialogue can be sure that their jointly co-constructed interpretation of an action represents a valid meaning, and not just a *folie-à-deux*. Here, we arrive at the concept of reality, which must always be presupposed and to which both partners have to relate in order to make themselves understood in the first place. Cavell (1998) points to the existence of a language community that predates both partners. For Bedorf (2003), a dyad as a dual union is faced by the danger of melding. It is only the third in a structurally conceived triad that can point the way beyond the immediate here and now of the encounter. Intersubjectivity can never succeed between just two, and, indeed, the third is always already present as someone who is excluded. The third also forms the locus situated between the self and other, in which a conflict is articulated. The third, then, emerges as a disturbing factor, which forces the system to continually engage in a new exchange (*ibid.*, p. 363). Spezzano (1998) takes up another aspect of this position, making reference to the "clinical triangle" in which we are always situated. The analyst is not only positioned in relation to a patient, but also to a virtual community of psychoanalysts, with whom he seeks an inner consensus in the application of theoretical concepts and the rules governing treatment practices.

The remainder that cannot be conceptualized intersubjectively: death drive, negativity, destructiveness vs. *non-conflictual socialization*

Intersubjective conceptions of human development tend to view it as relatively free of conflict. According to these conceptions, the formation of an individual identity is directly connected to social and interpersonal recognition. Many critics have argued that these theories ignore the insights about social non-conformity furnished by psychoanalysis, since no drive wishes or unconscious fantasies can ever be completely integrated into an individual or social identity. In fact, the phenomena of aggression, the death drive, and narcissistic omnipotence lead to a retreat from, if not a rejection of, intersubjectively shared reality, giving rise to a "remainder" that cannot be fully integrated or dissolved. This concept of a remainder complicates the engagement of psychoanalysis with intersubjective theories. Green (1999) terms the retreat from intersubjective shared reality the "work of the negative". Negative narcissism does not involve any ego investment that seeks unity with the object; instead, the negatively narcissistic subject seeks a zero level in the attempt to resolve the problems that result from his or her destructive strivings. Destructiveness is, thereby, dissociated from aggression, as the latter is still directed towards the object and can be connected to a positive narcissism.

Whitebook (2001) has argued that the intersubjective paradigm of psychoanalysis has so captivated the theoretical imagination that the truth content of Hobbesianism—that is, the reality of the individual's isolation, his dependence on drives, and his fundamental asociality—is in danger of being lost. In his critique of infant research, Whitebook observes that the development of the self cannot be viewed as being intersubjective from the beginning on. Despite the fact that an intersubjective self does emerge, we still have to assume the existence of a pre-social self (and, naturally, this pre-social self is an object of particular interest among psychoanalysts). This begs the question, however, of whether this pre-social self is not too loaded with critical meaning when it is seen as the bastion of resistance to its intersubjective formation and, consequently, its socialization. At the centre of the debate between Whitebook (2001) and Honneth (2001) is the question of whether we have to depart from the notion of asociality in the subject. Honneth asks, for instance, why social theory should only be considered critical when its premises of socialization theory work from the assumption of a structural conflict between the individual self and the social order that finds formal expression in a negativity of subjects.

Conclusion

As we have seen, under the rubric of "intersubjective theories" we find a number of quite heterogeneous psychoanalytic conceptions. They include, for example, North American approaches, which can be subsumed under the heading of "relational psychoanalysis"; South American perspectives, whose development was informed by family theory; and continental European theorizations, which combined an intersubjective psychoanalytic framework with certain conceptual traditions, pertaining to the self and the other, of continental philosophy . In this chapter, I have attempted to sketch these theoretical approaches, to offer a cursory discussion of each, and to critically compare them to one another. This process has shown that the comparison and exchange between these theoretically diverse models can help to correct one-sidedness, aid in forming clearer distinctions, and counterbalance the overemphasis of concepts that have superseded those which had previously been dominant.

Conceptually, the development of intersubjective theories has increasingly centred on the immediacy of the intersubjective encounter. Immediacy, processes of pure interaction, and the experience of present moments are all ways of formulating elements of the therapeutic relationship that are affectively significant, but which are experienced pre-verbally. It seems that philosophy has had less to do in bringing this about, in its phenomenological analysis of self and other, than have the results of infant research, which describe the interactive, pre-verbal emergence of the infantile self. The progress made in clinical theory is that this element can be conceptually amalgamated with, or added alongside, the analysis of transference and countertransference. Concepts of encounter and the relation of the self to the Other allow for the introduction of an excess of meaning into a theory of the therapeutic relationship, something that cannot be subsumed by the analysis of transference and countertransference, but which only emerges as present experience, and which must then be caught up with verbally, though the attempt can never entirely succeed.

CHAPTER TWO

From surgeon to team-player: the transformation of guiding metaphors for the analytic relationship within clinical theory

Introduction

Important innovations in psychoanalytic theory, such as the development of new concepts or the expansion of existing ones, have often been accompanied by changes in the metaphors used by psychoanalysts: for example, to visualize the questions and problems being addressed. These metaphors serve to illuminate and more clearly define the matter at hand by way of a comparison. Yet, the descriptive function of metaphors also carries with it the danger that the metaphor will assume a life of its own and be taken for the matter itself, thereby hindering rather than advancing the development of theory. In the following, I will address this and other problems by examining a selection of key images and guiding metaphors, taking Winnicott's famous figures of mirroring and potential space as my point of departure and from there moving on to explore other key metaphors that have arisen during the development of clinical theory in psychoanalysis.

I will begin with a few general observations regarding metaphorical thought and speech. This discussion will not attempt to encompass formal theories of metaphor, nor will it provide a comprehensive evaluation of the significance and function of the rhetorical figure in conceptual thinking, as it would be beyond the scope of this chapter to consider these topics adequately or to go into technical detail (here, I refer the reader to the relevant literature: Arlow, 1979; Buchholz, 1993, 1998, 2003; Haverkamp, 1996; Lakoff & Johnson, 1980; Wurmser, 1983.) Since, in everyday communication, the use of metaphors is so taken for granted, it is necessary in this discussion, before we try to consider metaphor at all, to become consciously and explicitly aware of what this peculiarity of language is and what it does. In a metaphor, an idea or image from one realm is conveyed into another, and in this way heterogeneous contexts are connected. When we look at different contexts simultaneously, we draw on their similarities, and the meaning from one area is carried over into the other. A metaphor's structure allows it to make visible what as of yet has not been fully conceptualized, and metaphors therefore serve as catalysts in the process of elaborating the implicit. In creating a comparison, a metaphor establishes a retroactive link to the experiential world (*Lebenswelt*); the metaphor provides an important motivating factor in the development of new theories and concepts (Haverkamp, 1996). We use metaphors both passively, as the medium by which we experience reality and the world, and actively, to construct that reality. Although many concepts therefore originate in metaphor, this origin is often forgotten or lost; the metaphorical element fades and the metaphor and the concept become identical. Metaphors can indeed illuminate and reveal certain aspects of an object, but since they rest upon comparison and partial similarity, they can also conceal or overshadow other aspects. As Nagel has argued (quoted in Wurmser, 1983), metaphors and models are at once an invaluable intellectual instrument and a treacherous epistemological trap, and nowhere is this double-sidedness more pronounced than in the development of scientific theories.

Metaphors are clearly of great significance in psychoanalysis. Indeed, some consider the entire field to be an essentially metaphorical enterprise (Arlow, 1979). One consequence of this is that psychic reality can be easily overdetermined by its broad associative intertwinings. This excess of meaning creates a fertile soil for the emergence of metaphors, and their capacity for both the representation and the figurative illustration of things makes them an ideal medium for the expression of unconscious fantasy life. The analyst can make use of metaphors to stimulate a patient's unconscious fantasies and assist in their articulation. Yet, metaphors pervade not only the clinical practice of psychoanalysis, but also its theoretical formation, by making mental matters capable of conceptualization and description. In his own theoretical work, Freud was a master of the device, drawing on an extremely broad range of metaphors. He writes:

> What is psychical is something so unique and peculiar to itself that no one comparison can reflect its nature. The work of psycho-analysis suggests analogies with chemical analysis, but it does so just as much with the intervention of a surgeon or the manipulations of an orthopaedist or the influence of an educator. [1919a, p. 161]

However, Freud was also aware of the limitations of such comparisons. Though Freud, in his writing, implicitly demonstrated the necessity of using metaphorical conceptualization in articulating the mental, he also explicitly warned against the danger of allowing metaphors to become reified.

The significance of the mirror and potential space metaphors in the formation of psychoanalytic theory

Freud famously used the metaphor of the surgeon to describe the proper role and comportment of the analyst. He advised that the analyst, while conducting psychoanalytic therapy, should model himself on this figure, a figure "who puts aside all his feelings, even his human sympathy, and concentrates his mental forces on the single aim of performing the operation as skilfully as possible" (1912e, p. 115). Freud argued that this emotional coldness produces the most advantageous conditions for an analytic cure. The analyst, he believed, should try to temper his or her own desire to cure the patient so that he or she will be able to display an open and unassuming demeanour when confronting analytical material in the session. Only from a stance of emotional coldness, said Freud, can "concealed unconscious material" (ibid.) be recognized by the analyst. In order to more precisely describe how the analyst should behave, Freud introduced two additional metaphors: the metaphor of the telephone receiver and the metaphor of the mirror. Just as "a telephone receiver is adjusted to the transmitting microphone", Freud said, an analyst "must turn his own unconscious like a receptive organ towards the transmitting unconscious of the patient". The analyst must "not tolerate any resistances in himself which hold back from his conscious what has been perceived by his unconscious" (this, of course, implies that the analyst "should have undergone a psychoanalytic purification" [*ibid.*, p. 116], that is, a self-analysis), nor, in fact, should the analyst share any of him or herself with the patient at all, but instead, as well as being "opaque to his patients," should be "like a mirror", which "[shows] them nothing but what is shown to him" (*ibid.*, p. 118). Freud employs these metaphors to express his conviction that, as a science, psychoanalysis can only be based methodologically on the interpretation of empirical evidence gained through observation. The metaphor of the mirror expresses the imperative to gain the most objective knowledge possible of psychic reality. In the years after these metaphors were introduced, they came to be accepted as definitions of the epistemological principles, as well as the therapeutic ideals, to which analysts should adhere, even though, in practice, such ideals were unachievable. Despite this discrepancy between practice and recommendation, however, psychoanalysis was slow to modify the conceptions of analytical practice contained in these metaphors.

In 1954, Leo Rangell used a different metaphor to recast the, by then, classical model for analytical treatment: the metaphor of the magnetic field. His main concern was to emphasize the analyst's position as a neutral observer and to differentiate between psychoanalytic and psychotherapeutic treatment techniques. Rangell describes the role of the analyst as follows:

> Let us consider that the mental apparatus exerts around it a field of magnetic energy. In psychoanalysis, the therapist takes up his position at the periphery of this magnetic field of his patient, not too far away, so that he is useless and might just as well not be there, nor too close, so that he is within the field interacting with it with his own magnetic field (he can err equally in both directions). Immune from repulsion or attraction (at least optimally, within the limits set by his own unconscious), he sits at the margin, like a referee in a tennis match, so that he can say to the patient, "This is what you are now doing, here is impulse, here defense, here resistance, here compromise formation, here symptom". [1954, p. 741]

In psychotherapy, however, the therapist does not simply remain on the sidelines. "He is, rather, generally on the court with his patient, interacting with him, the two magnetic fields interlocked, with the therapist's own values, opinions, desires, and needs more or less actively operative" (*ibid.*, p. 742). Psychoanalytic treatment, as depicted here, is a process; once set in motion, it keeps going like a chemical reaction until it reaches a final stage of dynamic balance (Freud himself compares the unfolding of transference to a chemical reaction (1916–1917, p. 183)). The analyst is solely concerned with the transference neurosis, and his two tasks are to first establish it and then to maintain the optimal conditions for its final and complete dissolution. In psychotherapy, however, the therapist intervenes in this ongoing process, bringing it "to an end at any intermediate point of stability" (Rangell, 1954, p. 743).

In this conception of the analytical process, the analyst nearly disappears as a factor influencing the patient's experiences. A clear line separates patient and analyst, one not unlike the classic border dividing the observer from the observed. The analyst, according to this formulation, should assume a position so that he or she can objectively observe the world of the patient as it unfolds in the analytical situation and uncover the fundamental conflicts underlying it.

In the decades since Rangell modified the classic model of the psychoanalytic process, that model has been subjected to such a sweeping critique that it is now considered outmoded. Clinical experience has revealed the interactive and intersubjective connection that exists between the analyst and the analysand, as well as the influence the two exert on each other. As a result of the acknowledgment of the analyst's contribution to the unfolding of the patient's clinical material, the scientifically sanctioned position of the analyst as an objective observer has been undermined to the point that it has nearly dissolved. The power that the analyst possessed in the classical model, which was to devise interpretations and to determine the unconscious source of the patient's material, has, thereby, been greatly diminished. I will return to this later, but I would now like to continue tracing the fate of the mirror metaphor.

Hoffman (1998) has subjected the metaphor of the blank screen to a fundamental critique, in which he argues that its definitional context has given rise to an asocial conception of the patient's experience in psychotherapy. If the analyst were to remain as passive and receptive as a mirror, he argued, the patient's productions would acquire an "organic-like momentum of [their] own" and follow their own "natural course". More moderate critics have argued that the mirror function does have a place in analysis but only in the context of the patient's neurotic transference, and that, additionally, the analysand will inevitably perceive many of the analyst's personality traits. To these critics, a friendly, natural, responsive attitude on the part of the analyst is beneficial for the unfolding of the transference, but this more open analytic stance, in which the analyst allows him or herself to be partially known by the patient, will not influence the neurotic portion of the transference, that is, the patient's distorted perception of the analyst. Incidentally, this division between transference as distorted perception and transference as accurate perception of the analyst has been met by an increasingly radical critique from newly emerging intersubjective approaches over the past thirty years. We now regard the patient's perspective of the analyst as but one of several relevant perspectives, each of which is thought to illuminate a particular facet of the therapist's involvement in the interaction. To use the term "distortion" is said to discriminate against the patient's perception. Even when the patient's view of the analyst is overdetermined by his or her experience of past relationships, this does not undermine its validity. In this conception of the analytic relationship, the metaphor of the analyst as an opaque mirror (blank screen) is replaced with that of the therapeutic space as an intersubjective field, a field within which both protagonists influence each other.

The comparison between an analyst and a mirror, however, encompasses a wider range of possible meanings than the one meaning we have discussed so far, which is that the two entities share the quality of being opaque, and Hoffman's critique of the mirror metaphor for seeming to describe, as well as mandate, a therapeutic relationship that is impersonal and unidirectional is, therefore, a narrow criticism. Hoffman fails to consider another similarity that the comparison can serve to highlight, which is that both analyst and mirror act as instruments of reflection, with the analyst in the sense that the patient's statements and depictions strike the analyst and pass through him before being bounced back. In this respect, the metaphor of the mirror contains the insight that another person is always needed for a person to understand himself or herself.

In the larger context of the Western world as a whole, the mirror has long served as a guiding metaphor to describe and map the process of self discovery, and within this larger context it has had two main trajectories of meaning: an active and a passive one. While in Freud's writing the mirror metaphor described passivity, and the image of the mirror invoked was the mirror as passive instrument supplying as undistorted a reflection as possible, in the writing of Winnicott and Green, among others, the mirror metaphor has come to describe a type of activity, and the image invoked has been one of a living mirror that actively adjusts to its objects. Such an active notion was prefigured as early as in the work of Lacan (1949), who describes the function of real mirror images in the emergence of a unified (if illusory) image of the self and of reflective capacity. Winnicott (1971), however, locates the mirror in the face of the mother. For the child, according to Winnicott, the mother's gaze becomes the mirror of the self. What the mother sees in the child is reflected in the expression the mother displays on her own face. In the mother's face, the child recognizes something that he or she has given the mother (what the mother has seen in the child), and then internalizes it as his or her own self-image. Winnicott uses the mirror function of the mother as a model for the psychoanalytic process:

> The glimpse of the baby's and child's seeing the self in the mother's face, and afterwards in a mirror, gives a way of looking at analysis and at the psychotherapeutic task. Psychotherapy is not making clever and apt interpretations; by and large it is a long-term giving the patient back what the patient brings. It is a complex derivative of the face that reflects what is there to be seen. I like to think of my work this way, and to think if I do this well enough the patient will find his or her own self, and will be able to exist and to feel real. [*ibid.*, p. 117]

Freud emphasized the opacity of the mirror in order to underscore the importance of detached observation in analysis— observation that is free from subjective falsification—and of the knowledge of the patient's mental experience that such observation affords. For Winnicott, too, the analyst's image of the patient should not be distorted by his or her subjective perception, and the analyst's "mirror function" is performed by his helping to reveal, or by his helping the patient to find, the patient's true self. This "mirror function" is not imagined to simply passively reflect back what is seen, but, rather, to actively capture the actual true self, and, by doing so, to enable the patient to become existentially aware of his or her self. Hence, the concepts of insight and self-knowledge are seen as having their basis in the early eye contact between mother and child.

Green (1975) also employs Freud's mirror metaphor. Like Winnicott, Green emphasizes the reflective function of mirrors. Green asserts that the mother performs a mirror-like function for the child by providing him or her with an object that the child can use to create an image of him or herself with continuity in time. Out of this process emerges something like an inner mirror of the self and a corresponding actual capacity for self-reflection. Green takes up a further element of the metaphor that had previously been neglected: the work of the mirror itself. Just as the father is absent in the reflecting gaze of the mother upon the child, yet also present in that the child is the figure of the union between mother and father, the analyst assumes the work of the mirror in processing and symbolizing the patient's diffuse discharge within himself. In this respect, the analyst lends form to the patient's experience and brings about a registration of experience that could not have arisen otherwise. In short, a meaning is created in the process that did not exist prior to the analytic relationship.

Kohut (1971) also adopted the mirror metaphor in outlining the treatment of narcissistic disorders. According to Kohut, during normal development a mother will reflectively react to the exhibitionistic displays of her child, and Kohut argued that analysts, while treating narcissistic patients, should try to simulate this early childhood interaction by establishing a mirror transference, in which the patient's grandiose self is echoed and confirmed. Kohut, like Green, used the mirror metaphor to describe a process of active engagement rather than simply passive reflection. The mirror metaphor describes the analyst's capacity to serve as a "therapeutic buffer", and to help the patient give form to the ego-dystonic narcissistic fantasies and impulses characteristic of the disorder, so that these fantasies and impulses can be integrated into a more coherent self.

In empirical infant research, the image of the mirror has largely lost its metaphorical meaning and acquired the status of a scientific concept. First appearing in descriptions of the "mirroring" process that occurs in early childhood, a process that is facilitated by the mother and that is crucial for childhood development, the image of the mirror has been further elaborated on in Stern's notion of "affect attunement" (1985) and the theory of affect mirroring in the work of Fonagy, Gergely, Jurist, and Target (2002). In order to understand the development of these concepts, we must first consider the spatial metaphors connected to the process of mirroring itself.

It was Winnicott (1971), primarily, who applied spatial metaphors to the psychotherapeutic process in his conception of the transitional object and transitional area. Winnicott identified three distinct realms of experience: the outer realm, formed by object relations and the satisfaction of drives; the inner realm, consisting of dreams, sleep, fantasies, and psychic reality as a whole; and, metaphorically located between the two, what he terms the potential or intermediate space, within which mother and child are simultaneously connected and separated, and the subjective and objective are undivided. In the context of the intermediate space, Winnicott speaks of a paradox that cannot be resolved and that we only ever perceive to be resolved mistakenly: our objective perception of mother and child and of the physical space between them does not allow us to observe directly the phenomena that occur in the intermediate space. As a tool to help us obliquely grasp these phenomena, Winnicott uses the metaphor of the potential space as an area of play. For him, the essential element of play is the attempt to externalize inner reality upon a real object. For this to succeed, the external object must comply, so that it can be shaped and controlled in accordance with the inner reality. The implication of comparing potential space to an area of play is that potential space is framed as a sphere of illusion. For Winnicott, the potential space as area of play becomes the central metaphor for the work of psychotherapy:

> The general principle seems to me to be valid that psychotherapy is done in the overlap of the two play areas, that of the patient and that of the therapist. If the therapist cannot play, then he is not

suitable for the work. If the patient cannot play, then something needs to be done to enable the patient to become able to play, after which psychotherapy can begin. The reason why playing is essential is that it is in playing that the patient is being creative. [1971, p. 54]

With the metaphor of potential space, Winnicott successfully formulates a condensed description of the creative therapeutic process as a paradoxical field of tension in which both therapist and patient are simultaneously connected and divided. The point of departure is no longer the two interacting subjects of the analytical dialogue; instead, it is their intermediate connection in the potential space of the analytic session. To put it in terms of the philosophy of dialogue, not the other but the "in-between" is the initial basis from which the subject takes shape (Theunissen, 1977). Ogden describes this as a dialectical connection between individuality and intersubjectivity, but he introduces a different term to describe this intermediate area: the "intersubjective analytic third", "to which analyst and analysand contribute and from which they individually draw in the process of generating their own experience of the analytic relationship" (1997, p. 720).

In their studies of affect regulation and mentalization, Fonagy, Gergely, Jurist, and Target (2002) refer back to Winnicott's mirroring processes and potential space. While Winnicott used these concepts, for the most part metaphorically, for Fonagy and his colleagues they are empirically verifiable concepts of development. The authors conducted research studying the early preverbal affect-regulative mirroring interactions between mother and child. They found that not only does the mother mirror the affective state of the child through her behaviour and expression, but she also and simultaneously identifies that affect as belonging to the child, distinguishing those affective displays that are meant to mirror the child's affect from displays that express her own affect by marking the former with added gestures, for instance, nodding her head, increasing her pitch, etc.; these markings, they found, allow the child to recognize such displays as referring to emotional states in himself. The reflection of the child's affects back to the child creates a social biofeedback mechanism, enabling the child to associate this marked expression of affect with his own inner affective state. This process also stimulates the formation of secondary representations of primary affective states. Here, two elementary modes of representation emerge: the psychic equivalence mode and the pretend mode. In the psychic equivalence mode, one's own thoughts and feelings are confused with, or taken for, an accurate reflection of reality. In the pretend mode, which is developed primarily in childhood play, these representations are separated from reality and regarded as purely the products of imagination. Both modes of mental representation must be integrated in the course of development, and this occurs primarily through repeated playful interactions with the most important others. Play furthers the capacity to distinguish, and to maintain a distinction between, pretend and psychic equivalence mode, while also enabling an inner exchange between the two. Within the context of play, the mother takes up the child's ideas as pretend mode, thereby reflecting the child's inner state in which these ideas are represented. At the same time, however, the mother maintains contact with reality and provides the child with connections between reality and fantasy. The authors, in describing the significance of this process for development, call on Winnicott's notion of intermediate potential space.

> The essence of the process is not simply play, but play that breaks away from psychic equivalence while retaining contact with reality. In other words, the child, using the parent's mind, is able to *play with reality*. [Fonagy, Gergely, Jurist, & Target, 2002, p. 267]

Fonagy and his co-authors' understanding of mentalization clearly influences their view of the psychoanalytic process, primarily in regard to the treatment of patients with serious developmental disorders. In their view, the central therapeutic goal of psychoanalysis is to get the patient to "mentalize affectivity" (*ibid.*, p. 315). The analytic setting serves "the purpose of focusing the patient's attention on his internal mental contents, which are to be externalized within the safe, reality-decoupled 'as-if' world of the analytic situation" (*ibid.*). The therapist uses mirroring interpretations or observations to externalize and regulate the patient's affects and, thereby, shares with the patient a corrective emotional and representational experience. This capacity for representation teaches patients to regulate their affects on their own. By learning

to "mirror themselves", the patients acquire the capacity to mentalize and modify their emotional impulses.

Let us return to the subject of metaphors and their importance
in the formation of theory. Holmes (2006) has compared the metaphors contained in Fonagy's model of the development of mentalization with those contained in Bion's model of thinking. Both
conceptualize the same or very similar processes. The mirror metaphor lends Fonagy's model of mentalization a predominantly
visual character. Bion's alpha-function theory and the container–
contained model of thinking are, by contrast, based on metaphors
of nourishment and digestion as well as their corresponding spatial
metaphors. The image central to Bion's metaphors is the
breast/nipple and the mouth. The role of the mother differs in the
two models. In Bion's model, she performs a relatively passive
function, assuming an attitude of reverie, and it is the child who
acts as the instigator; when the child cannot tolerate his or her frus-
tration, he or she instead projectively evacuates his or her undesirable feelings on to the mother, who absorbs them, like a container,
in order to detoxify them, subsequently returning them in a more
bearable form. For Fonagy, in the development of safe attachment
and of mentalization, the opposite is the case: the mother performs
an active function, actively trying to imagine the inner mental space
of the child and actively reflecting marked externalizations of the
child's affective states.

Here, I will conclude my brief theoretical history of the mirror
metaphor. It has a wide array of possible meanings, some of which
have been gradually worked out within psychoanalysis. Initially,
the metaphor of the mirror was used to bring out the analyst's
opacity and his or her quality of providing pure reprojections to the
analysand. In later occurrences of the mirror metaphor, the notion
of reflection was highlighted, and was incorporated into explanations of the emergence of reflective function within individuals and
the role of reflective function in providing individuals with a sense
of self. In neither case was the mirror as a metaphorical object
simply a two-dimensional surface. Metaphors and concepts with a
spatial character that have been invoked alongside the mirror metaphor have served to extend the metaphor of the mirror, particularly
through the notion of "potential space". Examining human development, self-constitution, and self-knowledge, as well as the thera-

peutic relationship and the function of the analyst, demonstrates the centrality of these metaphors in understanding psychic processes. These processes are perhaps best understood through metaphor, as opposed to through discursive concepts. It should come as no surprise, therefore, that Winnicott uses metaphors, specifically metaphors of mirroring and potential space, to understand the existential element of the self as well as the intertwining of fantasy and reality in the analytic relationship. In addition, Fonagy and others have offered impressive empirical proof of the way in which the capacity for mentalization springs from affect mirroring and play, and how mentalization processes are strongly tied to concrete experiences of interaction. The intermediate space of therapy in which two potential spaces overlap becomes the site of a transformative encounter. Were we to think of the therapeutic relationship solely as a medium of verbal exchange, this reality would remain beyond our conceptual reach.

Intersubjective/relational psychoanalysis and its contrasting metaphors

In scientific theories, metaphors play a formative role not only in producing ideas and concepts, but also in bringing about contrasts and oppositions. These theories themselves can have a metaphorical character, and when such theories are taken literally, they can turn into something like myth (Carveth, 1984). We find such constellations in modern intersubjective/relational theories. Adherents of these theories vehemently dissociate themselves from classical psychoanalysis, which, they argue, conceives of people as "isolated monads" whose inner world, though it is described as being always in the process of unfolding, is, however, only capable of being secondarily involved in relationships to others (Mitchell, 2000). The concept of the monad as invoked in these criticisms does not represent a traditional philosophical notion, but is used metaphorically. It is made use of in order to claim that, over the past several decades, psychoanalysis, in its study of the inner world, has neglected to examine relationality and the intersubjective nature of the analytic situation. Indeed, the aim of human development was long considered to be the autonomy of the individual. The psyche was, therefore, understood as the exclusive property of the individual, while exchange with others became a question of intention (Mitchell, 2000). Critics of psychoanalysis/adherents of intersubjective theories regard the notion of an "isolated mind" in psychoanalysis as reflecting the alienation of modern man, and declare the monadic view of the inner world to be a modern myth and a reified conception that serves "to disavow the exquisite vulnerability that is inherent to an unalienated awareness of the continual embeddedness of human experience in a constitutive intersubjective context" (Stolorow & Atwood, 1992, p. 22). Such a view of Freudian psychoanalysis is, however, itself a myth, which has been constructed in order to allow proponents of intersubjective and relational approaches to define themselves in opposition to it.

Almost all psychoanalytic schools have distanced themselves from the purely intrapsychic point of view and have increasingly embraced interactively orientated concepts. Countertransference, enactment, and projective identification have become guiding concepts in the field of psychoanalysis. The phenomenon of countertransference has, in fact, unfolded in a dynamic that has continually expanded the concept and made the analyst's subjectivity the centre of attention. This development has not gone far enough to satisfy relational theorists, however. Renik (2004), for example, in spite of the developments described above, accuses modern psychoanalysts of naïveté for failing to acknowledge that the analyst's estimation and understanding of the patient is "irreducibly subjective".

The central concept in modern intersubjective theories is "mutuality", a term used to characterize interaction in a subject–subject relationship. It is inevitable, these theories argue, that the analyst and patient will influence each other mutually and reciprocally. The analyst cannot remove himself from the mutually interactive events to which he is tied. If he becomes involved, as he must in order to perform the work of an analyst, he cannot at the same time also be detached enough to observe and work through his unconscious participation in what is taking place. The analyst is both a player on the field and a part of the field itself.

> Mutuality, in any relational model . . . becomes a central principle and a predominant area of investigation precisely because of the recognition of the analyst's participation and the inevitability of

mutual influence. . . . Analysis takes place between the patient and analyst as they analyze each other, even if often much of this analysis takes place implicitly or unconsciously, and even if the relative contributions of the two participants is not equal. [Aron, 1996, p. 127]

In many ways, the notion of mutuality, as it appears here, stems from Winnicott's conception of play and from the other metaphors used by Winnicott to describe the process of psychoanalysis. In modern intersubjective theories, interpretations are given a role similar to that given to what is metaphorically described as the transitional object: they are something that the analyst introduces into the transitional space of the analysis, and, like the transitional object, their primary utility is not found in any information they offer but in their function as a link to the analyst: "The interpretation can be carried around and sucked on when the analyst is away" (*ibid.*, p. 101). In addition, interpretations do not originate with the analyst or the patient, but, instead, emerge from the transitional space between them. The analyst can formulate interpretations ambiguously, so that it is unclear whose idea is being put forth.

The core metaphors in the intersubjective/relational model are "dialogue" (Mitchell, 1997), "collaboration", and, above all, "negotiation" (Mitchell, 1991; Aron, 1996). The latter is seen as an inherent feature of the relational model. It is argued that the dynamics of the therapeutic relationship would be better understood if we stop thinking of the relationship in terms of an individual's needs, wishes, and resistances, and, instead, consider it in regard to relational needs within a relationship. Desires and needs, according to this view, are not inherent and have no intrinsic meaning; they are, instead, embedded in a dyadic field. What is decisive in treatment, therefore, is not whether wishes are fulfilled or frustrated, but, rather, the way in which both participants negotiate them and whether or not the analyst can find a way to confirm and to share in the patient's subjective experience. In the course of analysis, both participants negotiate meanings that are co-created between them:

Therefore, who the analyst is, is to some degree determined by who the patient is. Since this interpersonal process is mutual and reciprocal, the patient continually influenced by the analyst and vice versa, one can legitimately claim that the very essence of who the patient and analyst are with each other is negotiated. [Aron, 1996, p. 140]

Winnicott's conception of mirroring, unlike his metaphor of transitional space, is left without a role in current intersubjective theories. Freud's concepts of the "blank screen" and the objectivity of knowledge, in contrast, do serve a function for intersubjective theorists, but not as part of the theories themselves: they are, instead, addressed by intersubjective theorists so as to be disputed, or as something that intersubjective theory can be defined against. The mirror metaphor, these theorists argue, obscures the idiosyncratic influence of the analyst, which, if it is not explicitly acknowledged, will not only still enter into the patient, but also additionally appear as something internal to the patient. The notion of the analyst as a "blank screen", for these theorists, is replaced by a conception of the analyst as someone who engages in "self-disclosure", and belief in the objectivity of knowledge as an analytic ideal is supplanted by a belief in the analyst's irreducible subjectivity, according to which even an approximation of objectivity is impossible. As a result of the influence of system theory and of the widespread conception of the analytic session as a bipersonal field, concepts such as reciprocity, negotiation, and co-construction between analyst and analysand have become predominant. Rangell saw the analyst as a type of referee who observes the intrapsychic play of the patient's structural elements. This notion of the analyst has since left the field, and now the analyst has come to be regarded as a team-mate of the analysand, the rules and "ways of playing", as well as the results/aspired outcome of therapy, as something to be worked out interactively by analyst and patient. The asymmetric positioning of analyst and analysand has been largely rescinded in favour of what is considered a symmetrical mutuality.

> In this way the two subjects of the analytic relationship sometimes risk collapsing into each other, with the subsequent decline of the analytic field towards non-specific aspects with negative implications and generating an increasingly symmetrical therapy. [Marzi, Hautman, & Maestro, 2006, p. 1308]

While the surgeon metaphor contained a conception of field-specific authority, and the mirror metaphor was associated with the possibility of an approximate, yet clear and somewhat objective, knowledge of the patient's (unconscious) complex of problems, these notions disappear in the new metaphors of relational theories. Dialogue and negotiation in a subject–subject relationship involve a shared production of the meanings of interactions within the context of the reciprocal involvement of both partners in the inter-action. Meaning is no longer found or discovered with the analyst's help; instead, it is created anew at the moment of interaction. The notion of the analyst's authority, based on the analyst's knowledge, is now considered outmoded. Demands for authenticity and self-disclosure now take centre stage.

These developments reflect social changes that have occurred over the past fifty years: they are expressions of the trend towards social and institutional democratization and the tendency towards more co-operative relations. Authority no longer goes unques-tioned: it is subject to criticism and is required to justify itself. The intersubjective positions described above owe a sizeable intellectual debt to postmodern thought, which questions the existence of objective knowledge and declares science to be but one socially defined version of truth. In a postmodern context, "grand theories" are abandoned in favour of conceptions of the world and reality that are explicitly regarded as constructions. According to this "con-structivist" view, identity and the self are not a unity, but a parti-tioned plurality of selves. Making fixed structures flexible and playing with reality are becoming new ideals. Against this back-drop, metaphors for psychoanalysis (and/or metaphors for the psychoanalyst) that ascribe authority to the analyst, such as Freud's metaphor of the analyst as educator or teacher, appear antiquated. My examination will turn to this subject in the following section.

Metaphors of the analyst's authority and power

In a 1974 paper, Loch described the analyst as performing a role similar to that performed by law-makers and teachers: like these figures, the analyst introduces into existing discourse a new language for the patient's behaviour and inner life that formulates unconscious processes, conflicts, and feelings. This creates a reality that can be shared by both the analyst and the analysand. The danger that arises from the analyst's giving voice to the patient's psychic reality in this way is that the analyst will become an authoritarian figure, invested with the power to impose, perhaps unintentionally and even automatically, his or her own points of view and values. Loch argues that this is avoidable if both the analyst and the patient identify with the analytic method and the zeal of discovery associated with it in their joint pursuit of a truth that is only to be gained through an interpersonal consensus. Therefore, all positions of power, and of authority, arising in the analytic process are themselves subject to methods of analytic examination. The analytic method, thereby, guards against the danger of being seduced into a narcissistic assumption of authoritarian attitudes. In this case, therefore, the analytic method performs a de-idealizing function.

In comparing Loch's position, which is surprisingly modern and constructivist for its time, to modern relational approaches, it is clear that the idea of an analytic method to which both analyst and patient are bound has given way to the recognition of the irreducible subjectivity of both and the inevitability of self-disclosure by the analyst. For the patient, the identification with the analytic method is replaced by a lasting identification with the patient's particular and individual analyst, a person in a unique position to recognize his own subjectivity. The analyst's authority is derived from his role as "an expert in collaborative, self-authorizing self-reflection" (Mitchell, 1998, p. 26). Open disclosure, by both participants, of the subjectivity manifesting itself in the patient–therapist interaction, is now seen as a necessary part of the analytic process. They each need the other in order to become aware of their own blind spots. Renik describes the position of the analyst as follows:

> The benefit of an analyst's willingness to self-disclose is that it establishes the analyst's fallible view of his or her own participation in the analysis as an appropriate subject for collaborative investigation—something analyst and patient can and should talk about explicitly together. [1999, p. 529]

Thus, the patient is now seen as a legitimate "interpreter of the analyst's experience" (Hoffman, 1998), a kind of "consultant", who helps the analyst more fully understand his own involvement

(Renik, 1999). Renik is an advocate of the somewhat radical policy according to which, in therapy, the analyst should be constantly prepared for, and willing to engage in, self-disclosure, a style of conducting analysis that he metaphorically describes as "playing one's cards face up". Renik sees himself as following a trend in contemporary psychoanalytic thought for critique of the analyst's authority. Within their respective social environments, Freud and his immediate successors were able to claim a high level of authority for their assertions because of science itself being accorded such a high degree of authority and prestige. The crisis of scientism and the postmodern critique of science have fundamentally altered this position. The cultural and historical contexts have been fundamentally transformed for both the analyst and the analysand. Psychoanalysis "can hardly survive in the monkish isolation traditionally generated by psychoanalytic pretensions of existing on a higher, or deeper, plane from the rest of humanity" (Mitchell, 1998, p. 4). Or, as Renik argues,

> The attitude toward self-disclosure . . . is consistent with any number of trends in contemporary analytic thinking that take the analyst off a pedestal and permit the patient greater authority. . . . More and more, we have been leveling the clinical analytic playing field. [1999, p. 523]

To remain within the semantic horizon of these metaphors, we can say that the analyst has become a team-mate and a team player.

The thesis of the analyst's irreducible subjectivity not only undermines his authority, but also his position as an objective observer. Because the analyst cannot make any objective statements about the patient's internal reality, it is argued, he is also not able to claim any authority for his interpretations, or to make any claims regarding their accuracy. The mind, it is believed, can only be created in the process of an interpreting construction, and does not exist independently of this construction. The interpretation itself comprises the very thing being interpreted (Aron, 1996). Conclusions or assumptions about a psychic reality that exist independently of their construction in the relationship are not possible.

This radically intersubjective position has posed a challenge to other psychoanalytic approaches, which have been forced to consider and sharpen their own understanding of the therapeutic relationship and the intersubjective involvement of the analyst. Out of this self-examination, what has been criticized above all is the thesis positing impenetrable subjectivity, and the various psycho-analytic tenets and assertions that depend on, or grow out of, this thesis. While an acknowledgement and formulation of the subjectivity of the analyst (as has been done within a number of clinical orientations) is regarded as a legitimate theoretical and clinical activity, considering this subjectivity as absolute is not: the proposition that knowledge is intersubjectively established and founded does not imply the second proposition that all objective knowledge is impossible. No matter how fragmentary or limited, the analyst's interpretations refer to psychic contents that exist independently of the process of their interpretation. (This critique has been formulated in various ways. As an example, I make reference here to Eagle, Wolitzky, and Wakefield [2001]; Friedman [1996]; Hanly and Hanly [2001]). Cavell (1998) has demonstrated philosophically that for us to even imagine a purely subjective point of view requires that we also assume the existence of a real world outside of that viewpoint, one whose qualities are independent of the qualities we perceive. That the discovery of repressed or split off mental contents often brings about a far-reaching transformation of a patient's perspective and conflicts is another argument cited to support the proposition that mental contents exist independently of the interpretation in which they are articulated. How, it is asked, could a patient find interpretations convincing when the analyst no longer assumes that there is an existing unconscious that his interpretations refer to, but, instead, regards the unconscious as simply a useful construction that assists the patient to understand his symptoms? Contrary to the view described above, Mitchell (1998, p. 25) advises limiting the analyst's role to a purely pragmatic one: he is merely to show the patient paths by which he can construe his own experience in potentially helpful ways, rather than attempting to bring the patient to a discovery of any "true" meaning.

One can agree with intersubjective critics that the analyst must demonstrate his authority and knowledge to the patient in order for his authority to be acknowledged by the patient, and one can also agree that idealizing parental transferences, which cause the analyst to (perhaps unwittingly) exert excessive power over the patient, should be analysed to correct this power imbalance. These recommendations are reasonable and perhaps necessary. What is surprising (and perhaps illuminating), however, is that these recommendations, which challenge the analyst's power and authority, coincided so well with pervasive social trends, which were moving in a markedly anti-authoritarian direction. It is as if these recommendations reflected, or resulted from, a larger anti-authoritarian social sentiment, and arose because the authoritative position of the analyst was itself regarded as suspect, part and parcel of an older patriarchal social order that required democratization. Using metaphors like "pedestal" and "higher plane" to describe the way analysts traditionally position themselves in relation to the patient, or to conventional wisdom, portrays the traditional analytic stance as suspiciously authoritarian without always necessarily providing arguments to substantiate this portrayal.

Metaphors of the intersubjective field and the Other

In this final section, I would like to make some observations about the metaphor of the field and that of the Other. (I presented these in greater detail in Chapter One of this volume.) Field theories lend themselves to conceptualizations of intersubjective experiences. The "field" that is invoked in field metaphors is the kind of field that results from the interaction of forces; such fields have a particularly dynamic quality. The prototypical example of this kind of field is the magnetic field. The structure of such fields is metaphorically compared to the structure of the relationship between analyst and analysand in order to bring out the intersubjective dynamic of this relationship. In the resulting picture of the analytic process, the participants in the process are no longer individuals; instead, what is presented is a "field" that, as a whole, as a dynamic totality, reacts to "forces". Since the 1960s, Baranger and Baranger have developed their own field-based conception of the analytic situation, drawing from Gestalt theory, as well as the further elaboration of Gestalt theory by Merleau-Ponty. They identify their conception as being the result of an application of Gestalt concepts, based, in addition, on Kleinian concepts of projective identification and, above all, on Bion's basic assumptions. Here, the "field" is much more than simply a product of interaction and a space of intersubjective relation. Not only does their field conception radically depart from the notion of both people as individuals (whom they do not regard as active subjects), but additionally, in their conception, the field is the sole object of investigation. The dynamics and power of this "field", in their conception, is determined by a "basic unconscious phantasy" that is

> not a sum or combination of the individual fantasies of the two members of the analytic couple, but an original set of fantasies created by the field situation itself. It emerges in the process of the analytic situation and has no existence outside the field situation, although it is rooted in the unconscious of the members. [Baranger, 2005, p. 63]

Because the field is the only possible object of study, the characteristics of the two members themselves can only be inferred through study of the field. Ferro (1999, 2005) has also formulated a bipersonal field conception of the analytic process: he conceives of the analytic environment as a kind of intermediate area in which scenes and characters are embodied and come to life. He connects this to ideas from Bion, primarily Bion's notion of beta- and alpha-elements, as well as his use of Italian narratology. In his conception, the "field" of which analysis is comprised is a "space–time-context, aiming to foster the narration of the stories that represent the 'alphabetization' of the proto-emotions within the couple" (2005, p. 94). All scenes and characters are a function of the field. Authorship can be clearly ascribed to neither the analysand nor the analyst (Ferro mentions the title of Pirandello's play, *Six Characters in Search of an Author*, as providing a kind of allegorical encapsulation of the conditions obtaining in analysis).

Strictly speaking, the ideas developed by Renik do not conform to the field theory template, but Renik does present the analyst as being subject to intersubjective forces (which can be said to define a "field"), forces that are beyond his control but that he can use to his advantage:

> Instead of the analyst as surgeon or reflecting mirror, our guiding metaphor might be the analyst as skier or surfer—someone who allows himself or herself to be acted upon by powerful forces, knowing that they are to be managed and harnessed, rather than

completely controlled. Of course the forces with which an analyst contends in his or her work are internal ones. [1993, p. 565]

The central problem emerging from such conceptions is that they limit what can be examined to that which both partners share and have in common. It follows that the individual and unique elements that are not activated in the intersubjective field become a blind spot. Likewise, otherness is theoretically undefined in these conceptions, and, therefore, is not included as a part of the relationship that is, or should be, examined. Yet, the individual is always more than the contexts in which he or she acts and experiences. Guiding metaphors that highlight or capture or privilege intersubjective organizational principles cause us to lose sight of the self as an autonomous entity which functions independently as author and actor. The individual is also, in reality, more than a mind co-constructed in the "here and now" of the analytic relationship. Taking this into account, Ferro seeks to supplement the conception of analysis as a horizontal field, existing in the here-and-now, with a vertical dimension, encompassing the transgenerational; "this is how time enters the consulting-room" (2005, p. 95). In this way, he attempts to develop a theoretical solution to a problem that faces all intersubjective field theories: how to conceptualize the individual history of the analysand and its determinative power. In so doing, however, he over-extends the field metaphor and falls back on a simple interpretation of the transference of the analysand. It is the temporal dimension that makes the characters three-dimensional: "from different temporal dimensions, demanding or needing, in any event, to be able to come on stage autonomously. At this point any interpretation made within the field becomes a transference interpretation" (ibid.).

Many intersubjective conceptions, especially those stemming from systemic theoretical thought, display a lack of an adequate understanding of the position of the other in an intersubjective relationship. The metaphor of "the one and the other" has been explained conceptually in continental philosophy as a phenomenological dialectic of self and other, and has given rise, more recently, to a number of psychoanalytic concepts. Notably, Lacan, invoking Hegel, Husserl, and Heidegger, described the "I" as being, from the beginning, internally divided. According to Lacan, the "I" can only encounter itself as an other within someone else, as first occurs, in a sense, during the mirror stage. This imaginary intersubjectivity is, however, more or less tied to the moment of mirroring, and the entrance into the symbolic order of language is required in order for this intersubjectivity to gain a foundation, since this foundation can only be based on recognition and communication.

Green (1999, 2000) draws on Hegel in asserting, and accounting for, an inherent human heterogeneity: this heterogeneity, he says, is a product of the alterity of the other. Ultimately, he claims, it is irresolvable: the other never fully merges with his or her function as the one who is the other person's other. Moreover, he also remains an other who is not constituted by this function. For Green, only with the advent of psychoanalysis—with its method of free association, its strategy of unfolding transference, and the analytic situation it created—has alterity become truly comprehensible and tangible. Psychoanalysis is a procedure that allows the self to be understood and returned to itself by way of a detour through the other. Incorporated into Green's conceptualization, alongside Hegel's philosophy of recognition, is Winnicott's mirror theory, according to which the mother provides the child with a mirroring response and, thereby, represents to the child the child's own self.

Conclusion

My deliberations in this chapter have been something of a whirlwind tour through modern psychoanalytic theories; I could not truly do these individual theories justice because I was concerned with one issue that runs broadly through all of them. The main issue I have focused on in my remarks has been the extent to which metaphors and corresponding analogies are used within these theories, and how these metaphors allow researchers to arrive at an understanding of psychological issues that could not be arrived at directly. In addition to their function of aiding understanding, however, metaphors steer and channel thought, and can therefore hide those aspects of the whole that lie outside of a given metaphor's field of meaning. Metaphors always carry an excess of meanings, that is, convey meanings that were not consciously intended to be conveyed by the author, but were perhaps determined pre- or unconsciously. Regardless of whether they were intended or not, however, these meanings are transported and retained by the containing metaphor in such a way that they can variously emerge and take shape over time, even if they were not identified or elaborated on when the metaphor was initially formulated; I have attempted to demonstrate this primarily by pointing to examples of the metaphors of the mirror, potential space, and play, in addition to tracing similar metaphors within the context of intersubjectivity.

CHAPTER THREE

Psychoanalytic theories of personality, adolescence, and the problem of identity in late modernity

Introduction

Social developments have accelerated at such a rapid pace since the 1980s that many cultural theorists have discerned a break in the general course of modernity, so that a new designation is required for our present age. Philosophy and the social sciences continue to struggle to understand and categorize the present. The erosion of social structures through rapid economic and technical developments has led to the dissolution of former identity-guiding social roles and schemata, entities that had previously helped the individual to construct a somewhat coherent identity. Today, lifestyles have become increasingly atomized, as freedom of choice and the right to individuality and self-realization emerge as guiding principles. In *Civilization and its Discontents* (1930a), Freud described how the civilized man of modernity had obtained a greater degree of security by learning to accept limitations to his freedom and to relinquish a good portion of his possibilities for happiness. In contrast, Bauman (1997) takes the view that the "Discontent in postmodernity" arises from individual freedom itself, noting that our values have changed to the point that security, or the desire for security, is regarded primarily as an obstacle in the search for happiness and pleasure. Today, the position once occupied by reassuring identity formations is increasingly assumed by more open, experimental, and sometimes fragmentary self-designs. Indeed, social science researchers have claimed that a new social personality type has emerged: the "protean being", the "modular man", a figure characterized by "drifting" (I am referring here to Bauman, 1997; Giddens, 1999; Rosa, 2005; Sennett, 1998). Ties to places and to other people have started to come undone, as have the long-term commitments they entailed. Despite the scepticism with which a psychoanalyst might regard such descriptions of the modern self, these claims are not without a certain cogency. Psychoanalysis's own image of man has undergone various shifts in emphasis over the past forty years, for instance, from the focus on the autonomy of the ego to object-relations theory and self psychology. The field has also taken a narrative–constructivist turn, and today is experiencing a shift toward the relational and intersubjective. These changes were and are not only the result of clinical and theoretical developments within psychoanalysis, but have also come in response to the evolving position of the individual in late modern society. In the following, I will outline the changes that have been undergone by psychoanalytic concepts, especially in regard to personality development, and I will focus my attention on the evolving understanding of adolescence and identity formation.

Erikson's conception of identity and the autonomy of the ego

Introduced into psychoanalysis by Erikson, identity is a limit-concept that can be defined both sociologically and psychologically. As a psychological concept, "identity" represents the bridge between the intrapsychic and the intersubjective. The concept of identity has the advantage of containing two aspects of the self: the autonomous aspect and the belonging aspect. The concept thereby conjoins internal core structures within the individual with external social structures and concepts, and provides a link between inner personal development and external social development. Erikson traces the sense of a personal identity to two concurrent perceptions: the direct sense of one's own sameness and continuity over time, and the perception that others also recognize this sameness and continuity. In Erikson's view, identity formation is, in fact, linked to a series of human epigenetic developmental stages. Even as a child, one is already trying to find oneself, identifying with primary objects and claiming their characteristics as one's own. For a long time these identifications can remain disconnected or contradictory. However, by late adolescence the individual should have been able to bring about a relatively stable integration.

> The final identity that is fixed at the end of adolescence is superordinated to every single identification with individuals of the past; it includes all significant identifications, but it also alters them in order to make a unique and a reasonably coherent whole of them. [Erikson 1959, pp. 112–113]

Normally, by the end of late adolescence, a stable social, professional, and heterosexual identity has emerged, along with a readiness to assume the responsibilities of a career, enter into relationships, and become a parent. This development is made possible by a sense of affective safety in the individual, which is brought about via the example provided by other adults, and it is spurred on by the testimony of adults that growing up is a meaningful pursuit and that the future holds prospects for adequate satisfaction and fulfilment. The young person, therefore, tries to find a place in society, a "niche", something that is both clearly defined by external structures (or within external social arrangements) and, at the same time, seemingly made just for him. Here, identity is conceptualized as if it were property that one acquires, owns all one's life, and uses in order to progress along a path paved by society. Seen from our current perspective, such a model of stable identity formation seems both antiquated and somehow inadequate. At many points, Erikson's work focuses on, or is based on, observations of American society in the 1950s and 1960s, particularly that portion of society defined as "white middle class"; here, indeed, identity formation among young people followed the kinds of predetermined paths that characterize stable societies. In his model, for the most part, the concept of professional identity is given the greatest weight within the larger concept of identity, and other aspects of identity, such as social or intimate relationships, are accorded little significance in comparison. At some points, however, his definition of identity is much more open and compatible with contemporary concepts. Erikson positioned himself within the framework of American ego psychology, but his conception probably fits better within later notions of self, and within object-relations psychology (Wallerstein, 1998); even though he assumes that individuals, for the most part, achieve a harmonious adjustment, he also recognizes breaks that occur during identity formation, breaks that stem from the affinities and conflicts that arise between nature and culture, the individual and society.

The ego psychology of the time was primarily concerned with the autonomy of the individual and his disentanglement from infantile relationships. Ego psychologists tended to exclude the significance of being recognized by others, and of having a sense of belonging, in the formation and stable maintenance of identity, that is, of the balance between inside and outside, between the self and the world of objects, although these were issues that were central for Erikson. Indeed, proponents of ego psychology dismissed his conception of identity as vague and obscure, and as being more sociological and phenomenological than psychological or psychoanalytic. For ego psychologists, the concept of identity primarily served as a description of an inner coherence of psychic structures and personal identity. Jacobson (1964) understood identity as the capacity to establish and maintain a highly individualized, yet coherent, unity for the entire organization of the psyche, a capacity that must contend with the psyche's increasing structural complexity, as the psyche separates itself from the environment (perceiving itself as different from its surroundings) but still retains the same sense of continuity and purpose. Here, identity hinges on the ability to maintain an optimal secondary autonomy of ego and superego in dealing with reality, drives, and intersystemic conflicts. Just what this unified sense of identity seeks to accomplish, however, is left unspecified by Jacobson, nor is the question posed, as Jacobson is concerned solely with the autonomy of the individual, seeing the goal of development as a disentanglement from dependencies. Erikson's detailed consideration of the anchoring of identity in processes of recognition by significant others and society is absent from Jacobson's conception. Later conceptions of identity, such as those formulated by Kernberg, Modell, Schafer, and G. S. Klein, also concentrate on the stability and inner coherence of the self, issues primarily of importance for patients with severe personality disorders.

In research on adolescents conducted within the context of ego psychology, the concept of identity has also had little impact. Drawing on the work of Mahler, Blos (1979) sees the adolescent process as a second stage of individuation. Mahler conceives òf development as a process of increasing detachment from the mother, with a transition taking place in the small child from dependency to independent functioning. This process continues during adolescence via a gradual inner disengagement from the powerful primary objects. In almost all theories of ego psychology, therefore, self- and identity-development is seen as a break from infantile dependencies, and it is this break, it is thought, that leads to the emergence of an autonomous personality, so that the individual is able to enter into personal and intimate relationships without becoming entangled in larger conflicts of dependency.

Psychoanalytic and social science critiques
of the autonomous subject

Ego psychology's depiction of human development elicited a great deal of psychoanalytic and social scientific criticism in the decades following 1960, during which new developmental concepts led to important modifications of earlier views on adolescence. One such criticism targeted the constraints of its gender specificity, since the then-dominant paradigm of adolescent development was the juvenile male. The exclusion of female development, it was claimed, led to an overemphasis on problems of drive control, rebellion, superego battles, and the significance of adolescent ideologies, while problems of attachment, intimacy, and care were neglected. Further, because, in the account given by ego psychology, autonomy was presented as the goal of development, this account also presented the need for attachment as a residue of childhood dependency and an immature phase of development, but, as Gilligan argued in her 1980s' work on female development (1982, 1988), there is another state, besides independence, that can be thought to lie opposite from dependency, which is isolation. A (perhaps provocatively worded) summary of the differences critics identified between male and female adolescent behaviour (differences because of which, they argued, ego psychology's male-centric account is limited) might go as follows: in order to free themselves (from dependency), boys fight battles in the name of abstract principles of justice, while girls are more likely to be involved in conflicts of loyalty, which they seek to resolve by talking and negotiating in order to maintain relationships; much more so than boys, girls develop an ethics of care that underscores the importance of responsibility and responsiveness in relationships. I will not go further into research on female development, which has been conducted primarily by feminist theorists and by those working in gender research, but it is important to emphasize that, through the integration of aspects of female adolescent development into the general psychodynamic developmental picture, attachment and family belonging have been accorded a greater developmental significance. In response to a concept of development according to which initial dependency is transformed—through processes of detachment and aggressive undernourisment—into autonomy and the capacity for mature adult relationships, a new understanding of development has emerged, and the interchange and competition between these two conceptions has remained fruitful. Within the new conception, relatedness serves as a *leitmotif*, and attachments are seen as continuous (though changing) rather than subject to substitution and termination (through separation) (Gilligan, 1982).

The integration of female development into models of adolescence took place slowly, over the course of decades, while new avenues of investigation stemming from object relations theories, self-psychology, and infant research had a more rapid influence on developmental models and gave rise to a new paradigm. Above all, research in attachment theory shows that adolescent autonomy does not come at the expense of attachment relationships with parents, but, rather, that it develops against the backdrop of secure relationships with them. More specifically, attachment theory anchors the search for autonomy in the exploratory system, whose activation is closely tied to a fundamentally positive relationship to one's parents. The attachment and exploratory system, to which the sexual system is then added, fuel adolescent development. The attachment function of the parent–child relationship is then carried over into new affectively significant and intimate relationships with peers (Allen & Land, 1999; Ammaniti & Sergi, 2003).

Drawing on self psychology, Galatzer-Levy & Cohler (1993) claim, in their far-reaching developmental psychology of the self, that dependency on significant or important others is a constant throughout one's life. Due to social developments in the 1970s and 1980s, they argue, modern adolescence is no longer a phase of uncertain transition, but is, instead, almost entirely socially constructed. Young people are confronted with patterns of behaviour and demands they are expected to fulfil in order to assume the tasks and responsibilities of an adult. Adolescence is also no longer a phase of emotional turbulence, during which the child breaks away from infantile dependency relationships in order to become an independent adult; rather, it has gone from being a phase of chaos to a time of transformation, in which dependencies develop into more mature and complex forms of mutual reliance between growing adolescents and their parents. They argue that the developmental schema of separation and individuation is based on a dogmatic assumption: that object loss is a necessary catalyst for development. Contrary to this assumption, they assert that the separation of an adolescent from their parents is normally not a complete break. Solidarity, not conflict, is what characterizes the relationship between generations of adults, and this solidarity, in most cases, has already begun in late adolescence. Only in certain pathological family structures is the long dominant notion of adolescence as a period of upheaval still valid. Here, complete separation is often the only course that will allow the adolescent to develop successfully. As with self-psychology, modern theorists of intersubjectivity also accuse classical psychoanalytic theorists of viewing human beings as isolated monads who can only be brought into relationships with others secondarily (Mitchell, 2000), and charge that the privileging of independence as a developmental goal reflects cultural norms more than it does the true psychic needs of young people; throughout all developmental phases, they argue, human experience is continuously tied to a constitutive intersubjective context.

There is no doubt that the new intersubjective paradigm has the potential to be enormously fruitful in the effort to understand the development of the self. One drawback of these theories, however, is that they tend towards a rather flattened out view of adolescence and a simplification of its meaning. Indeed, within these theories, fundamental insights into the connections between sexual matura- tion, autonomy, and relatedness are lost or neglected. These theo- ries call the human capacity for inner autonomy into question, and the opposition between individual interests, drive wishes, and social demands—an opposition that arguably provides much of the energy required for individual formation of identity—is largely ignored. The significance and power of instinctual impulses is also doubted, though these impulses, one might argue, are the primary force compelling the adolescent to denounce or reject the former security granted by familial structures, and produce consequences (such as the decentring of the self and even, potentially, the alien- ation of the young person not only from attachment figures, but also from their own body) that are still in striking evidence. In inter- subjective accounts, the role played by these impulses is largely taken over by abstract thought. The acquisition of this capacity in adolescence forces the self into a process of restructuring its world of relations. Moreover, in these theories, adolescence loses its socially innovative function, which stems from generational conflict and the detachment from parental authority, a function that Freud himself was early in emphasizing (1905d).

Transformations in social structure since 1970

As I have argued above, many of the new psychoanalytic theories can only be adequately understood, and their origins and develop- ment accounted for, in the context of certain transformations in social structure that have occurred since the 1970s and 1980s. I would now like to expand my discussion somewhat to consider these social changes themselves. Beginning in the 1980s, an age-defined popula- tion category emerged that, in the quality of its relationship to the rest of the social environment, was and is without historical prece- dent: the category of socially regulated post-adolescence. The post- adolescent does not make a complete transition into adulthood; rather, he or she gains independence socially, mentally, and sexually, yet does so without financial independence: "Maturity is determined here according to the criterion of competent participation in the sphere of consumption, no longer primarily in terms of whether or not one has a job" (Shell-Jugendstudie, 1982, p. 102, translated for this edition). This phase is often prolonged well into one's thirties. Post-adolescence is characterized by three possible constellations or channels of activity: (1) enrolment and participation in extensive training programmes and postgraduate education; (2) unemployment; and (3) involvement in a firmly established alternative or sub-culture within a large city. This latter path, in particular, enables the individual to delay their entrance into adult life, given that a suitable infrastructure has been developed within the alternative community, one that allows members to support themselves without entering the conventional working world.

This social development has complicated the process of identity formation, and made identity disorders harder to diagnose, because this post-adolescent phase itself readily pointed to a sense of ambivalence. This extended ambivalence, in keeping with Bernfeld's conception of prolonged adolescence (1923), it could be a creative moratorium, yet might just as easily become a dead-end psychosocial development in the sense of Erikson's notion of identity diffusion (Bohleber, 1987). Through empirical research, Erikson's student James Marcia (Marcia, 1994, Marcia, Waterman, & Matteson, 1993) then made a surprising observation: In a 1984 study, in which he used his operationalized concept of identity to conduct interviews first undertaken with a group of young adults twenty years earlier in exactly the same way methodologically with a similar group, he found that the percentage of young people and young adults who could be classified as experiencing identity diffusion had increased from 20% in the 1960s to 40% in the 1980s (a state of identity diffusion was assumed if the young person exhibited an avoidance of commitments and had neglected to undergo an active and future-orientated experimental phase). These findings have been confirmed by additional studies (Kraus & Mitzscherlich, 1998). Clearly, the conclusion to draw from this study is not that, in the span of twenty years, young people have become 20% more pathological. Marcia, instead, explained the shift he observed as reflecting a fundamental functional transformation in the processes of identity formation themselves. He argued that a new, unprecedented form of identity diffusion had emerged. To distinguish this form of identity diffusion from more pathological variants, he called it "culturally adaptive diffusion". He considered this diffusion of identity to be a rational (or, at least, tactically advantageous) response to the social conditions young people were encountering, conditions which seemed to favour non-commitment and indifference (in fact, as noted elsewhere, young people in this period did and do take advantage of opportunities, with the difference that, in doing so, they do not close themselves off from other opportunities [Kraus & Mitzscherlich, 1998, p. 160]). Marcia thereby normalized the concept of identity diffusion. These results showed quite clearly that identity development can no longer be considered an epigenetic developmental task that is completed at the end of late adolescence. Instead, it is, to a much greater degree, a never-ending project. Although perhaps the social world confronting young people in the 1950s was a thoroughly organized social world, since the 1970s it has changed dramatically. If the search for one's identity is in part a search for a place in society, then, today, this task is not bound up in any specific life stage, but extends across the entire life process (Keupp et al., 1999).

In order to understand this shift more fully, we have to consider the larger social transformations that have occurred, transformations that have brought about a historical period variously described as "late modernity", "second modernity", and "postmodernity". Rapid economic and technical development have, objectively, led to an expansion in the number of options available for courses of individual action, and have resulted in the dilution, or even the dissolution, of earlier stable identity-guiding social roles and schemata. Reassuringly solid identity formations have been increasingly supplanted by more open, experimental, and fragmentary self-designs. As a result, the number of possible lifestyles has greatly multiplied, and the gender roles that are available have been dramatically altered and made more flexible, developments that allow more scope for processes of reflection and self-discovery. The possibility of greater individualization has added a potent impetus to the pursuit of self-fulfilment and authenticity. These changes are generally understood as processes of social liberation, whereby the individual gains in competence and ability to shape their own life course. At the same time, however, social science research has revealed the contradictions and ambivalences inherent to these changes.

For Michel Walzer (quoted in Keupp et al., 1999), while the advent of these new social opportunities is a positive development in the sense that it more closely aligns society with a state of true freedom, and allows the pursuit of happiness to proceed with fewer constraints, it also has the negative consequence of an increase in feelings of worry and dissatisfaction as transience and uprooted-ness become more widespread and pronounced. Honneth (2002) describes another cost that this access to new opportunities incurs. According to Honneth, precariousness and ambivalence are inher-ent features of individuation in its modern form: while there is an increase in external opportunities and options, the individual is also (and perhaps consequently) expected to achieve more, and to do so alone, whereas in the past, though an individual's actions were more circumscribed, their expected output was more firmly fixed and defined. Moreover, increasingly, there is a tendency towards social isolation, as social networks are, to a growing extent, com-posed of loose connections between anonymous social contacts. All of these developments have intensified the crisis of adolescence since the 1970s. A paradox of this development, Honneth observes, is that the individual's desire for self-realization has increasingly been transformed throughout the past thirty years into an institu-tional demand. While he acknowledges that the working world has become more democratic, the expectations faced by the individual have become more onerous: individuals must present themselves as biographically flexible subjects who are always open to change. This implicit but pervasive demand—that the individual must be himself, or become himself—can become too much for the psyche to bear, and the growing force of this demand, it has been argued, has led to an increase in the occurrence of depressive illnesses (Ehrenberg, 1998).

Ambivalence in the modern individual is further induced as a result of exposure to the standardized identities and biographical models of biographies and identities that are produced by the advertising industry and spread by the media. The individual is conditioned to measure himself against these models, and strives to realize these models in himself. This urge, however, runs against another desire, the desire for originality, so that an internal tension is introduced. Illouz (2006) has examined what we might call the consumption-orientated co-opting of emotions. She argues that the wish for self-realization has been transformed from a personal to cultural category. Personal narratives are now performed and articulated in a broad range of social spaces (self-help groups, talk shows, counselling, therapy, and, most recently, the Internet), and, within these narratives, personal suffering is presented as part of a never-completed process of self-realization. In all of these spaces the self is performed, staged, and realigned. In the past twenty years the public sphere has been transformed into an arena in which psychology helps in putting private life, emotions, and intimacy on display. Private experiences are recast as material for public discussion. The constant demand for self-transformation and self-realization extends into the realm of consumption. Emotions are evaluated, inspected, discussed, negotiated, and quantified. Illouz describes these conditions as creating a state of "emotional capitalism" which pervades all social relations: emotions are verbally managed to an unprecedented degree, and intimate relations become moulded according to standardized models, as a result of which individuals' capacity for closeness in relationships is weakened, and the ability to speak about specific and unique aspects of individual relationships is diminished. The individual's imagination is overrun by standardized constructions spread via the media. The co-opting and exploitation of the emotional sphere, however, is not total. It, too, inherently possesses a dynamics of ambivalence, which the individual can use to reflect upon himself, gain emotional competence and enter into communicative contact with others. Emotional capital serves, then, as a resistant form of self-realization, and cultural techniques for standardizing relationships can lead to the liberation of identity formations. Whether or not this occurs, however, also depends on one's reserves of conscious and unconscious emotional ideas of a future life developed in one's early family environment.

In general, the modern feeling of being "disembedded" (Giddens, 1999) from a stable cultural framework and from an enduring matrix of traditions has led to a diminished sense of security and the rise of social situations that require the individual to assume an attitude of openess. The ambivalence and ambiguity that characterize this experience of disembeddedness create a space in which the adolescent's search for his own path and for innovative and personal solutions for his own identity formation can be successful.

Modern society is not monolithic, but, instead, consists of various subcultures, of rival and conflicting social, cultural, and political movements, each of which seeks to push the larger society in a particular direction. Such social movements can assist adolescents and young people, as these young people pursue their own development, by providing role models and ideals that can be identified with and on to whom wishes can be projected (Frosh, 1991). Wishes, ideas, and convictions can be tested against reality as a result of which they are modified, weakened, or rejected. Once transformed through this interaction, they can be re-internalized by the individual. The diversity and contradictory nature of social forces and tendencies is also reflected in the multiple identity elements that exist in the individual, a multiplicity that works against clear-cut self-definitions. The multiplicity of these movements offers both an opportunity and a risk.

In the light of these observations, the psychological question arises of how an integration of plural identity segments can come about and how the individual is to arrive at a feeling of coherence and integrity. The classic psychoanalytic theories of personality identify the incoherencies and inconsistencies that occur in the human self as the result of conflicts and oppositions between different mental structures, the consequences of which are repression, splitting, and projective identification. However, in order to address the modern problem of identity, further psychoanalytic conceptions of personality are needed that are open to multiple configurations of the self. This is connected to the question of whether the sense of unity of the self is an illusory feeling that we generate because we need it, or whether it should be understood as anchored in a core self that controls the integrity and continuity of the sense of self. In the following, I briefly present four views that address this question.

More recent psychoanalytic theories of the self and identity

For Strenger (1997, 2002), the cultural developments of the last decades have undermined the notion of a biologically predetermined mature personality. In modern liberal societies, he argues, pluralistic frameworks have developed, which, housed in various subcultures, centre on particular ideals of accomplished individuality. The psychoanalytic conception of developmental phases or steps that one is internally compelled along is cast into doubt by Strenger. At present, he argues, a new type of ideal of individuality has come about, one not bound by traditional models of gender roles or of personal identity, but that adheres, instead, to multiple constructions of individuality, life phases, gender roles, sexuality, conceptions of the family, etc. Whereas, previously, self-experimentation was a task of adolescence, enabling the adolescent to find himself and his place in society, today this experimentation has become a standard part of normative life expectations. The search for individuality is now experienced by many people as a fundamental existential need that must be fulfilled in order to give their lives a sense of authorship. Cultural changes are also reflected in the pluralism that now exists among psychotherapeutic schools of thought, manifested, above all, in the rise of constructivist and intersubjective theories. Strenger (perhaps radically) regards these separate therapeutic schools as comprising nothing more than separate cultural traditions, each revolving around their own particular ideal of individuality, with no criteria by which to favour one or the other; there is the Freudian ideal of stoic self-control, the Winnicottian ideal of spontaneity, and the Bionian ideal of the capacity to bear a lack of knowledge. From these psychoanalytic traditions, he observes, cultural and therapeutic practices emerged that helped the individual to shape the self according to the ideal of accomplished individuality contained within each tradition.

Like other postmodern thinkers, with whom he finds himself in agreement in many regards, Bollas (1992, 1995) no longer views the self as phenomenologically unified. One reason for this is the old philosophical insight that we cannot perceive ourselves equally as well as others can. The self needs the object as a counterpart in order to experience itself. The object thereby obtains a subjective meaning, while the self, in turn, is simultaneously processed and transformed by objects. The function of objects is assumed not only by significant others, but also material objects, landscapes, artworks, musical compositions, and works of literature. These objects give shape to the texture of the self. Like Winnicott, Bollas also conceives of the self as a kernel, one's idiom, which has to be released and which we cannot think but only feel and be somewhat vaguely aware of. This core is an innate mental organization, nourished by early themes of identity inscribed by the mother. For Bollas, the theory of id was a crucial first step in conceptualizing an important "itness" to us, our idiom, something that drives consciousness. It is "our mystery" (*ibid.*, 1992, p. 51). This gives rise to an early figuration of the personality that is reliant upon deciphering its personal code through objectifications. Bollas sees dream work as the model for his conception of self-experience. In dreaming, we lose our self in an archipelago peopled by beings, roles, and objects. In a similar fashion, the dream work of one's own life can be understood: "we dream ourselves into being by using objects to stimulate our idiom, to release it into lived experience" (*ibid.*, p. 53). This gives rise to a multiplicity of residues of extended unconscious experiences, which cannot be integrated representationally in the form of an active subject, but, instead, form an organization of the self assembled from thousands of experiences. They cannot be explicated or represented as a unity, but only as a psychic texture. For Bollas, the notion of a unified self is an illusion. He views such a totality as a projection, or at most as a creation assembled from the manifold meanings of the psychic texture. To this degree, a holistic self is always a type of false consciousness stemming from the individual's wish for unification and integration. Bollas turns this long familiar goal of human development on its head. He does not consider the goal to be increasing adjustment to reality, as in ego psychology, but the dissemination of the self into the world of objects. Hence, increasing mental complexity heightens our capacity to "scatter our being throughout the object world" (*ibid.*, p. 65) and to seek objects that stimulate one's own idiom.

While Bollas proceeds from the assumption of a core self with an inherent unconscious message that can only unfold and be experienced in the world of objects, other conceptions deny that the self has any essentialist character and instead think that it has a narrative structure. This story forms the interpretative framework for the understanding of human existence. The self is either itself narratively structured, or it subjects its experience to a deferred narrative structuring. The findings of cognition research support the notion that the self can support itself on a protonarrative structuring of non-verbal actions and events (Bruner, 1990; Polkinghore, 1998; Stern, 1995). In this way, the self shapes the actions and events into

a temporal whole in the form of a story. For the subject, it assumes
the function of lending meaning to one's own actions and life experiences, while also providing the self with an integrating identity.
Attachment research has provided interesting confirmations of this
(Dornes, 1998; Fonagy, 1996). Using the Adult Attachment Interview, it was found that, despite her own bad childhood experiences, a mother's capacity to narrate a coherent, plausible, and
emotionally balanced story about her experiences with her own
mother can be taken as a prognosis for her ability to enable her own
child to develop a secure attachment. For Schafer (1976, 1992) this
narrative construction is not a reflexive procedure that first comes
about after the fact; instead, human experience is *a priori* verbally
and narratively constructed and we have no access to its underlying reality. Language creates the world of which it speaks (as in
Spence, 1982). Further, Schafer does not believe in a unified, lasting
self that can be experienced directly, without mediation by language and narrative. His criticism of existing notions of the self and
identity centres on their essentialist character. The self is not a
concrete mental formation, which exists in nature and might somehow be directly observed, either objectively or empathetically;
rather, it is a construction built by observers in the form of narration. This gives rise to not one, but an entire series of different
stories about a cast of various selves. The plurality of narrative
selves is bound together by the subject, who acts as narrator. As if
condensed to an Archimedean point, this subject as narrator then
represents the whole. The more a story meets the criteria of stability, coherency, and comprehensibility, the more it reflects a person's
identity. Self-narratives assume the function of mental integration,
but no longer culminate in a notion of the self as an organic whole.

Modern intersubjective theories also see individuality as something that emerges from the interaction of two or more subjectivities. The paradigm of these theories stems from modern infant
research, which considers the self to be created in the interaction
between mother and child, with its structural formation dependent
upon the success of "matching", in other words the fit between
mother and child. Both in infancy and in the course of further
development, the experience of the self cannot be separated from
the intersubjective fields in which it is always embedded. Therefore,
intersubjective theories do not assume a self that becomes unified

and autonomous in late adolescence, as this would require it to remove itself from its intersubjective relatedness to such an extent that it could be independent of them. For these theorists, this would lead to a return of the conception of an "isolated mind" that they so fiercely battled in countering the ego psychology school of psychoanalysis. Instead, they speak of multiple selves, which are activated according to a given situation. Here, the synthesizing function of the ego, the trend towards unification in which Freud found the power of Eros to be at work, has become fundamentally obsolete or deemed an illusion. Readily apparent, however, is the impact of postmodern thought, which is based on the assumption that we can never ascertain reality with absolute certainty, but that we only have constructions of it at our disposal, which vary according to the perspective and context of the observer. For Howell, for instance, the self is "plural, variegated, polyphonic, and multivoiced" (2005, p. 38). In her view, humans' intersubjective–relational perspective is most readily connected to the notion of a dissociative mind. Indeed, not only the traumatized mind, but the human mind *per se* is of a dissociative nature: "The relational self and the dissociative mind are interlocking constructs" (*ibid.*, p. 3). In keeping with this view, dissociation also advances from a cause and marker of polypsychism to becoming a main mechanism supplanting repression. Seen as models, intersubjective approaches assume horizontally ordered self-states, separated by dissociation. In this respect, dissociation represents the possibility for remaining in a relationship, while also allowing for separation from other relational self-states. However, dissociation can also be a pathological defence mechanism that leads to the collapse of relationality. In the model of classical psychoanalysis, however, psychic processing is ordered vertically. Undesirable parts of the self that cannot be integrated into a unified self are repressed and pushed into the unconscious. Mental integration, as conceptualized in ego psychology models of personality, is criticized by Howell as "monolithic". At most, integration consists of a "harmonious interaction among the multiple self-states" (2005, p. 218).

Thus far, I have presented some of the more recent psychoanalytic theories of the personality, which emphasize the complexity and plurality of the self and its unity, even if only recognized, if at all, as an illusion that is psychologically necessary. Either the self shrinks into a kernel that scatters itself in objectifications or a wide range of narrations, or it consists, at best, of a not entirely contradictory ensemble of self-states. As different as they are, these theories reflect the changes people have gone through in late modernity and have, thereby, greatly removed themselves from the notion in ego psychology of an autonomous and relatively integrated personality as the ultimate goal of development. But has the "the trend towards unification, towards synthesis" of the ego (Freud, 1926e, p. 196) really become obsolete to the extent that these theories of personality would have us believe? The search for coherency and stability, and the related question of one's own identity, can be easily settled theoretically, but, in practice, it remains a problem, primarily for those in late adolescence and for young adults. I will now turn to a conception of identity that attempts to address the questions raised here.

The concept of identity today: autonomy vs. relatedness

I shall sketch the outline of a modern conception of identity in connection with the adolescent restructuring of the personality. To me, the concept of identity has the advantage of taking note of a subject that has to engage with contingency, difference, and alterity, experiences that lead an individual to be concerned with developing a coherent and stable sense of self. Indeed, identity is based on a person's experiences of crisis, which force the individual to assure himself of his sense of self. The prototype of such an experience is adolescence. This phase represents a convergence of many of the problems we have already addressed, not only those facing the individual, but also psychoanalytic theory itself.

First, however, I would like to return to Erikson's concept of identity, which Wallerstein (1998) has subjected to a recent re-evaluation. He demonstrates that Erikson formulated his concepts in the language of ego psychology, though they did not really fit within it. With the demise of ego psychology, he argues, Erikson's concept of identity was also damned to psychoanalytic limbo, in which it remains to this day, despite its central relevance for the theoretical architecture of contemporary psychoanalysis; indeed, his notion of identity is a precursor of modern theories of object relations and the self, as well as of intersubjective approaches in psychoanalysis. When freed from its ego psychological limitations and the then current essentialist understanding of the self and identity, his concept of identity can be seen to include a modern theoretical notion of object relations and intersubjectivity. Such an updated concept of identity, if further developed and purged of substantialist elements, might help us to do justice to the problem of the self in late modernity. Although Erikson thought of identity as the creation of an individual and rather integrated whole, at the same time he also emphasizes the importance of the recognition of significant others. Both dimensions, self-definition and relatedness, as well as their dialectical interaction, are implicitly included in his model of identity (cf. Blatt & Levy, 2003).

The experience of identity takes place as an inner process of comparison of images of the self or patterns of action, which are then examined to see if they can be considered as being compatible with fundamental self-representations. This inner process is based on the capacity for self-reflection. In recent years, its emergence has been depicted in depth, primarily in the work of Fonagy, Gergely, Jurist, and Target (2002) on mentalization. Mentalization is based on the intersubjective exchange between mother and child, in which a preverbal regulation of affect is apparent in their mirroring interactions. When the mother mirrors the affective state of the child in her behaviour and expression, she simultaneously marks it through distinguishing features of perception such as nodding her head, raising the pitch of her voice, etc., which help the child to recognize it as a reflected emotional "as-if" expression of his self and to distinguish it from a direct self-expression of his mother. In the mother's conspicuous mirroring of the child's inner state, the child is prepared for the knowledge that the mother symbolically represents his or her intention. In this way, the capacity is developed within human development for reflecting actions, feelings, and thoughts. They are not only experienced directly, however, as the child learns to think of himself or herself as a being who feels and thinks. The reflexive capacity of the self forms the core of its structure, thereby also eliciting a rudimentary feeling of identity. This basic form could be summarized with the idea of "I am that which my mother sees in me". This is a reflection of one's own self in an object that is, in turn, connected to an act of recognition by the object. In this respect, identity is always founded intersubjectively and is also internalized as just such a reflective dialogue.

Thus, while self-reflection and a sense of identity are formal structural capacities, they also bear the imprint of the early relationship between mother and child and its subsequent history. This stems from the fact that the mother's reflection of the child's intentions also contains her conscious and unconscious perceptions about her child, for whom they become a deep-seated identity theme which is inscribed into the self as a motif for self-expression (Laplanche, 1992; Lichtenstein, 1977; Winnicott, 1971).

Building on this basic structure, I define identity as an ever-incomplete psychic construction that consists of reflective processes of comparison. Here, the central representations of the self are compared with social roles, actions, feelings, narratives, and dreams. While self-representations are indeed organized psychodynamically in an interactive, generalized context and shaped by its transmitted meaning, they are not confined to it. In this respect, the formation of identity is a deferred act, which is preceded by an external or internal mental action. The ego thereby oscillates between central self-representations and ideas cathected in a trial identification in order to determine whether, and to what degree, a sense of identity can be brought about. The superego and ego ideal also take part in this examination, which can become conflictual if unconscious contents are also touched upon. The criteria in this process of comparison are again the maintenance of coherency, stability, and integrity. This structure of identity work is related to Winnicott's notion of transitional space, in that it assumes a medial position between the inner world and external reality and belongs to both. Bollas (1992) expresses a similar idea in stating that we are all "intermediates". In this sense, identity work is a regulatory activity of the ego, which seeks to create a balance between external expectations, social roles and expectations, and inner reality, identifications, and the derivatives of unconscious fantasies and idiosyncratic basic experiences. Identity is, thereby, also related to the unconscious as the Other and the non-identical. The sense of identity attempts to control the hierarchical organization of self-representations and to regulate the dynamic processes at work between the ego, id, and superego; it can, however, also be passively subjected to them and go missing for a time, when an experience becomes foreign and incapable of integration (Gedo, 1986). The process of inner balancing is based on an affectively anchored pre-representational sense of a core self that, in essence, is made up of preverbal experiences of mother–infant interactions and information from inside the body, particularly from biologically based affects. This affective core self "guarantees our continuity across development in spite of the many ways we change" (Emde, 1983, p. 165). Basic experiences, especially if conditioned by trauma, can also assume the character of an identity theme that the individual will have to work through for a lifetime. This inner balancing is also founded on a lifelong basic polarity between "being together-with" and "being distinct from" (Sander, 1995). From infancy onward, interactive regulations and self-regulating processes remain linked throughout our entire lives (Beebe & Lachmann, 2002). Blatt and Levy (2003) also emphasize the synergistic interdependence of the two fundamental developmental processes of relatedness and self-definition.

While a sense of identity is the leading regulatory principle shaping the experience of identity, it also results from it. (I have described the feeling of identity and its development in detail in Bohleber [1992]) If we view a sense of identity as the result of such an inner balance, we no longer reify it as an ever-available consciousness of a unified whole or tie it to a self-representation that it might somehow engender. Rather, the experience of identity is much more a means of giving a specific form to the relationship with one's own self and its objects. It proceeds as a dialogical process of comparison, in which the subject allows its self to "pass through" the object, so to speak, and reflects this operation metacognitively on a higher level. Zima (2000) also conceives of identity as, in essence, dialogical, requiring an encounter with the other in order to prevent the subject from becoming overly rigid or from being absorbed and lost within the other. Instead of a feeling of identity, we should perhaps refer to it as a sensation, since this feeling is fleeting and purely of the moment, so that, in order for it to be sensed, a repetition of the inner process of comparison is necessary. Lichtenstein calls this the "dilemma of human identity":

> Identity as experience of the pure actuality of being remains indefinable, unworldly. Any definable identity requires that we

perceive ourselves as objects, which means equating identity with the identity given to us as social roles, losing thereby the sense of identity as pure actuality of being. A psychological study of the problem of human identity must accept this dilemma as the basic phenomenon of human identity. [1977, p. 166]

For Lichtenstein, the two types of identity experience are mutually exclusive, as only one can ever be available at any one time. I disagree, however, and find that, at its core, identity is, in fact, the result of a comparison. Metaphorically speaking, while Lichtenstein places identity experience solely on one side of the scale, I position it in the middle as a process of balancing. Such a definition of identity does not allow for concretely conceiving of the unity of the subject, nor for deconstructing it as an illusion. Instead, this definition enables us to think of identity as a process seeking and resulting in an inner equilibrium, in which the subject appears as an open system of relations whose attempts at mental integration go on for a lifetime.

Conclusion

First, this survey of developments in psychoanalytic theory throughout the past forty years shows how mental development has been increasingly located within an interpersonal matrix, a shift set in motion by object relations psychology, attachment theory, and research in infant development. If the goal of development in ego psychology was considered to be the autonomy of the mature personality, then today such notions have been displaced by the recognition of the lifelong embeddedness of the self, as well as its development in satisfying interpersonal relationships. The two are dialectically related. The concept of identity provides a commensurate description of this complex organization of the self in its developmental stages by its poles of autonomy and relatedness.

Second, within psychoanalysis, individuation and the formation of identity through the severing of infantile dependencies once represented a central theoretical principle. Although theoretical developments have departed from this position, it is still often evident as a conceptual model in the implicit theories psychoanalysts employ in discussions or publications of case material. Thus, it is said, for example, that separation leads to self-reliance and external and inner autonomy. Further, in late adolescence, it is held that separation becomes "dominant as a vital need". Likewise, reference is made to the necessity of a repeated break from parental objects. Metaphorically, this gives rise to the perception that the inner representation of one's own self has to separate itself from parental object representations in order to gain greater self-understanding. Yet, it would seem that recent insights into early development and the resulting developmental paradigms demonstrate that "separation" has long been idealized by psychoanalytic developmental theory as a path to inner autonomy and led to an overemphasis on aggression involved in processes of separation. Of course, it is precisely in late adolescent identity conflicts that we often find a basic disorder resulting from an unsuccessful early separation from the primary object; later, these patients are often unable to adequately distance their self-representation from their primary object's area of influence. They are left with a very limited capacity to play with independent self-conceptions in "transitional space" (Winnicott) and to then try them out in external reality in order to gradually acquire a more stable sense of identity. Yet, apart from this basic disorder, is it not often the case that what we have to deal with is not a separation from parental figures, but, rather, a transformation of inner object relations? And could not such a revised theoretical conceptualization, with a notion of identity that does not have to play off "to be alone with oneself" against "belonging to", help us to more fully understand many late-adolescent conflictual structures?

Third, in our globalized world, migration has become the fate of many, forcing those affected to bid farewell to their former way of life, remove themselves from their interpersonal and cultural embeddedness, and adapt to, and integrate within, a new social context. Usually, they are subjected to a type of culture shock and an increasing feeling of identity discontinuity, as the confirmation provided by their familiar environment, which is so crucial to identity, is at first absent (Garza-Guerrero, 1974). New self-representations come about, which at first cannot be integrated with the old and often exist split off from each other. The experience of identity oscillates between these representations. If, at first, the old ones provide more affective support, in time this will be inverted, especially if the old experience of identity is not idealized in memory. Gradually, an experience of identity can emerge that rests upon an integration of the old self-representations with the new. Theoretical difficulties arise, however, if identity is seen as analogous to a substantial unity; in that case, reference is made to a "solid hybrid unity" or a "mixed-identity", or the new identity is viewed as a loose aggregation of various selves (see Akhtar, 1999). If identity is not reified but, instead, understood as a process, one in which the feeling of identity, based on a core self, results from a process of comparison and balancing between central self-representations and other representations, social roles, actions, and external objects, then such a concept of identity can help us to more adequately theorize and understand the psychic transformations that many people have to go through in a globalized world.

PART II

TRAUMA, MEMORY, AND HISTORICAL CONTEXT

CHAPTER FOUR

The development of trauma theory in psychoanalysis

Introduction

The catastrophes of the twentieth and twenty-first centuries, wars, the Holocaust, racist and ethnic persecution, as well as the increase in social violence and the newly developed awareness of violence in families, and maltreatment and sexual abuse of children, have made the development of a theory and technique of traumatization and its consequences an urgent task in psychoanalysis.

On the one hand, we are faced by the task of gaining as comprehensive an understanding as possible of the destruction and consequences of violence and traumatization; on the other, the therapeutic concepts of psychoanalysis have to be re-examined to determine the extent to which they are suitable for the treatment of trauma.

For a long time, trauma and its consequences, political and social violence, was not accorded the status that it should have been in psychoanalysis. Clinical and theoretical assessments of it were often characterized by a peculiar ambivalence. One of the main reasons for this is that clinical theory in psychoanalysis increasingly focused on the here and now of the transference–countertransference relationship and thus on the meanings that unfold in the psychoanalytic encounter within the treatment situation. The current intersubjective, constructivistic, and narrative theories conceive of the perception of oneself and of the outside world as being complex and undetermined. Their meaning is created anew in the intersubjective relationship between the analyst and the patient. Thus, experience is regarded as an ongoing intersubjective and interpretative process. Childhood experiences and the determining force of the past become vague for the most part. The physicality of all human experience also disappears, for it cannot be totally subsumed by a model of social constructivism, nor can it be defined entirely in terms of social and intersubjective categories. This one-sidedness of postmodern intersubjective theories becomes especially evident in the treatment of trauma, for the trauma breaks through the protective shield that is formed by the psychic texture. It is indelibly recorded in the body and has a direct effect on the organic substrate of mental functioning. The quality that is specific to trauma, which has to be adequately described in psychological terms, lies in the structure of the perceptual processes and of the affects as well as in the experience that the psychic space has been broken through and symbolization is destroyed. The traumatic experience is essentially one of "too much".

This brief overview already gives an indication of where one emphasis will lie in my presentation of the development of theories about trauma, which is in the conjunction of hermeneutic and psycho-economic conceptualizations. The question of what forms the core of the traumatic experience psychologically is another main concern of this chapter. Trauma and its consequences have met with increasing scientific interest in psychoanalysis in recent years. The psychoanalytic literature on trauma has grown so much in the meantime that I cannot even begin to attempt to give a complete overview of the works on trauma theory. My choice of literature is guided by the emphasis I have chosen for my discussion; I will not be able to deal with works that are concerned more specifically with issues involved in the treatment of trauma patients.

Sigmund Freud and the development of a psycho-economic model of trauma

During the early period of his practice, in the treatment of female patients who had developed hysterical symptoms, Freud was confronted with episodes of sexual seduction in the post-puberty phase of their development. In his estimation, however, these episodes were not sufficient to explain the illness. His patients' accounts of having been sexually seduced in childhood led Freud to assume that a pre-pubertal sexual trauma was involved, a genital stimulation of the child by an adult, but which it could not experience as sexual. It was not until a second seduction after puberty and sexual maturation, with the ability to experience it as such in the meantime, that the early experience now took on meaning, in a deferred action (*nachträglich*). It is through the association with the acute experience and the overstimulation that this first experience develops its traumatic effect, which forces the individual to defend against remembering it and make it unconscious. If this defensive process fails, a hysterical symptom formation opens up as a way out.

According to Blass and Simon (1994), Freud always had doubts about his seduction theory. What seemed to be a sudden withdrawal of his theory had by no means been a sharp break and shift, they claim. Freud's theoretical thinking was more like a serpentine path that was traversed only with great difficulty over the course of twenty years. For a long time, Freud continued to be plagued by the problem of whether a seduction had actually taken place. In his letter to Fliess on 21 September 1897 (Freud, 1985, pp. 265ff), he mentions a number of reasons that caused him to give up his theory of seduction: for one thing, he was not having the success in his analyses that he had anticipated with this explanation; for another, the frequency of hysterical neuroses would force him to go back and conclude that there was massive widespread sexual abuse in families. The third reason that Freud mentions lies in the nature of the unconscious material itself. Since there are no indications of reality in the unconscious, he says, there is also no way to distinguish between truth and fiction that has been cathected with affect. Consequently, he was forced to assume that his female patients' accounts did not involve real experiences, but fantasies. This turn in his theory is said to have come about as a result of his discovery of the Oedipus complex and unconscious fantasies. Blass and Simon (1994) contend more precisely, and rightly so, that, contrary to this generally purported assumption, it was not the discovery of Oedipal fantasies that was the decisive reason, but the realization that a fantasy may be perceived as a reality, and that fantasies can have the same influence on us as real events. As a result, Freud had to proceed from the assumption of a rather complex interaction of evidence, theorizing, and fantasy, both in himself and in his patients.

Even though Freud characterized the change in his theory as a "collapse of everything valuable" (Freud, 1985, p. 266), this formulation did not correspond to his clinical reality. Grubrich-Simitis (1987) speaks in terms of a countercathexis against the trauma model; indeed, Freud "catapulted himself away from it". In reality, however, she says the newly found drive model and the trauma model were not antagonistic, but mutually complementary. Again and again in his writings Freud comes back to the traumatic genesis, and also to sexual abuse, which he never gave up as one of the causes of neurotic illnesses. As Grubrich-Simitis emphasizes, Freud was always afraid that the trauma model, which was more agreeable by comparison, might be inclined to jeopardize the radically new, forever disagreeable, and more difficult, more improbable drive model.

As Freud now saw it, "in the world of the neuroses it is psychical reality which is the decisive kind" (1916–1917, p. 368). He came to the conclusion that a traumatization could also emanate from internal sources. He regarded some phase-specific infantile drive manifestations, anxieties, and conflicts as prototypical internal conditions that could infuse an experience with traumatic consequences under certain external circumstances. The First World War forced Freud and his followers to deal once again with the traumatic neurosis and the pathogenic effect of factors in the outside world. A psycho-economic dimension came to the fore:

> It is as though these patients had not finished with the traumatic situation, as though they were still faced by it as an immediate task which has not been dealt with; and we take this view quite seriously. It shows us the way to what we may call an *economic* view of mental processes. [*ibid.*, p. 275]

In *Beyond the Pleasure Principle* (1920g), he developed this view further through the model of the shield against stimuli (*Reizschutz*). This shield is broken through in the traumatic experience, in which the onslaught of quantities of excitation is too great to be mastered and psychically bound. The mental apparatus regresses to more primitive modes of reaction. The compulsion to repeat revives the traumatic experience in an effort to abreact the excitation in this way, or to bind it psychically and thus reactivate the pleasure principle again. But the trauma is not just a disturbance of the libidinal economy, it is also a radical threat to the integrity of the subject (Laplanche & Pontalis, 1988). In *Inhibitions, Symptoms and Anxiety* (1926d), Freud describes the ego as being absolutely helpless in view of an unbearable excitation in the traumatic situation. The ego, which normally develops an anxiety signal when in danger, is now flooded by automatic anxiety. A traumatic situation can occur due to excessive internal instinctual demands as well as external, real experiences. However, Freud never precisely defined the relationship between the external event and the internal processes. What was decisive was the "too much", the excess stimulation and a paralysed ego, which was not able to discharge the accumulation of excitation or to bind it mentally.

Fenichel (1937, 1945) also defines trauma as an excessive quantity of excitation that cannot be bound, so that the traumatic effect of an event depends on how unexpectedly it occurs. In addition to discharge and binding, anxiety is central to Fenichel's model of trauma. Traumatically excessive anxiety, real anxiety, and conscience anxiety represent a genetic series of development, and the psychoneuroses are derived from the traumatic neurosis in this way. The more psychic energy has to be invested to uphold earlier repression, the less the ego can bind quantities of excitation and the more susceptible it is to traumatization. In a state of helplessness, the ego regresses to a more primitive passive–receptive form of coping with reality. Fenichel created a purely psychoeconomic model of discharge for trauma, in which the traumatic situation is then conceptualized only as an excessive quantity of excitation. Whereas, in Freud's theory, the object was at least still present as one that was missing in the ego's traumatic state of helplessness, with Fenichel, anxiety and helplessness are all there is, which he sees as shutting down the overwhelming flood of stimuli.

In the theoretical discussion of psychoanalysis during the time thereafter, trauma became marginal in relation to the drive-related conflicts and the fixations of the libido. Works that had to do with trauma confirmed Freud's formulations, but did not go beyond that. (Furst [1967] provides a more detailed presentation of these works.) It was not until the studies on the early development of the child since the 1950s that new insights on the conception of trauma came to light.

Ferenczi and the development of an object relations model of trauma

One exception in this development was Sándor Ferenczi. He was convinced that the traumatic element in the pathogenesis of the neuroses was being neglected. The disregard for external factors, he contended, led to wrong conclusions and premature explanations based on inner dispositions of the neurotic phenomena. It was the change in his therapeutic stance that enabled Ferenczi to gain a deeper understanding of traumatic disorders. He gave up a distanced analytic stance because he realized that with traumatized patients in certain situations it is therapeutically necessary to be absolutely honest, to admit mistakes, and also to reveal one's own feelings. Ferenczi recognized the effect of lies and deceit as a traumatizing factor and the danger of this being repeated in the therapeutic situation. The trust created through this honesty is what makes the difference from the traumatogenic past and enables it to be worked on therapeutically. For Ferenczi, consequently, it is not just the relationship to the object that has a traumatogenic effect, but also, and in particular, the communication embedded in it: disappointment, breach of trust, and denying or trivializing what has happened create a feeling of insecurity in the child with respect to what it has perceived. The words of the traumatizing love-object and language are assigned a significant role here as traumatogenic factors. Ferenczi anticipated many later insights that were gained in trauma research: the destructive effect of the trauma, which produces a dead ego fragment and agony; the enactment, by means of which a trauma is expressed in treatment; the splitting of the ego into an observing agency and a relinquished body; the numbing

and the blocking of affects, and, especially, the effect of the aggressor's silence and speechlessness on the traumatized child. Ferenczi
further described an emergency reaction by the child, who, in its
tremendous fear, helplessness, and defencelessness, is forced to
identify with the aggressor for its own inner survival. Above all, his
work on the "Confusion of tongues between adults and the child"
(1933) is an analysis of traumatic disorders that is still modern, but
met with a lack of understanding and rejection within the psychoanalytic community of the time and was long disregarded.
Ferenczi's studies on external traumatizing conditions and their
internalization by the individual were forgotten for a long time.

* * *

Since the 1950s, psychoanalysts have been examining deficient
conditions in the early mother–child interactions and their traumatic effect on the child, and various terms have been introduced
for this: "strain trauma" (Kris, 1956; Sandler, 1967), "silent trauma"
(Hoffer, 1952), "cumulative trauma" (Khan, 1963), "deprivation
trauma" (Bowlby, 1973). All of these studies moved the child's
objects and relationship to them into the centre of attention.
However, this posed the risk of an overly broad concept of trauma
that could be applied to all kinds of deficits in the mother–child
relationship, thus jeopardizing its specificity.

With the development of object relations theories, other model
conceptions entered the discussion. The so-called one-person psychology and purely quantitative considerations about an unbearable quantity of excitation flooding the ego were rejected. It was no
longer a single event, such as an accident, that is the paradigm;
rather, the object relationship becomes the basis for trauma theory.
Balint (1969) was the first to follow in Ferenczi's footsteps and describe it in those terms. Whether or not an event or a situation has a
traumatic effect depends on whether an intensive relationship
existed between the child and the traumatogenic object. The object
relationship itself thus acquires a traumatic character. This view of
the way in which childhood traumata occur proved to be very fruitful. As confirmed by later studies (Steele, 1994), in cases of maltreatment or abuse it is not primarily the physical injury to the child that
causes the traumatic disorder; rather, the most pathogenic element

is that of being mistreated or abused by the person whom one actually needs for protection and care. Moreover, this object relations theoretical approach also opened up the view that, in the case of a severe traumatization, it is not just the internal object relationship that is damaged or falls apart, but also the internal, protecting, safety-providing communication between self- and object representations. This gives rise to islands of traumatic experiences that are encapsulated and / or split off from internal communication.

From the scotomization of sexual abuse to the recovered memory debate

Although psychoanalysts dealt with the pathogenic effects of developmental deficits in children, the traumatic reality of sexual abuse and incest was largely disregarded. The reasons for failing to give adequate consideration to traumatic phenomena in psychoanalytic treatment have to do with scientific methodology and practice. Analytically, it proved difficult to distinguish between unconscious fantasies and repressed memories. This lack of differentiation then made it difficult to perceive the reality character of childhood experiences and to acknowledge the influence of traumatizations. Another reason for the reservations about regarding memories as storing life experiences was that psychoanalysis, but also cognitive psychology, had repeatedly shown how much perception is infused with fantasies and wishes, and how memories are always reworked, depending in part on the context in which they emerge into consciousness (Person & Klar, 1994). This is why the attention of most psychoanalysts was focused on examining the unconscious fantasies as well as the libidinal wishes contained in them, and on how these organize the clinical phenomena and the narrative of the patient. These observations, however, have to be supplemented in order to explain the long and persisting theoretical and clinical neglect of sexual abuse. Among the ranks of the psychoanalysts, to a large extent the concern prevailed that dealing with real incest could put the central role of the Oedipus complex in question. The oedipally orientated presumptions on the part of many analysts then meant that, in cases of patients who had experienced sexual abuse, attention tended to focus more on the child's seductive behaviour than on what the adult had done to the child. Furst (1967) noted, as a result of several studies on children's experiences with incest, that they had condoned, provoked, or even offered themselves for the sexual contact with adults. Moreover, they had rarely suffered from guilt feelings or emotional disorders because of it. A similar view can already be found in the writings of Abraham (1907a,b), who assumed in cases of patients suffering from hysteria that, as an effect of traumatophilia, they had unconsciously provoked a sexual trauma when they were children. According to Good (1995), Abraham wanted to develop Freud's views about infantile sexuality further and find an explanation for those cases in which a sexual trauma had actually taken place. This caused him to have a conflict with Freud. Abraham later relativized his position.

Since the 1980s, there has been a change of attitude within the psychoanalytic community with regard to the question of sexual abuse and the treatment of incest victims. Clinical practice has done more to deal with this kind of traumatization, research on it, its theoretical formulation, and therapeutic treatment. An increasing number of studies on this subject have appeared in the psychoanalytic literature (Hirsch, 1987; Kluft, 1990; Kramer & Akhtar, 1991; Levine, 1990; Shengold, 1989; Sugarman, 1994).

In recent years, a scientific and socio-political debate has developed, especially in the USA, about the validity of memories of a childhood trauma, especially if these reappear in the course of a psychotherapy after having been repressed for a long time in adulthood. The scientific debate revolves around the question, among others, of whether there is a special traumatic memory in which memories are preserved differently from those in the explicit autobiographical memory. This idea has been advanced in particular by van der Kolk and his colleagues in various studies (summarized in van der Kolk, 1996). According to this theory, traumatic experiences are encoded specifically due to the hyperarousal. Integration and interpretation with the help of the semantic memory is interrupted, and the experience is stored as a state of affect, as somatic sensations, as smells, sounds, and as visual images. The result is a non-symbolic, inflexible, and unalterable content of traumatic memory. Its reappearance depends on the occurrence of certain stimuli that are associated with the original traumatic scene. One aspect of van der Kolk's hypothesis that remains contradictory regards the extent to which these traumatic memories are "etched onto the mind" (1996, p. 297) and cannot be changed through later experience.

Although comprehensive research has been done in the meantime on the question of forgetting and remembering again, the scientific problems in this area are extremely complicated and there is currently no consensus about how a forgotten or repressed memory can come back again, and whether traumatic memories are processed differently. A more detailed criticism of the hypothesis of a special traumatic memory can be found in Brenneis (1997), and in Fonagy and Target (1997). Although it is generally agreed that traumatic memories can be forgotten, one of the main arguments against the assumption of a special traumatic memory is that the essential content of traumatic events in the majority of cases is most definitely remembered by means of the autobiographical memory. Generally speaking, peripheral details are forgotten and distorted (Schacter, 1996). This is also true of early memories, which may go back as far as the third year of life. It also does not seem very likely that sensory fragments that are stored or encoded in the implicit memory are exact replicas of the earlier experience. Rather, it has to be assumed that these memories are not invariable, and are subject to mental processing.

A reconstruction of traumatic experiences from such re-emerging sensory impressions, images, enactments, and affective states through the therapist, which then reactivate memories of forgotten experiences with sexual abuse in the patient, entails many imponderables and unverified assumptions unless it is backed by extra-therapeutic confirmations: (1) there can be no perfect fit between the explicit, autobiographical memory and the implicit memory; (2) memory is vulnerable to suggestive influences that need not even be consciously exerted; (3) still debatable are the observations presented by Brenneis (1997), as well as Fonagy and Target (1997), that, in the case of all recovered memories of sexual abuse reported in the psychoanalytic literature, there are no confirmations that go beyond that or are brought by the patient from outside the therapy (also see Good, 1994). Kluft (1999) contradicts this emphatically, citing his own published case material, among others, for which external confirmations exist. (4) Some psychoanalytic case reports on individuals who report abuse also make questionable assumptions. In them, traumatic memories are attributed a special quality that allows their historical reality to be recognized. This special quality is found by Davies and Frawley (1994) to lie in the dissociative states: the "therapist must accept, work with, and even encourage the dissociated states into which the patient enters during treatment. It is through these states that the truth unfolds" (p. 94). For Person and Klar (1994), the intensive affect-charged quality of these memories, their visual and sensory form, as well as their invariability, are signs that they are true. Such assumptions can lead to illusory conclusions, especially if no alternative hypotheses are considered. Therapist and patient then come to agree that certain memories are authentic, whereas in reality it is a matter of screen memories (see Good, 1994, 1998). The fact that there is presumably no such thing as a specific traumatic memory whose contents come closer to historical reality can lead one to withdraw entirely from historical reality and confine oneself to the notion that only a psychic reality is to be found behind the recovered memories. Fonagy and Target (1997) write, "There can be only psychic reality behind the recovered memory—whether there is historical truth and historical reality is not our business as psychoanalysts and psychotherapists" (p. 216). In other words, they go to the opposite extreme and classify the distinction between fantasy and reality, which is so important with regard to trauma, as irrelevant.

War neuroses

At the International Psycho-Analytical Congress at Budapest in 1918, a symposium was held on the psychoanalysis of war neuroses, with papers by Ferenczi, Abraham, Simmel, and Jones. These were published in 1919, and Freud wrote an introduction to them in which he speaks of an ego conflict between the old, "peaceful ego" and the new, "warlike ego". The former feels that its life is threatened by the rashness of the latter. Because of this "shape assumed by the ego itself", that which is feared, and is an external force in the case of the traumatic neuroses, becomes an "internal enemy", none the less (Freud, 1919d). After the outbreak of the Second World War, Kardiner reassessed his experiences and observations in the treatment of war veterans from the First World War and published them in 1941. The nucleus of the traumatic neurosis, he claimed, is a physioneurosis, with a chronic extreme physiological excitation. Further characteristics are a fixation on the trauma, with an altered conception of the self in relation to the world, an atypical dream world (nightmares with threats of destruction, dreams with little symbolic content, with guilt reactions), ego constrictions, chronic irritability, startle reactions, and a tendency towards explosive–aggressive reactions. Simmel had also already gathered abundant experience with war neuroses in the First World War. He now (1944) interpreted them in the light of the new ego psychology. The type of traumatic situation, he says, is what causes the traumatization in a given case. Simmel distinguishes between traumatic neuroses in peacetime and in war. The decisive difference from other traumatic neuroses lies in the fact that the soldier develops a "military ego". He has to function as part of a unit and has to replace his civilian superego with obedience to his superiors. Thus, he regresses psychically to a parent–child relationship. His superiors guide him and thereby convey to him security and protection against an unknown reality. If this identificatory tendency is disappointed by the superior, the soldier feels as if he were being abandoned by his parents. The disappointment of trust becomes the trauma-provoking factor because the superiors have lost their function as an internal source of protection. It is this internal situation that first allows the external perilous situation to become traumatic. In this way, Simmel acknowledges the special role of the object in the traumatic situation.

Moses (1978) took Balint's object relations theoretical approach further in his study of the war neuroses. He claimed that the purely energetic view of trauma as overwhelming the stimulus barrier had distorted the psychoanalysts' view and kept them from seeking further mechanisms that serve to counteract the susceptibility to mental breakdown. Moses finds them in the development of the self, in a realistic sense of self-esteem that is not determined unconsciously by omnipotence and denial of one's own vulnerability, in the capacity to control affects, and in the feeling of belonging to a primary group. These factors are based in early childhood, and they are the reason for the different degrees of vulnerability for traumatization in adulthood.

After the First World War, and also after the Second World War, the lasting effects of war traumatizations were forgotten again. It was not until after the Vietnam War that large-scale studies of the long-term psychic effects of war were conducted at the urging of the veterans' associations in the USA. In 1980, this resulted in the introduction of a new diagnostic category, "post traumatic stress disorder" (PTSD), in the official psychiatric nomenclature (see Herman, 1992; van der Kolk, McFarlane, & Weisaeth, 1996a). This innovation led to a wave of intensive psychiatric, psychological, and neurobiological research, the findings of which also had an influence on the psychoanalytic discussion of traumatic disorders.

The consequences of the Holocaust and their significance for trauma theory

With the mental consequences of the Holocaust for the survivors and subsequent generations, an extreme traumatic reality necessarily forced its way into psychoanalytic theory. After the survivors were liberated from the concentration camps, however, it took a relatively long time before the suffering of the victims, with some exceptions (Friedman, 1949), came to the attention of psychoanalysts. In the omnibus volume of Furst (1967), for example, no mention is made as yet of the Holocaust as a trauma.

One reason for this was the passage of the laws on indemnification for the victims of National-Socialist persecution in the Federal Republic of Germany (West Germany). They stipulated that a connection had to be established between their persecution and their current symptoms by means of medical and psychiatric examinations. In addition to psychiatrists, psychoanalysts were also engaged to provide expert opinions, many of whom were either survivors themselves or had been able to emigrate in time. Their pioneering works yielded fundamental scientific insights into the mental disorders of the survivors. (An in-depth presentation is provided by Bergmann and Jucovy [1982] and Grubrich-Simitis [1979].) The trauma theory that had been common up to then proved to be unsuitable to grasp the specific symptoms and the experience of the survivors. This kind of traumatization, with its immeasurable human suffering, was something new and could not be adequately described with the usual diagnostic categories. It was not a matter of a single incident breaking through the stimulus barrier, as in the case of shock trauma, for example, but of extreme and constant stress. The months or years of constant terror, the physical cruelty, the agonizing hunger, the helplessness and dehumanization, the loss of family, witnessing torture and murder, all of this far exceeded what the psyche could endure. The clinical manifestation of the traumatic effects revealed a certain uniformity and was largely independent of the pre-traumatic personality and its conflicts. I can only go into a few of the works on the effects of the Holocaust, which have sharply increased in number in the meantime.

Hoppe (1962, 1965, 1968) diagnosed a chronic reactive aggression, in addition to manifold psychosomatic reactions and illnesses in the survivors. The massive aggression, deemed by many researchers as being at the centre of the survivor syndrome, was turned against oneself and led to somatizations and to the often described chronic reactive depression. A far-reaching loss of self-esteem went hand in hand with a withdrawal from the outside world and apathy. The depth of the depression was determined by the extent of the narcissistic regression, which could lead to withdrawal of the object relations and to a disintegration of the libidinal and aggressive drives. Eissler (1968) characterized this as progressive "narcissistic depletion".

At the 25th International Psycho-Analytical Congress at Copenhagen in 1967, a symposium was held for the first time on the psychic problems of survivors. Niederland reported there on his clinical experiences in the diagnosis and treatment of Holocaust survivors. He (1968, 1981) coined the term "survivor syndrome", a typical psychopathological state that occurred after a longer period of time spent in a concentration camp, regardless of the person's age, sex, individual and socio-cultural background. The overall condition was dominated by a chronic state of anxious, bland depression. At the symptom level, there were multiple physical complaints, severe sleeping disorders and nightmares in which the past was relived, social withdrawal and chronic apathy, alternating with short-lived outbursts of rage, affective numbing, and the inability to verbalize the traumatic experiences. One of the main characteristics described by Niederland is a form of unresolved grief and mourning and a feeling of guilt about having survived (survivor guilt). Surviving itself became a conflict and was experienced as a betrayal of one's dead parents and siblings.

In Krystal's estimation as well (1968, 1988), the conventional economic view of trauma, with its assumption of excessive quantities of stimuli and its passive model of the stimulus barrier, also results in misleading constructions about affects and trauma. Whether or not a psychic trauma takes place depends entirely upon whether a given internal or external danger is subjectively deemed to be inescapable. If this is the case, the subject surrenders to a traumatic state, which is determined by an altered state of consciousness. Krystal refers to this as the "catatonoid state", which acts as an affective and cognitive filter. The paradox of the traumatic state is that the numbing and blocking of affect are experienced as a relief from the painful affects of anxiety. Various authors recognize in this an adaptation to the unbearable situation (Hoppe, 1962; Grubrich-Simitis, 1979; Niederland, 1981). As Krystal sees it, the catatonoid state introduces a process that leads to a "robot state". The submission involves a form of surrender and a splitting of the self into an observing part and a different part, the body, which the ego sacrifices. This is followed by a paralysis and numbing, which blocks all of the pain reactions and affective manifestations, and the cognitive processes become increasingly constricted until only a residue of the self-observing ego is left. This can end in psychogenic death. Krystal described the course of a general traumatic process, which can come to a standstill at certain points with varying degrees of intensity. Even after the end of the traumatizing situation, the traumatic reactions still persist: the cognitive–affective constriction remains; the catatonoid reaction turns into depression; stimuli that are associated with the traumatic experience are avoided and lead to pseudophobia. Nightmares, reactive aggression, and anhedonia are further effects. Krystal interprets the unusually high rate of psychosomatic diseases among the survivors as regressive phenomena of expressions of affect and as post-trauma alexithymia. He described the post-trauma alexithymia at the same time as Marty and de M'Uzan (1963) discovered it in psychosomatic patients.

Keilson (1979) conducted a large-scale, long-term study with Jewish war orphans in the Netherlands, most of whom had survived the horror in hiding places. He investigated the impact of the extreme stress situation on these children's development, finding that one and the same traumatic situation had different effects, depending on the children's age. Keilson coined the term "sequential traumatization" for this. The long-lasting extreme stress situation is structured in different phases. The nature of these sequences in each case had clinically and statistically significant differences in terms of the effects. The better the adoptive parents understood the children during the third post-war period, the more the effect of an unfavourable second sequence (the actual traumatization) on the child's development could be influenced. The deficient ability on the part of adoptive parents to grasp the meaning of the trauma for the affected child and deal with it in an understanding way proved to be a traumatogenic factor. Keilson, thus, empirically describes the significance of the object relations and of the communicative aspect for the impact of traumatizations.

Bergmann (1996) compiled some of the factors (listed below) that forced psychoanalysis to see the essence of trauma with new eyes after the Holocaust.

1. The question of pre-traumatic personality often played no role in the case of survivors of the Holocaust. The duration of the incarceration and the atrocities they had witnessed or experienced were much more important. The traumatization was so massive that there was no regression to an earlier psychosexual stage; instead, the mental structure itself was destroyed.

2. The need to mourn had transformed the inability to do so into melancholy.

3. The ability to speak and act metaphorically was lost. Unlike psychosis patients, the resulting mental concretism existed only partially. This led to an important discovery: that the survivors exist in a dual reality. In everyday life, they behave in accordance with reality. But, from time to time, the psychic reality of the Holocaust breaks through and disrupts their lives. In some areas of the psyche, the trauma destroyed the ability to distinguish between fantasy and reality.

4. In many cases, years and even decades lay between the liberation from the concentration camps and the outbreak of the traumatic neurosis. As long as life was difficult and uncertain, the effect of the camps often seemed to remain latent. This latency proved to be one of the main characteristics of traumatic disorders.

5. The traumatizations that were suffered exceeded the survivors'
    ability to process them mentally and also intrude into the lives
    of the subsequent generation. (I cannot go into any of the
    research on the transmission of traumatic effects of the Holo-
    caust to the next generation here, for space reasons.)

The consequences of the Second World War and the discussion of trauma in post-war Germany

Millions of people in Germany were affected by the mental and
emotional consequences of the Second World War, soldiers by their
war experiences, the civilian population, women and children, by
the bombings of their cities, fleeing, etc. These experiences must
have been present in the psychoanalytic psychotherapeutic treatments of the post-war years, either consciously or repressed,
denied, and split off, but represented in symptoms and through
derivations of them in their minds. This fact did not lead to research
or reflection on traumatic experiences and their effects on any large
scale. Although such symptoms and consequences were described
in individual case reports that were published from time to time,
they were not recognized as being traumatic, nor were they treated
as such.

The after-effects of the war on the psyche of individual Germans
were mixed with their involvement in National Socialism and its
crimes and with the repression of guilt and responsibility. This also
had an impact on memory and the process of coming to terms with
reality and the consequences of the war. Alexander and Margarete
Mitscherlich, in their famous study (1967), analysed the social
processes of repression and denial that resulted in an inability to
mourn, defences against remembering, and a derealization and
emotional numbing, as well as a general immobilism. The Mitscher-
lichs base their analysis on Freud's conception of mourning, without taking recourse to a theory of trauma. Today, we can assume
that an inability to mourn, affective numbing, and immobilism may
also be consequences of traumatizations. Considering whether a
traumatic disorder is being presented does not mean substituting
the question of guilt and responsibility and the necessary distinction between victim and perpetrator. Trauma is an empirical—

clinical term and can help one to understand the situation at that time in a more comprehensive, differentiated way. (I go into this in more detail in my work on "Trauma, Trauer und Geschichte" [Trauma, mourning and history], Bohleber, 2001).

Only Alfred Lorenzer took up trauma theory at that time and developed it further (Lorenzer, 1965, 1966, 1968a,b; Lorenzer & Thomä, 1965). Lorenzer and Thomä also noted at the beginning of their study that there was not yet enough observational material to describe the clinical syndrome of traumatic neurosis, even though it was of considerable social and political significance, and debate over the term "trauma" was one of the major tasks of psycho-analysis. The patients presented by the authors were severely trau-matized by the war: loss of eyesight from a phosphorous grenade during a bombing raid; loss of a leg or an arm from exploding grenades; a daring soldier who suffered various injuries and had to endure life-threatening operations. In all of these cases, the patient presented symptoms of anxiety neurosis some 15–20 years later. A precise examination clearly showed that this long, symptom-free interim phase proved in actuality to be a "silent illness phase" in which a rigid defence constellation on the surface conveyed the appearance of a pseudo- or supernormality. The traumatic loss of a part of the body is simultaneously acknowledged and denied by means of a split in the ego. It is "not important". It is not until a later exposure to mild traumatic stress internally related to the first traumatic situation in terms of the "experience theme" that this defence organization breaks down, giving way to a massive trau-matic reaction. Lorenzer (1966, 1968a) brings these psychodynamic insights regarding the two-phase defence and symptom-free inter-val to bear against psychiatric experts who did not want to recog-nize such a latency period for the traumatic reaction in the case of Holocaust survivors and, instead, diagnosed the disorders that appeared later as a predisposition that was not due to trauma, which meant that a survivor's claim to some form of compensation was denied. These works by Lorenzer are relatively unique in the German psychoanalytic literature of the 1960s and even into the 1970s. Although many international studies, especially on the consequences of incarceration in concentration camps, had been published in the German periodical *PSYCHE*, the subject of trauma was hardly noted by German psychoanalysts. Further milestones

are the works by Grubrich-Simitis in 1979 on extreme traumatization, and by Simenauer (1978) and Rosenkötter (1979, 1981) on the
transgenerational effects on the second generation. Space does not
permit a discussion of any of the newer research on the traumatic
effects of National Socialism and the Second World War on the next
generation. (See Bohleber [1997b].)

More recent object relations theoretical approaches to trauma theory

The extreme trauma of persecution from the Holocaust led to a
further development of the models in trauma theory, for the scale
of this trauma could not be adequately described with the economic
model of the protective shield that is broken through. Laub developed an object relations theory conception further in various studies (Laub, 1998; Laub & Auerhahn, 1991; Laub & Podell, 1995) with
regard to its communicative function in the traumatization process.
Central to the Holocaust experience is the collapse of the empathic
process. The communicative dyad between the self and its good
internal objects breaks down, with absolute inner loneliness and the
most extreme hopelessness as a consequence. The traumatic reality
destroys the empathic protective shield that was formed by the
internalized primary object and destroys the trust in the continuous
presence of good objects and the degree to which one can expect
empathy from one's fellow human beings, in that others will recognize the basic needs and respond to them. In the trauma, the internal good object falls silent as an empathic mediator between self
and environment (Cohen, 1985; Kirshner, 1993). The loss of the
empathic inner other destroys the ability to relate the trauma. It
cannot be incorporated into a narrative. It is only in the presence of
an empathic listener that the fragments can grow together into a
narrative and the story can be verified. Distance is created through
narration. The traumatic event and experience become a testimony,
and are thus re-externalized to some extent. This is also why the
recording of video interviews with survivors has a therapeutic
effect (Laub, 1992).

These object relations theory conceptions of trauma contain
various fruitful and further-going aspects. There are three aspects
that I want to highlight in this connection.

1. The internal loss of any and all objects that give empathic meaning in the traumatizing situation leads to the projection of the need for empathy to the perpetrator and to its malicious internalization. Amati (1990) described this process in the case of torture victims: the torturer constantly occupies the patient's inner world. The malicious persecuting object takes the place of the internal objects and determines the inner dialogue. The traumatized person later tries to escape from it, in order to put earlier pre-traumatic objects back in place (Ehlert & Lorke, 1987; Ehlert-Balzer, 1996).

2. The traumatic situation and its effect destroys the ability to symbolize it and grasp its meaning (Grubrich-Simitis, 1984). The trauma becomes the "black hole" in the psychic structure. Unintegrated trauma fragments later break into consciousness again and overwhelm the ego, which, however, cannot structure and integrate these fragments. They cannot be incorporated into a superordinate meaningful narrative without help. Since the traumatic experience disrupts the network of meanings for a human being, it is impossible to describe in a way that is bound to meaning. The support that meanings give no longer exists at this moment, the traumatic experience cannot be "contained". In order to describe this psychologically, we have to resort to metaphors. The metaphors most frequently used for this are "foreign body", "hole" (Cohen, 1985; Kinston & Cohen, 1986), "gap" (Caruth, 1995) in the psychic texture, "crypt" (Abraham & Torok, 1979), or the "empty circle" (Laub, 1998).

3. So-called "man-made disasters" such as the Holocaust, war, ethnic persecution, torture, are aimed at annihilating the historical–social existence of the human being. This is why an individual cannot integrate the traumatic experience into a superordinate narrative in an idiosyncratic act; aside from an empathic listener, a social discourse about the historical truth of the traumatic events is also needed, and about its being denied and warded off. The victims are also witnesses to a special historical reality. The acknowledgement of causation and guilt is what first restores the interpersonal framework and, thus, the possibility to understand the trauma in an adequate way. Only in this way can the undermined understanding of the self and the

world be regenerated. Victims are often at the mercy of their own doubts and uncertainties regarding the traumatic reality they have experienced. If defensive tendencies dominate the way society comes to terms with the disaster, the victims often feel excluded and blocked out or left alone with their experience, which undermines their feeling of security again, makes them vulnerable to retraumatizations, or condemns them to remain silent since they could never expect to meet with understanding.

Baranger, Baranger, and Mom (1988) offer an important criticism and supplement to these more recent object- and communications-theory approaches. They acknowledge the widening of knowledge that object-relations theory has brought in the understanding of the pathogenic role of trauma, but criticize the fact that the concept of trauma has become less distinct as a result. These newer theories run the risk of dissolving the link between the traumatic situation and anxiety, they claim. This is why the authors apply the economic aspect of anxiety as a central fact of the trauma. Anxiety, as they say, is the touchstone that helps us to distinguish between what is traumatic and what is merely pathogenic. They go back to Freud's concept of "automatic anxiety". In contrast to signal anxiety, in this case the individual is at the mercy of a nameless danger that cannot be localized, the nature of which is not known to him. This anxiety is so primitive that it can only be described in economic terms. The stimulus barrier is broken through and quantities of excitation that are not processed lead to mental disorganization and complete helplessness. They refer to this situation as the "pure trauma". The traumatized person tries to tame the pure trauma and mitigate it by giving it a name and putting it into a causal system of action that can be understood. What is paradoxical about it is that the trauma is actually incidental and foreign, but as long as it remains foreign, it will be revived and recur in the form of sudden repetitions, without its being understood. Since the human being quite generally cannot live without explanations, he tries to give the trauma an individual meaning and historicize it with this in mind. These historicizations after the fact are usually screen memories. It is the task of the analytic process to recognize these screen memories as such and reconstruct the authentic story, whereby the historicization is open-ended, basically endless. Baranger, Baranger, and Mom warn against the vast no-man's land of this "nameless trauma", which the analyst does not enter without risk. One of the dangers, they say, lies in hasty and erroneous historicizations, which can bring the analysis to a standstill, allowing the transformation of the trauma to slip back into a repetitive circular pattern again.

Integration of the psychoanalytic trauma models

According to Baranger, Baranger, and Mom (1988), we can only adequately get at the core of traumatic experience if we also take the overwhelming destructive anxiety into consideration. This anxiety can only be described in psycho-economic terms. If the authors postulate a "pure trauma" in theory, then this also means, on the other hand, that a psycho-economic model alone is not sufficient, for there is no trauma without a remnant of internal structures that give meaning. That which is experienced as the unexpected initially stands on the ground of what can be expected, which is what gives it meaning and from which it sets itself off. The massive traumatic experience then shatters this basis by destroying the confidence in the common symbolically mediated world, which binds us preconsciously and which we take for granted in all interactions. In that sense, the trauma represents a crux for all hermeneutic-narrative and constructivistic theories. What these can no longer grasp, especially in cases of massive traumatic experiences, is the breakdown of the constructive process itself, with which we generate meanings. Moore (1999) offers an interesting possibility for the solution of this problem within constructivistic theories. The destructive element, the immediate traumatizing violence, eludes the giving of meaning. What remains is a "too-much", excess, a massive surplus, which breaks through the psychic structure and cannot be "contained" by meaning. Krystal seems to be describing much the same thing with his term "surrender". This is why a psycho-economic conceptualization is needed, in addition to an object relations theory conceptualization.

In particular, the experience of being overwhelmed should also be mentioned here, in addition to the unexpected intrusion into the human being's nexus of psychic understanding. The recurring intrusion of fragmented traumatic memories can also have a retraumatizing effect because this, too, has the quality of being sudden and immediately overwhelming. Yet, it is not the temporal aspect that is ultimately decisive, but the fact that the intruding re-experience cannot be taken up by meanings and, consequently, the individual is again helplessly and passively at the mercy of the event. It is not until afterwards that the traumatized person tries to assign meaning to what happened and thereby establish a connection for himself. The intrusion has two faces, in the sense that it can serve the process of mental integration and the discovery of meaning, but can also be disruptive and overwhelming.

Traumatized patients often report feeling that time is standing still, or that their internal clock stopped on the date they were traumatized. They still have a sense of objective time, but not for their own development and lifetime, especially not for their future. Such a disturbance in the sense of time or feeling for time is also inherent to the repetition compulsion. Memories, nightmares, and flashbacks have such a quality of immediacy that it is as if the event had just taken place. They demonstrate to the affected person that time does not go by. Traumatized people anticipate further disasters and their perspective on the future is limited in scope; some report that they just live from day to day. Basic trust also affects their sense of time, and with its destruction by the trauma, time also gets out of hand for the traumatized person. These dysfunctions in the perception of time and the feeling for time, on the one hand, have to be described in psycho-economic terms as a change in the function of perception due to overstimulation, but, on the other hand, the distortion in the perception of time and feeling for time also serves the attempt to bring about an understanding of the whole by looking for "omens" to help them gain a retrospective control over what intruded upon them so suddenly.

Therefore, from the standpoint of metapsychology, the psychoanalytic theory of trauma needs both models, the hermeneutic object relations theoretical model as well as the psycho-economic one. At the psychic level of experience, the psycho-economic model for which the shock trauma is paradigmatic emphasizes the experience of being overwhelmed and an excess of violence, anxiety, and stimulation that cannot be bound mentally. The passiveness and helplessness that necessarily result can lead to an internal surrender. Object relations theory models, with the collapse of the internal supporting object relations, put the feeling of utter abandonment and the disruption of any and all affective bonds and internal communication at the centre of attention, as a result of which the trauma cannot be integrated through narrative.

Problems in the definition of trauma

As one can gather from the discussion so far, trauma is not a precisely defined concept in psychoanalysis. In the course of its development, many different forms of traumatization have been described, related to a variety of external events, such as: seduction trauma, sexual abuse, war trauma, extreme trauma, deprivation trauma, silent trauma, stress trauma, and cumulative trauma, among others. If only because of this breadth of phenomena, it could not be assumed that the effects and consequences of trauma were homogeneous. Moreover, the term had more or less lost its specificity and could often no longer be adequately distinguished from other pathogenic causes and severe frustrations or mental stress. During the 1980s, a working party on "Conceptual research, based at the Sigmund Freud Institute in Frankfurt under the direction of Joseph Sandler, examined the range of meanings covered by the concept of "trauma", assuming that, from the standpoint of its meaning, it can be regarded as the prototype of an elastic term (Sandler, Dreher, & Drews, 1991). The study showed that distinctions between the various dimensions of trauma and their interaction were fuzzy at best. Yet, a distinction has to be made between the process of traumatization, the traumatic state, and the pathological changes that remain afterward. Aside from massive or extreme traumatizations, not every traumatic situation has the same kind of effect on all people. This means that a trauma, as far as its effect is concerned, can, as a rule, only be defined in retrospect from its consequences for the psyche. Predispositional factors have to be taken into account as well.

Trauma is a concept that links an external event with its specific consequences for the inner psychic reality. In that sense, it is a relational concept (Fischer & Riedesser, 1998). This dual relatedness of the term is also what makes it fuzzy. Therefore, it seems advisable to define the relationship between the two determinants more precisely in order to counteract the dissolution of trauma as a concept. I agree with A. Freud, Furst, Krystal, and Cooper, among others, who are in favour of a narrow definition of trauma. Cooper (1986) defines trauma with reference to Freud:

> a psychic trauma is any psychological event which abruptly over-whelms the ego's capacity to provide a minimal sense of safety and integrative intactness, resulting in overwhelming anxiety or help-lessness, or the threat of it, and producing an enduring change in the psychic organization. [p. 44]

A major factor in this definition is the sudden, disruptive, uncon-trollable aspect of the traumatic event and the experience of a "too much" that renders one helpless. The traumatic experience con-fronts the ego with a *fait accompli* (Furst, 1978, p. 349). The ego's reactions are too late in coming. They do not come in response to an impending danger, but only after this danger has become reality and the ego has been passively put at its mercy. For Krystal, that which is often characterized as psychic trauma in the literature is actually just a trauma-like situation that does not expand into a traumatic situation. In order to distinguish this from the actual trau-matic process, with specific pathological consequences, Krystal (1978) speaks of "catastrophic trauma". For him, the central factor is the *experienced* helplessness. It is not the traumatic situation itself that triggers this helplessness, but its subjective evaluation. Whether or not this is accurate is initially irrelevant for the mental reaction. If the danger is regarded as unavoidable, the helplessness changes into an inner sense of giving up on oneself. For Krystal, this experience of having the defence function, as well as the expressive function of anxiety, overwhelmed and its inhibition is the actual traumatic event.

For the ego, it is impossible to integrate the traumatic experi-ence into the psyche. The assignment of meaning is interrupted because the coincidental and unexpected nature of the event can-not be absorbed by existing structures of meaning. One lasting effect, which is important for the definition of trauma, is that basic trust is destroyed, resulting in an enduring disruption of the understanding of oneself and the world (Fischer & Riedesser, 1998). Trauma is not just a relational term because it connects inside and outside, but also because, in trauma, a fundamental holding object relationship breaks down.

CHAPTER FIVE

Remembrance, trauma, and collective memory: the battle for memory in psychoanalysis

Introduction

Psychoanalysis began as a theory of trauma. To cite Freud's famous dictum, when hysterics suffer from reminiscences, it is memory that possesses a pathogenic quality. Freud abandoned the quest to uncover traumatizing infantile sexual scenes when he abandoned his seduction theory, and, thereafter, psychoanalysis began to undertake a broader exploration of psychic reality. With the concept of transference, Freud discovered a new dimension of memory: its repetition in behaviour. Although he continued to think that the goal of the treatment was to bring repressed memories of early psychic life to consciousness, psychoanalytic clinical theory subsequently took a different course, because the transference concept contained a particular dynamic of its own. The prevailing therapeutic relationship increasingly merged with the transference concept and, with the recognition of the countertransference, took a further specific step away from the past and towards the here-and-now of the analytic relationship. Remembering individual life history thereby lost its central therapeutic importance.

However, there was one domain in which it continued to be a crucial issue: in the treatment of people who had been traumatized. Freud was certainly constantly concerned with trauma, which the catastrophe of the First World War and the approaching barbarism of National Socialism turned into a particularly pressing issue. However, Freud never systematized his theory of trauma. Moreover, he consigned certain problems—such as post trauma dreams and traumatic neurosis—to a dark domain that he did not wish to probe any further. Thus, a trauma theory long remained a *desideratum* of analytic research and the concern with political and social violence, as well as with their consequences, did not achieve the status in psychoanalysis that it should have done. One key reason for this was the almost complete separation of psychic and external realities within psychoanalytic theory. Most analysts more or less exclusively directed their attention to the inner world and to the question of the influence of unconscious phantasies on perceptions and the shaping of internal object relationships. Incorporating external reality would have been widely interpreted as an attack on psychic reality and the importance of the unconscious. This attitude became most strongly apparent in the understanding of sexual abuse (Simon, 1992; see also Chapter Four in this volume).

The catastrophes and extreme experiences that people suffered in the twentieth century turned trauma into the century's hallmark. As a result, the century was marked by a growing need to investigate and understand the phenomena, not only in psychoanalysis, but also in the other human sciences. The psychic consequences of both world wars entailed a special therapeutic and theoretical concern with these traumatizations, but the interest proved to be short-lived each time. It was only after the Vietnam War, for example, that post traumatic stress disorder was adopted as a diagnostic category in the psychiatric nomenclature, giving rise to a wealth of research into this syndrome. At the centre of this hallmark of the twentieth century, however, stands the Holocaust, as the National Socialist crime against humanity. The transportation to concentration camps and the murder of millions of Jewish people wreaked unimaginable destruction and suffering on the victims. The therapeutic assistance given to the survivors involved a confrontation of extreme experiences and effects that had never been known before. Trauma, and being overwhelmed by its remembrance, was not only a concern for the surviving victims, but also had specific consequences for their children and their children's children. At the same time, those belonging to the culpable population were confronted with an unprecedented criminal history with manifest consequences that extended to their children and their children's children. Their actions, and the defensive repudiation of guilt and responsibility, as well as their denial and forgetting, left their mark not only on individual and family memories, but also on the collective memory of post-war German society, in which the painful, shameful memory of the criminal history for which they were responsible led to the unfolding of a specific set of dynamics over the decades. Thus, the Holocaust turned remembrance into a special moral requirement in Germany.

These introductory comments are intended to outline the framework for my next observations. These are concerned with the concept of memory, as well as with remembrance and reconstruction in psychoanalysis and their particular significance in traumatizations and their treatment. I conclude with a discussion of the dynamics of trauma and remembrance in relation to collective memory.

Freud's theory of memory and its therapeutic function

As I have said, Freud was constant in his view that bringing repressed memories of early psychic life into consciousness was the goal of analytic treatment. One reason for this is to be found in his theory of memory. According to Freud, perceptions are stored in the memory as memory traces. They are certainly copies of the original impression, but they are not preserved as isolated elements as they would be in a primitive engramme theory. In Freud's view, there are several superimposed systems of memory that order the same memory trace, which is stored several times in duplicate, in accordance with specific principles. The first memory system associates the elements using the principle of simultaneity in time; subordinate systems represent them according to other forms of concurrence, such as relationships of similarity (1900a, p. 539) or contiguity (1899a, p. 307). (In the *Standard Edition*, "Kontiguitätsassoziation" is translated into "associated by continuity".) Memories of past impressions and experiences can, in principle, be retrieved intact. In reality, however, this is not generally the case, because unconscious wishes connected with elements of memory entail displacements and repressions. The re-emergence of memories is, thus, linked to the destiny of the drive wishes. For Freud, then, the authenticity of memorial reconstructions of childhood scenes are significant in so far as only an analysis of the processes that distort them can bring to light the unconscious wishes. (Freud [1899a] provides an exemplary description of this [cf. Hock, 2003].)

In "Remembering, repeating and working through", Freud describes the aim of analytic treatment as "filling in gaps in memory" (1914g, p. 148) by overcoming the resistances to repression. The patient has to remember specific experiences and the affective impulses that they evoke, because it is only in this way that he can be convinced that what appears to be reality is, in fact, "a reflection of a forgotten past" (1920g, p. 19). It is not the events or facts in themselves that are remembered, but their psychic processing. Freud refers very generally to "psychic events", such as the patient's childhood defiance towards his parents' authority. For him, the historical truth of memories also consists precisely in this, rather than only in an accurate reproduction of objective facts. Freud celebrates it "as a triumph for the treatment if he can bring it about that something that the patient wishes to discharge in action is disposed of through the work of remembering" (1914g, p. 153). This does not always succeed, because forgotten and repressed material is frequently repeated as an act rather than reproduced as a memory. Here, the repetition compulsion takes over from the urge to remember and the transference becomes its arena. Its interpretation then leads "to the awakening of the memories which appear without difficulty, as it were, after the resistance has been overcome" (*ibid.*, p. 154). Freud, as he writes in "Constructions in analysis", later became more cautious with regard to awakening memories. We are indeed seeking "a picture of the patient's forgotten years that shall be alike trustworthy and in all essential respects complete" (1937b, p. 258), but, in some cases, it is impossible to go beyond constructions. These certainly produce an '"upward drive" of the repressed that strives "to carry the important memory-traces into consciousness" (*ibid.*, p. 266) but is often obstructed. The process of becoming conscious then extends only as far as the patient's "assured conviction of the truth of the construction" (*ibid.*, p. 266). As this return to Freud's theory of memory shows, he regards memories as a revival of mnemic residues that are conceived as images of earlier psychic processes. It is only by lifting the repression and working through the conflicts that the past can be reproduced, but this is without any remodelling in consciousness being experienced through the revival (1923b, p. 20).

Freud never unified his theory of memory. In addition to the predominant conception outlined above, there are some alternative concepts and models that paved the way for some later developments.

1. If a memory is reproduced as an act through repetition, it is integrated into a behavioural context with its own meaning in the present. The present, therefore, not only has the function of awakening the memory and thus the forgotten past material, but also forces the past psychic occurrence into the present structure of events, shapes it, and thereby transforms its meaning. The past experience is actively incorporated into the context of the current life experience. Freud, therefore, also refers on occasion to a remodelling process that applies to memories. Thus, in a letter of 6 December 1896 to Wilhelm Fliess, Freud says that from time to time memory traces undergo "a *rearrangement* in accordance with fresh circumstances—to a *retranscription*" (Freud, 1985, p. 207, original italics). This retranscription is the psychic achievement of successive stages of life. In puberty, for example, phantasies develop concerning childhood, and memory traces undergo "a complicated process of remodelling" (Freud, 1909d, p. 206, n. 1). Quindeau (2004) bases her conception of memory on passages of this kind in Freud, which lend themselves to a constructivist interpretation. These alternative concepts paved the way for a modern understanding of memories as constructions that are influenced by the present.

2. This premise of a retroactive remodelling of memories is related to Freud's concept of deferred action (*Nachträglichkeit*): through a frightening or confusing event after the period of sexual maturation, an earlier childhood scene with sexual content that could not originally be integrated into a meaningful context

retroactively (*nachträglich*) accrues a traumatic effect. Impressions from the pre-sexual period thus attain "traumatic power at a later date as memories" (Breuer & Freud, 1895d, p. 133). This conception of deferred action (or retroactive resignification) was predominantly expanded upon in French psychoanalysis, where it was the foundation of the theory of *après-coup*: the retroactive attribution of new meaning. The concept was largely detached, however, from its causal connection with two temporally separate life-historical scenes and the temporal sequence was expanded into a "reticulate relation" (Green, 2001, p. 36).

The "colonization of the past"[1] by the present in contemporary psychoanalytic clinical theory

In this section, I will describe the fate of memory as a curative element in the development of clinical theory, while restricting myself to some principal mainstream positions and leaving aside some of their offshoots. In ego-psychology, the main focus in analytic work gradually shifted away from remembering life-historical events, and towards reconstruction. Through its connection with an unconscious phantasy, a psychically significant childhood event forms a complex dynamic pattern that is repeatedly psychically reintegrated and accordingly remodelled in the course of later development. The goal of reconstruction is to comprehend this pattern and its superimposed revisions on the basis of material from the analytic session, in order to be able to trace the development in reverse back to the original event and its associated unconscious phantasy. The real long-term repercussions of this dynamic complex are understood as a causal history. Remembrance and reconstruction acquire therapeutic evidential status through the identification of their direct causal connection with the continuing psychic effects of the event (Arlow, 1991; Blum, 1994; Kris, 1956).

This view of the therapeutic efficacy of remembrance and reconstruction has been dealt a massive blow by the emergence of the more recent forms of object relations psychology and the move towards narrativism and constructivism. According to the narratological view, we never make contact with the *actual* memory, only with its description by the patient. The truth does not, therefore, exist as something hidden that can be found, but is constantly integrated into a narrative that only acquires truth status when it acquires plausibility for the patient, giving hitherto unconnected fragments of a life narrative a more coherent meaning (Spence, 1982). In the transference relationship, early forms of experience are more or less incorporated into a narrative framework. Historical clarification cannot proceed by uncovering the past, since this would be tantamount to destroying the present. For Schafer (1982), the transference is not a time machine for returning to the past (Freeman, 1985), but the outcome of a necessarily circular progression. The present and past are reciprocally constructed. As in the hermeneutic circle, we constantly see the past through our preconceptions of the present, which are, in turn, shaped by the past. In this conception of memory, the discovery of real events disappears from view. Historical truth is replaced by narrative truth. The framework of narrative reality becomes all encompassing and the connection with the real world goes unmentioned. The fundamental problem with these narratological and constructivist conceptions of psychoanalysis consists in their exclusion or obscuration of any connection with the reality behind the narration.

In the development of analytic technique, investigating the transference–countertransference interplay has evolved into the main therapeutic focus. An increasingly subtle perception and formulation of psychic microprocesses as they unfold in the dynamics of the therapeutic relationship also incorporated emerging life-historical material. It had long been known that memories could not be understood in isolation from the context of their emergence. However, it was then shown how strongly the emergence of memories was driven by an evolving, unconscious dynamic in the transference–countertransference relationship. Furthermore, the analysis of earlier disorders sheds light on the extent to which auto-biographical material could be distorted and misrepresented by splitting processes. Moreover, where psychic triangulation is deficient, the psychic space that is the prerequisite for any interpretive discussion of memories is often lacking.

Most markedly in British psychoanalysis, primarily within the Kleinian school, therapeutic activity has changed into an analysis of internal object relationships in the here-and-now of the transference–countertransference. The patient unconsciously shapes the relationship with the analyst in such a way that his or her inner world is transmitted as a "total situation" (Joseph, 1985) from past to present. The present is, in fact, explicitly stated to be a function of the past. This is understood to mean that the present more or less completely contains the past and that this develops in the here-and-now of the analytic relationship. In terms of treatment technique, the past has lost any autonomous meaning. With the interpretation of the transference in the here-and-now of the analytic situation, past and present are interpreted simultaneously. The two are more or less intermingled. Any reconstructive recourse to the historical past tends to be suspected as a defensive manoeuvre. If it still serves any purpose at all, a reconstruction merely conveys to the patient a sense of his own continuity and individuality (Birksted-Breen, 2003; Joseph, 1985; Riesenberg-Malcolm, 1986).

As this brief overview demonstrates, in most current conceptions of the treatment, the process of remembering and reconstructing past events in the patient's life history has been marginalized and classified as being of secondary therapeutic importance. Recent cognitive and neuroscientific research into memory seems to provide some findings and hypotheses that can be regarded as external confirmation of this viewpoint. Clinical models formulated on this basis assume that real early object relationships are stored in non-declarative implicit memory as "implicit" or "procedural" memories (as already described in Sandler & Sandler, 1998) or as "implicit memory-objects" (Pugh, 2002, p. 1388). They influence current experience and behaviour without representing the past in the form of consciously accessible memories. They re-emerge in the transference as acted-out implicit relational schemas (PCSG, 1998). Autobiographical and episodic memories, by contrast, are stored in declarative memory.

Whereas Freud worked from the premise of a unified memory system, today object-relational patterns or transference enactments and autobiographical memories are localized in two fundamentally different types of memory process. The connection between a behavioural repetition of old relational schemas in the here-and-now and the remembering of life-historical events largely seems to break down (Fonagy, 1999, 2003; Gabbard & Westen, 2003). In this view, psychic change occurs through the interpretation and influencing of mental models of object relationships that are anchored in implicit memory. Autobiographical remembrance becomes merely a secondary phenomenon. However, these new conceptions seem to throw the baby out with the bathwater, by declaring life-historical remembrance and the possibility of a (at least approximate) reconstruction of historical reality to be therapeutically insignificant. Psychoanalysis, originally undertaken in order to discover repressed childhood memories, is now in danger of becoming a treatment technique that actually fades out history (see also Kennedy, 2002).

In fact, contrary to the claims of these modern theories, the "there-and-then" is neither absorbed into the "here-and-now" nor into the transformation of a memory by the dynamics of the present situation. The present transforms the memory of the past, but the memory retains an autonomous status, nevertheless. Even if Freud's theory of the memory trace has become obsolete and the metaphorical comparison of the analyst's work with that of the archaeologist is no longer considered apposite, the metaphor of the trace still conveys something that derives from clinical knowledge. The "trace" concept accords the past an element of autonomy that is left out of account by modern theories of memory based on transcription and construction. On the one hand, unfulfilled promises concerning abandoned life plans or the enigmatic messages of the other (Laplanche, 1992) attest to the autonomous hermeneutic status of the past; on the other hand, traumatic memories can exercise a distressing power and intrude violently into the present life context without being transmitted with it. Trauma is a brute fact that cannot be integrated into a context of meaning at the time it is experienced because it tears the fabric of the psyche. This creates special conditions for its remembrance and retroactive integration into present experience. I discuss these questions next, beginning with a few systematic observations concerning the modern view of memories.

Memories between past and present: findings from studies in cognitive science

In the past few decades, there have been ground-breaking discoveries in the cognitive sciences and neurosciences that have vastly expanded, if not revolutionized, our knowledge of the brain's functioning. The topological storage models have been replaced by a much more dynamic and flexible view of remembrance and memory. Today, we no longer regard memories as stored impressions or traces that will be reawakened by recall and returned to consciousness. The remembrance process involves a more complex interaction of present life circumstances, that which we expect to remember, and material that we have retained from the past. Cognitive researcher, Schacter, writes,

> Our memories work differently [from the way a camera records]. We extract key elements from our experiences and store them. We then recreate or reconstruct our experiences rather than retrieve copies of them. Sometimes, in the process of reconstructing we add on feelings, beliefs, or even knowledge we obtained after the experience. In other words, we bias our memories of the past by attributing to them emotions or knowledge we acquired after the event. [2001, p. 9]

According to "embodied memory" theory, memory is a constructive and adaptive process, through which the whole organism interacts with the environment and connects past experiences with analogous new situations through sensorimotor co-ordination in a continual process of recategorization (Leuzinger-Bohleber & Pfeifer, 2002). The neuroscientific data concerning the construction of memories has now led some to conclude that the truth question (as it relates to the correspondence between memories and past events) has become obsolete. Memories are conceived of as narrative constructions containing gaps that have arisen as a result of forgetting, which are then filled by narrative to produce a meaning that corresponds to the ego's present situation (according to Welzer, 2002). In this view, too, there is a danger that the difference between remembrance and interpretation is almost completely eliminated.

A closer analysis of the empirical research into autobiographical memory lends scant support to this theory, however (with reference to the descriptions in Granzow [1994] and Schacter [1996]). Moreover, the theory appears to make no distinction between genesis and validity. Even if the brain constructs memories, a distinction should nevertheless be maintained between the process of emergence and the result; otherwise we are subscribing to a genetic fallacy. Empirical studies provide no direct answer to the question of the precision and reliability of autobiographical memories. This controversy erupted particularly violently during the scientific and social debate concerning memories of experiences of sexual abuse. The work of Loftus and Ketcham (1994) demonstrated that suggested misinformation can have a long-term influence on memories. Other studies on suggestibility, however, have provided strong evidence that memories of real events are characterized by more varied and detailed representational images than those that are merely suggested (Schacter, 2001). Shevrin (2002) emphasizes that misinformation certainly influences the reporting of memories, but does not necessarily change the memory trace itself. Experiments have shown that genuine memories leave behind a "sensory signature" that is absent from so-called false memories. In the study of this debate and the further empirical studies that have emerged from it, one may well be struck by the impression that conclusions are being prematurely drawn here in favour of the unreliability of memory. I agree with Shevrin's view that

> we need a theory of memory in which motivational and cognitive factors can be independently assessed and their interactions investigated. In what way do real perceptions of significant others become distorted under the influence of desires and wishes that cannot be given expression? It is from this point of view heartening that there is evidence that despite suggestion and misinformation the original perceptions need not be erased; they are retrievable once the misinformation, the distortions, have been identified, for example, in the transference. [2002, p. 138]

Studies which are of particular relevance to my theme have demonstrated that the precision of a memory is often directly proportional to the emotional excitation caused by an event. The emotional intensity and personal significance, as well as the surprise element and general consequence of an event, are key determinants. Experiences in which all of these factors are present in great intensity can be remembered for longer periods, with greater precision, and in more detail. (Empirical studies of so-called flashbulb memories, described by Granzow [1994] and Schacter [1996], are notable in this respect.) Intensive visual representation plays an essential role here.

These factors have an even stronger influence on the registration of traumatic experiences. Undoubtedly, the connections between memory and traumatic events are even more complex than those connecting memory and non-traumatic emotional experiences. Opinions concerning the nature of these connections are divided, however. One set of arguments suggests that traumatic memories cannot generally be retrieved coherently at first. The event is said to be represented in implicit memory, and explicit memories were, therefore, temporarily lacking, as for example in psychogenic amnesia. Its existence is considered to be a sign of traumatic experiences. The findings of empirical studies do not generally confirm these arguments (I am basing my argument here on Kihlstrom [2006], McNally [2003, 2005], Schacter [1996, 2001], and, above all, on Volbert [2004], with reference to excerpts from her summary). Rather, they substantiate the view that memories of acutely stressful and traumatic events are predominantly highly detailed, extremely constant, and, as far as can be judged, also relatively reliable. As with other memories, mistakes and mechanisms of forgetting can certainly occur over the course of time. From a neurobiological perspective, a pre-attentive subcortical emotional evaluation of detailed stimuli takes place with events of a high affective intensity. Activation of the amygdala leads to an improvement in the memory's performance. The strong, intensive excitation increases the remembrance of core features of the event. Key aspects of the event and its experience are relatively well retained, whereas details that are unconnected with the core of the event are less so. The determining factor here is the ego, which must, at the least, still be able to maintain its observational function during the traumatic event. Laub and Auerhahn (1993) classify memories on a continuum of psychological distance from the trauma. In severe traumatizations, the observing ego can even break down, with the result that memories are only very distant and fragmentary. Psychogenic amnesia can also occur as a consequence of traumatic events. This is more rare, however, than is assumed in some studies. Similarly, repressed or dissociated memories can re-emerge and be verified by external confirmation, although we also encounter the opposite: re-emergent memories that cannot be confirmed. I cannot agree with Brenneis (1999), who classifies the re-emergence of traumatic memories after a reconstruction as an artefact that originates from the emotionally charged therapeutic dynamics of the present but, rather than being interpreted as such, is shifted as a reconstruction into the past with suggestive effect. Although Brenneis goes on to restrict the scope of this line of argument, on the whole, I agree with Kluft's (1999) criticism of it. From their fourth year of life, children can remember traumatic events well and their descriptions of the key events are generally reliable. The question of whether a higher incidence of amnesia must be assumed following acutely stressful experiences in children is beyond the scope of this discussion (see Gaensbauer [1995] on the inner representation of traumas in the preverbal developmental period).

These research findings point to the conclusion that traumatic memories constitute a special set of experiences that are prioritized for encoding and are generally preserved in detail and with great precision over a long period. However, they are not fundamentally different from other memory processes; therefore, it seems that memory mechanisms form a set of neurocognitive processes in which the processes of encoding, consolidation, and retrieval are specifically assembled (Volbert, 2004, p. 138). This means that the deposition and retrieval of traumatic experiences are exempt from the usual process of retranscription and transformation of memories by each present situation. With traumatic memories, the function of the present as the hermeneutic lens through which the past is perceived and structured can only operate in a very limited way.

Psychoanalytic theories of traumatic memory

The above-described findings from cognitive and neurobiological studies suggest that, in principle, we certainly cannot assume that a different form of processing occurs with traumatic experiences to that which occurs with non-traumatic experiences. Nevertheless, some deviations in the registration must be expected, as well as an obstruction of the normal course of psychic processes. When traumatic events are retained consistently, in detail and relatively precisely in the memory, it is primarily a case of facts that are remembered initially rather than a description of the psychic reality of traumatic experiences. How is the inner experiential core of these experiences of horror, pain, loss, and mortal fear that upset the psychic equilibrium to be described in psychoanalytic terms? What is the role of the affects, defensive manoeuvres, and unconscious phantasies that come into play? Before discussing this in further detail, I will briefly introduce the two main models of trauma that are encountered in psychoanalytic theory and which form the basis of the subsequent discussion.

Sigmund Freud's psycho-economic model of trauma

Breuer and Freud (1895d) conceived of the traumatic memory as a foreign body in the psychic tissue, which unfolds its effect there until it loses its foreign-body structure through an affective remembrance and abreaction of the trapped affect. Freud went on to develop this model from a psycho-economic point of view in *Beyond the Pleasure Principle* (1920g). Here, the foreign-body concept is conceptualized as a quantum of excitation that cannot be psychically bound and that overwhelms the ego, breaking through the protective shield. The force of surging quantities of excitation is too great to be mastered. In order to accomplish the task of psychic binding, the psychic apparatus regresses to more primitive modes of response. Freud introduces the concept of the repetition compulsion in order to describe the special nature of this experience, which lies outside the dynamics of the pleasure–unpleasure principle. Through the repetition compulsion, the traumatic experience is actualized in the hope of thereby psychically binding the excitation and setting the pleasure principle back in motion, as well as its associated forms of psychic response. Trauma not only disturbs the libidinal economy; it also threatens the subject's integrity in a more radical way (Laplanche & Pontalis, 1988).

In *Inhibitions, Symptoms and Anxiety*, Freud (1926d) falls back on the concept of automatic anxiety that he developed for the actual neuroses. The excessive quantity of excitation in the traumatic situation gives rise to a massive surge of anxiety. It floods the ego, which is defenceless against this onslaught, and renders it absolutely helpless. Automatic anxiety has an indefinite quality and lacks an object. In a first attempt at mastery, the ego attempts to convert the automatic anxiety into signal anxiety, which makes it possible for the absolute helplessness to be transformed into an expectation. The ego thereby develops an inner activity and "repeats it [the trauma] actively in a weakened version, in the hope of being able itself to direct its course" (*ibid.*, p. 167). The situation of external dangers is thereby internalized and acquires significance for the ego.

> On the other hand, the external (real) danger must also have managed to become internalized if it is to be significant for the ego. It must have been recognized as related to some situation of helplessness that has been experienced. [*ibid.*, p. 168]

The anxiety is symbolized and no longer remains indefinite and objectless. The trauma thus acquires a hermeneutic structure and becomes possible to overcome. Baranger, Baranger, and Mom (1988) have rightly emphasized this economic aspect of automatic anxiety as a key element of the traumatic experience. They characterize the anxiety situation, with its psychic indeterminacy and objectlessness, as the "pure trauma". The traumatized person attempts to control and alleviate the pure trauma by giving it a name and incorporating it into a comprehensible causal system of behaviour. The authors indicate the paradox that the trauma is actually intrusive and alien, but, as long as it remains alien, it is revived and falls into repetitions without becoming comprehensible. Since human beings cannot generally live without explanations, they attempt to give the trauma an individual meaning and to historicize it. These retroactive historicizations are mainly screen memories. It is the task of the analytic process to identify these screen memories and to reconstruct the authentic history while the future historicization remains unconcluded.

Freud (1926e) repeatedly describes the helplessness experienced by the ego as the consequence of an object loss. If the mother is missed, the infantile ego is no longer entirely helpless because it is able to cathect the mother's image. In the actual traumatic situation, however, there is no object available to be missed. Anxiety remains the only response (*ibid.*, p. 203). This form of complete loss of internal protective objects constitutes the foundation of the second model of trauma.

The model of trauma in object relations theory

With the development of object relations theories, quantitative considerations, concerning an intolerable mass of excitation that floods the ego, were rejected. The paradigm for the model is no longer an isolated experience with a shock impact, such as an accident, but the object relationship. Ferenczi (1949; Dupont, 1988) anticipated many insights of later research into trauma. Balint (1969) was the first to follow him in this respect. He emphasized that the traumatogenic quality of a situation depends on whether an intensive relationship has developed between the child and the object. The object relationship itself thus acquires a traumatic quality. As later studies (Steele, 1994) confirm, it is not primarily the child's injuries from physical force that produce a traumatic disorder; rather, the most intensely pathogenic element is mistreatment or abuse by the person whose protection and care is needed. This viewpoint broadens the understanding of psychic reality in a traumatic situation. The greater the trauma, the more severe is not only the damage to the internal object relationship, but also the breakdown in the protective, stabilizing internal communication between self- and object representations. This gives rise to isolated fragments of traumatic experience that are cut off from the internal communication.

The object relations theory approach to trauma theory was further developed by research into the severe traumatizations that were suffered in the Holocaust. A key psychic consequence of such experiences is the breakdown of the empathic process. The communicative dyad between the self and its good internal objects breaks up, resulting in absolute internal isolation and the most intense desolation. The internal good object falls silent as an empathic mediator between self and environment and the trust in the continual presence of good objects and the expectability of human empathy is destroyed (see Cohen, 1985; Kirshner, 1994; Laub & Podell, 1995). This conception gives a better understanding of the experiential core of severe traumatizations. It consists in a domain of experience that is almost incommunicable: a catastrophic isolation, an inner abandonment that not only paralyses the self and its possibilities of action, but annihilates it, accompanied by mortal fear, hatred, shame, and despair. Or, as Grand (2000) expresses it, a dead, quasi-autistic region of a non-self arises in which there is no available other capable of empathy.

These conceptions in object relations theory represent a major advance in the understanding of trauma. Nevertheless, we require both the object relations theory and the psycho-economic models to conceptualize the severe traumatic experience that demolishes the foundations of expectability and destroys the trust in a shared, symbolically mediated world that preconsciously connects us. To that extent, trauma represents the sticking point of all the hermeneutic–narratological and constructivist theories, which cannot account for the breakdown of the construction process by which we generate meanings. (Moore [1999] offers an interesting possible solution for this problem within constructivist theories.) The destructive element, the direct traumatizing force, remains something excessive, a massive surplus that ruptures the psychic structure and cannot be bound through meaning.

The intractability of traumatic memories: the problem of reconstruction, narration, and mental integration

I have concluded from cognitive psychological studies that traumatic material, although certainly modified, is neither encoded nor retrieved in a completely different way from non-traumatic material. Before further examining these facts psychoanalytically, I will describe a conception of trauma that holds that traumatic experiences are stored in a different way, on account of the surplus of an excessive excitation associated with them.

On the basis of their research, van der Kolk, McFarlane, and Weisaeth (1996) hypothesize a specific trauma memory that preserves traumatic memories differently from the way in which explicit autobiographical memory stores memories. The intense excitation splits the memory into various isolated, somato-sensory elements: into images, affective states, and somatic sensations, as well as smells and sounds. Van der Kolk, McFarlane, and Weisaeth consider that these implicit memories accord with actual experience, but they cannot initially be integrated into a narrative memory in this form. As a result, the content of traumatic memories is non-symbolic, inflexible, and inalterable, because the self is disengaged as the author of experience during the traumatic event. The essence of this view is that trauma is effectively characterized by an atemporal and simultaneously literal precision in the memory. The inalterable precision of the memory seems to attest to the existence of a historical truth that is not altered or transformed by subjective meaning or by the individual's cognitive schemas, expectations, and unconscious phantasies. The autobiographical symbolic meaning is eliminated, which, according to Leys (2000, p. 7), reveals the mechanistic–causal foundation of many current theories of trauma.

This model of trauma memory is open to the criticism that stressful emotionally significant events can usually be retained and explicitly remembered in the long term (although psychogenic amnesia unquestionably does occur). (Space precludes a detailed critique of this model of trauma memory here, see Leys [2000], McNally [2003], and Volbert [2004].) Although the thesis of a special trauma memory is certainly adopted by some analysts (e.g., by Person & Klar, 1994), it leads to a series of suppositions that are scarcely psychoanalytically tenable. Indeed, it can be assumed that the integrative functions of the memory are disengaged by the excessive excitation in the traumatic situation, giving rise to a dissociated self-state involving depersonalizations and derealizations. Altered states of consciousness also frequently appear, and traumatic memories can irrupt suddenly into consciousness when this encapsulated self-state is activated. However, these intrusions are not pure repetitions, because flashbacks can be modified by external social influences. Lansky and Bley (1995) have also indicated that chronic post trauma nightmares not only reproduce affect-charged memories and visual repetitions of traumatic scenes, but also undergo a dream-work.

These facts support the psychoanalytically based thesis that, while traumatic experiences and their memories are subject to specific psychodynamic restrictions and operations, they are not completely excluded from the associative stream of psychic material or from any transformation by conscious and unconscious phantasies (this has been emphasized by Oliner, in particular, 1996). As described, in contrast to other experience, Freud does not define the psychic trauma in terms of general characteristics of psychic material, but as a form of "outside–inside" that has formed like a "thorn in the flesh" (Laplanche, 1976). Freud describes traumatic material as a foreign body in the psychic tissue, but goes on to qualify the metaphor thus:

> In fact the pathogenic organization does not behave like a foreign body, but far more like an infiltrate. . . . Nor does the treatment

consist in extirpating something—psychotherapy is not able to do this for the present—but in causing the resistance to melt and in thus enabling the circulation to make its way into a region that has hitherto been cut off. [Breuer & Freud, 1895d, pp. 290–292]

Traumatic memories unfold their own dynamics. As an isolated, encapsulated "inside", they elude any adaptation through the associative connections that result from new experiences or through repression. Such transformations come into effect only in a very limited way, if at all, for these encapsulated domains, resembling foreign bodies, have some specific characteristics. I have selected three of these for examination, but I must stress that I cannot provide any extensive description of the phenomenology or symptomatology of traumatic states here. I am dealing here only with some specific psychic operations:

1. A regression to omnipotent thinking as a defence against intolerable helplessness is frequently encountered. By blaming themselves for what has happened, traumatized people convert their sense of having been passively at someone's mercy into a sense that they themselves have caused the traumatic situation (see Oliner, 1996). At the moment of the traumatic event, a long-standing and repressed threatening phantasy, inner conviction, or central anxiety representation can also emerge and fuse with the intruding traumatic material. (Similarly, from a Kleinian point of view, Garland, 1998.) This gives rise to split-off convictions or screen memories.

2. The paralysed psychic activity of the traumatized self freezes the mental sense of time, producing an internal, temporal standstill. It is often described as a sensation that a part of the self has been left behind and stays more or less the same because it can no longer be exposed to life. It is also described in terms of "standing aside", or a "darkened existence". Langer refers to the state of a "uniquely imprisoned persistence" that "cannot overflow the blocked reservoir of its own moment" (1995, p. 16) Others simply say that their inner clock stopped at the moment of traumatization.

3. In the traumatic situation, the person affected can often no longer maintain the boundaries between himself and the other.

Overwhelming excitation and intense anxiety damage the sense of self and bring about a self–object fusion as the core of the traumatic experience, which is difficult to resolve and persistently impairs the individual's sense of identity.

I cannot further describe these psychic operations in traumatically induced split-off domains. They serve my purpose of illustrating what is meant by the psychic reworking of traumatic memories. I am, thus, adopting a midway position between the polarized viewpoints of empirical trauma researchers for whom traumatic events are precisely replicated in the memory and those viewpoints that only consider the trauma within the context of the general functioning of psychic reality. Neither position seems to me to be tenable on its own.

If the reworking of traumatic memories is now to be considered, the question arises as to whether a therapeutic reconstruction of traumatic events is possible or necessary. Traumatic memories are often activated in the analytic treatment by enactments in the transference relationship. The reality of the trauma and its associated affects (specifically, its historicization) must be discovered, even if only in a fragmentary or approximate form. This discovery is a necessary prerequisite for elucidating and comprehending its secondary revision and transformation by unconscious phantasies and meanings that contain guilt feelings and punitive impulses. Phantasy and traumatic reality are, thereby, disentangled and the ego gains an alleviating context of understanding. Historicization also involves recognizing the traumatic fact and understanding the individual experience and the emergent long-term consequences. When such a reconstructive interpretation succeeds, astonishing improvements in the condition of patients frequently occur, who then speak of a sensation of psychic integration, which is a sign that the self-organization is restructuring itself. If an encapsulated traumatic part of the self becomes permeable again, it can also be better interconnected associatively. An inaccurate reconstruction will be ineffective, however, no matter how meaningful it may appear to be.

What are the underlying reasons for this? A reconstruction must accord with the reality of the patient's trauma and grasp the reality that caused the traumatization. It is necessary to recognize what the patient has suffered, to articulate screen memories and split-off convictions, and to understand and interpret them in connection with the traumatic events. The interpretation must account for the elements that were already set or inherent in the traumatic experience itself, along with their secondary development of meaning. However, when the transference–countertransference is analysed only in the here-and-now of the analytic situation, and meaningful narratives then emerge without any reconstruction of the causative traumatic reality, these narratives run the risk of failing to distinguish between phantasy and reality. In the worst-case scenario, they risk retraumatizing the patient.

The representation of traumatic memories: generational and collective memory

Disasters that are defined as man-made—such as holocaust, war, and political and ethnic persecution—involve specific means of dehumanization and personality destruction that are used to annihilate the victims' historical and social existence. It is beyond an individual's capacities to integrate such traumatic experiences into a narrative context that is purely personal; a social discourse is also required concerning the historical truth of the traumatic events, as well as their denial and defensive repudiation. Generally, only scientific explanation and social recognition of causation and guilt will be able to restore the interpersonal context, thus opening up the possibility of finding out what actually happened at the time in an uncensored way. This is the only way that the shattered understanding of the self and the world can be regenerated. If defensive impulses predominate in society, or rules of silence prevail, traumatized survivors are left alone with their experiences. Instead of drawing support from other people's understanding, they are often dominated by their own guilt, which they rely upon as an explanatory principle. Present day Russian society, in which there is a notable absence of public debate about Stalinist terror, provides a pertinent example (Merridale, 2000; Solojed, 2006). The lack of a collective framework for discussion and of structures and reference points that could lend some security means that many victims still believe that they themselves are guilty and cannot understand, for example, the significance of the purges and their politics.

Traumatized individuals are not only victims of a destructive political reality, but are also its witnesses. They certainly often find themselves in a situation in which hardly anyone is willing to hear their testimony because listeners do not want to be burdened with feelings of fear and pain, anger and shame, or to feel afraid, or reproached with guilt. The historian Boll (2001) has shown from contemporary witness interviews with Holocaust survivors and those politically persecuted by National Socialism and Stalinism that the non-communicable quality of experiences is much too quickly cited in relation to traumatized people, which is, in fact, nothing but a rationalizing justification that predicates the reluctance to hear of those around them on the reluctance to speak on the part of the victims of persecution. The boundaries of what can be said are, therefore, always also connected with social restrictions, reinterpretations, and the imposition of taboos. There are things that can be neither spoken about nor endured, as well as the overwhelmingly senseless suffering, which imposes extreme burdens that the traumatized person does not wish to confront again by relating the events. They can also be impossible to talk about because the material of traumatic experiences and memories cannot be forced into a narrative structure, which would distort the core and the truth of the experience. I conclude by explaining this complex structural relationship between individual and collective memories of traumatic events in more detail in relation to the Holocaust and the Second World War.

The Holocaust is still the central focus of cultural memory in many societies. The dimensions of this genocide of the Jews broke the usual bounds of understanding and interpreting remembrance, memory, and historical insight. Attempts at remembrance are constantly overwhelmed by the immensity of the crimes, the immeasurable suffering, the unspeakable horror, and a merciless industrial machinery of destruction, which pose a challenge to cultural memory to this day. Even now we are at pains to explain the radical destructiveness of National Socialism and to gain a precise understanding of its criminal core and genocidal dimensions. Friedländer (1997) and others have indicated the paradoxical fact that Auschwitz occupies a much more prominent place in historical consciousness today than in past decades. The historian Berg refers to the overpowering repercussive impact of the actual events over the decades that "became the true guide, slowly and retrospectively shedding light on the event itself" (2003, p. 10). This view of the historical repercussions is related to the psychoanalytic under-standing of trauma, particularly the retroactive discovery of mean-ing and historicization. Various historians have also advocated adopting the concept of trauma in historical theory. The question is, thereby, certainly posed as to how the authentic collective experi-ence of a trauma is to be appropriately described, so that the horror of the experience and the shocking, brutal, meaningless fact of the trauma is not subjugated to defining historical categories that elim-inate the traumatic nature of the event. As Rüsen writes, the Holocaust

> destroys interpretive defining concepts when they are existentially related to the deepest layer of human subjectivity in which identity is rooted . . . this disturbance is difficult to endure. Nevertheless, it must become part of the historical culture if this is not to fall below the threshold of experience that the Holocaust in its return through memory to the experience of the past . . . objectively deploys. [2001, p. 214, translated for this edition]

What Rüsen stresses here is the need to return to the witness's indi-vidual memory in order not to neglect the catastrophic and trau-matic experiential quality in the process of historical description and classification. After contemporary witnesses have died out, summoning their history of persecution and suffering into memory takes over, even if the intolerable nature of the survivors' traumatic primary experience cannot be transferred into the remembrance of those who were not directly concerned.

In Germany, we could not restrict ourselves to keeping alive the memory of the victims and the crimes they suffered; we also had to incorporate the committed crimes that had to be accounted for and their perpetrators into the work of remembrance. Historians refer here to "negative memory" (Knigge & Frei, 2002). Remem-brance and its defensive repudiation, as well as the question of guilt and responsibility and their denial, thus set in motion a specific transgenerational dynamic in German society, which created a special meaning as a form of memory for the conception of the generation (Jureit & Wildt, 2005). In the predominant remembrance strategy of the generation whose members were involved as active perpetrators or as supporters and fascinated observers of National Socialism, their own participation was broadly denied. They turned themselves into the victims of Hitler and a small group of fanatical followers and culprits. The sufferings of the actual victims, in so far as they were perceived at all, were counterbalanced with their own victim groups, the prisoners of war, the war wounded, refugees, and victims of forced migration.

In their famous study, *The Inability to Mourn*, Mitscherlich and Mitscherlich (1975) described remembrance pathologies in post-war German society. They understand the defence against remembering the criminal and horrific events as a self-protective repudiation of a melancholia that would have set in absolutely inevitably if Germans had truly confronted their bond with Hitler and their burden of guilt. Through the omnipotently manifesting narcissism and National Socialist ideals, fellow humanity and the capacity for empathy with the victims were expelled from the self and destroyed. For Mitscherlich and Mitscherlich, the treatment of this pathology lay in a work of mourning that, in common with Freud, they understand as a work of remembrance that must serve the processing of guilt. The focus of their analysis was the pathology of the ego-ideal and the superego.

However, even from the case material described, there emerges a hidden subtext that reveals yet other conditions within this collective pathology. Accordingly, much of the symptomatology of the patients of Mitscherlich and Mitscherlich would today be interpreted as post trauma disorder. The rapid and successful reconstruction of German society in the 1950s and 1960s took place against a background of not only repressed guilt, but also an underlying trend generated by the preceding extreme exercise of violence and the traumatizing experience of violence, through the effects of war, bomb attacks, and migration. We encounter here a complex context of crimes, war, responsibility, trauma, and remembrance. As we know today, emotional rigidity, derealization of the past, and repression of the individual's own actions are also direct consequences of traumatizations, which impair the capacity to engage reflexively with the past. The moral problem of the repudiation of guilt is associated here with a remembrance pathology of traumatic origin. The apologetic victim-consciousness that members of the perpetrating generation retroactively created for themselves was fuelled from both sources—the defensive repudiation of guilt and the traumatic experiences themselves.

The next generation grew up in the shadow of this lie that was lived by their parents, who defined themselves as victims. The silence concerning their own participation and gaps in family biographies had produced a hazy and partly distorted sense of reality in the children. The parents' repudiated self-reflection also frequently prevented a critical engagement with National Socialist ideals and moral concepts to which they had subscribed. Many assured themselves of their validity through a narcissistic function-alization of their children, in whom any different kind of attitude was fiercely attacked. The way in which this second generation engaged with their parents then demonstrated a specific "split memory" pattern (Domansky, 1993), which is important for under-standing the subsequent development. Fathers fell under more or less wholesale suspicion of culpability in their children's eyes. In opposition and counter-identification, the children turned to the victims of this generation of fathers and perpetrators. Many engaged in political and scientific projects that undertook to explore and reconstruct the history and role of the victims. However, a public debate with the parents' generation often ended at the front door of an individual's own family. The silence and denial had certainly been broken on the general social level, but, nevertheless, it persisted on the individual level. It appeared to be too painful and too closely connected with catastrophic anxieties to venture there. As psychoanalytic treatments of members of this generation showed, their unconscious emotional bond to the parental repre-sentations of their early childhood, in many cases, had outlasted all subsequent debates concerning the parents' involvement in National Socialism. The representation was frequently split into an idealized father-image from early childhood and an image of the compromised father who had participated or been directly involved in crimes. Although they had moved a long way from the fathers' world in terms of their ego identifications and their conscious attitude, they could not overcome the splitting of the father image. The positive bond remained in the unconscious, but created a conflict of loyalty that led to respecting rather than ques-tioning the parental taboos. The striving for truth and the discovery of silenced and denied history were, thus, often combined with simultaneous defensive processes. Thus, the ego was constantly exposed to the danger of unconscious complicity with the parents and their attitudes.

For members of this generation, recognizing and working through this psychic configuration became an extremely painful process that, in many cases, nevertheless, dissolved hidden bonds of unconscious complicity with their parents and created some distance through a more independent perspective. This form of resolution was again made possible and eased by a simultaneous process of general social discovery and working through of taboos, myths, and legends about the crimes and the culprits. Defensive repudiation and remembrance constantly proved to be combined. As in a rising spiral, reality and its summoning to memory constantly had to be helped into its rightful place. In the course of this development, the rigid boundary between public and family remembrance also became more fluid. Questioning surviving members of the parents' generation and researching their culpable involvement produced many documentary testimonies as well as literary elaborations of family history from the 1990s onwards.

However, in many cases, clarification and reconstruction has so far only been possible in a very fragmentary way, since the parents' silence could not be broken or the children instigated the clarification too late rather than within their parents' lifetimes. Family secrets could then no longer be brought to light. Abraham (1987) refers to a ghost that can thus become lodged in gaps in family memory and goes on working unconsciously. Even when these facts have fewer pathological consequences, many members of the second generation must, nevertheless, live with an inescapable ambivalence, regardless of whether and to what extent their parents were involved in National Socialism and its crimes. The third generation is currently defining itself in succession. It takes its own, more independent, view of the events and the family involvements. We, nevertheless, encounter here the same loyalty conflicts within families, albeit in a milder form.

Conclusion

The development of analytic technique moved the analysis of the here-and-now of the therapeutic relationship increasingly to the

fore. Bringing memories to consciousness and life-historical reconstruction shifted to the margins. To a great extent, only the process
of working through present experience in the therapeutic relationship is now regarded as curative. Thus, the past disappears from
view, both in its determining significance and as a hermeneutic
counterpart to an understanding of the present. In the burning-
mirror of an analytic process understood in this way, the variety,
complexity, and intractability of a real history evaporates into a
relational thinking in which history is forgotten. The power of the
past, the repetition compulsion, and the return of the repressed are
themes of psychoanalytic thought that have more or less disappeared from the clinical debate.

Trauma, with its long-term consequences and its remembrance,
is opposed to this development in clinical theory. It forms a kind of
dissociated foreign body in the psychic–associative network. In this
split-off domain of the self prevails a specific dynamic that
constantly confronts the self with the experience of entrapment in
the force of the repetition compulsion. In order to be able to integrate this domain and resolve this dynamic, it is necessary to
remember and reconstruct the traumatic events in the analytic treatment. The returning power of the same is thereby historicized,
inner and outer acquire another context of understanding, and the
self regains a sense of psychic agency.

However, traumatic reality not only brings theoretical convictions into question, but also confronts us with the horror, cruelty,
and mortal fear that must come up for discussion. This arouses
defensive repudiation and avoidance not only in the traumatized
person, but also in the analyst, so that, in many cases, traumatic
experiences in analytic treatments do not receive the therapeutic
status that is actually their due. Far too little attention is often
devoted to the specific processes of defence and stabilization. The
victims of war, persecution, and other forms of political and social
power are simultaneously its witnesses. The confrontation with the
Holocaust, with the immense crimes, the unspeakable horror, and
the immeasurable suffering of the victims, threatens to overwhelm
remembrance and instigates avoidance strategies and a reluctance
to know among those not affected. The problem also arises for
collective memory and historical description of how to avoid
subjecting the Holocaust to defining categories that eliminate the

horror and the traumatic nature of the events. However, it is not only the victims, but also the perpetrators and the crimes that must be incorporated into the remembrance. Remembering crimes unfolds a special set of dynamics. So, in post-war German society, the defensive repudiation of guilt and responsibility by members of the generation involved in National Socialism introduced remembrance strategies that damaged the children's sense of reality and set in motion a transgenerational dynamic with specific identification processes.

Confronting these problems of a multi-faceted traumatic reality on the individual and social level and making them productive for theoretical and clinical debate also means battling to restore memory to its rightful place in psychoanalysis.

Note

1. This expression originates from Nietzsche and the reference is drawn from Assmann (1998).

CHAPTER SIX

Traumatic memories, dissociative states, and reconstruction

Introduction

Ground-breaking advances in modern cognitive sciences and neurosciences have led us to revise our understanding of memories. We can no longer think of them as impressions or traces that are then reactivated by recall and returned to consciousness. We now know that the process of remembering involves a much more complex interaction between present life circumstances, that which we expect to remember, and the material itself that we have retained from the past. In light of this new knowledge, memories must be seen as (re)constructions of the past that are co-determined by the present and are continually reconstructed anew from their stored key elements. When retrieved, they are supplemented by emotions, convictions, or knowledge obtained since the remembered event itself (Schacter, 2001).

In contrast, traumatic memories are not shaped by this transformative power of the present. The excessive arousal in a traumatic situation significantly alters processes of encoding, storing, and, later, consolidating a memory and its recall. Hence, a traumatic memory is subject to little or no revision or transformation by one's present circumstances. As long as they are not subject to amnesia, traumatic memories are generally preserved with great precision and permanence. This is caused by their unique manner of storage: excessive arousal presumably causes the integrative functions of memory to be overwhelmed and shut down. A dissociated state of self emerges in the process, whereby the traumatic memories are encapsulated and isolated from the remaining flow of consciousness. In the following, I would like to examine more closely these dissociated states of self that stem from traumatic experiences. Thus far, psychoanalysis has paid far too little attention to them.

On the concept of dissociation in psychoanalysis

In psychoanalytic treatment, we often encounter adult patients who have undergone a trauma in childhood, though this is not readily apparent in their symptoms. In treatment, one inevitably encounters parts of the psyche that are like split-off states of the self and which, when activated, give rise to a severely altered state of consciousness in the patient. The way in which patients describe these states varies, but they all refer to the loss of their previously familiar sense of self. The inner affective relationship to oneself and objects is lost, leaving the patient feeling alienated, frozen, petrified, and, in extreme cases, even outside of oneself. Descriptions of this feeling point to the existence of unintegrated states of the self, which are often experienced as unbearable.

These states are triggered by stimuli connected to an earlier trauma or to the sudden entrance of conflictual thoughts associated with the traumatic event. Their sudden intrusion into consciousness is overwhelming and often shocking, reducing the ego to a state of passive helplessness: it can neither gain control of the situation through self-reflection nor dissolve it. The patient feels imprisoned, having given up hope of finding a way out of this state, or fears further fragmentation of the self. If bodily experiences are seen as the cause of the trauma, patients often report that being held in someone's arms or, conversely, deliberately subjecting themselves to physical attack, can help them to feel themselves again. Likewise, patients often describe self-injurious behaviour, such as cutting oneself, as a means of relieving this state of the self. As one female patient reported, it is as if a pressure is being released and the feeling returns that one can sense oneself again. In other cases, patients require the affectively perceptible presence of the object and the reconstruction of the triggering situation in order to move beyond this frozen state. Such a psychic reorganization is often characterized by the way in which it suddenly appears, as if in a switch process with a pronounced "on-off" quality.

The significance of these altered states of consciousness has yet to be adequately addressed within psychoanalytic research. In the early days of psychoanalysis, Breuer and Freud concerned themselves with abnormal states of consciousness and their dissociation in order to characterize split-off groups of ideas in cases of traumatically determined hysteria. In becoming dissociated, these ideas form a double consciousness and cannot be connected with the normal state of consciousness by means of association (Breuer & Freud, 1893a). Janet formulated a concept of dissociation as the splitting of consciousness. In certain individuals, the personal self is weakened by a genetically determined lack of sufficient psychological binding energy. In the wake of a trauma, this primary weakness of mental integration has significant consequences, as the individual lacks the psychological strength necessary for integrating the traumatic experience into consciousness. Memories and their associated feelings are, therefore, dissociated from conscious awareness and control of the self (Nemiah, 1998). While Janet's concept was descriptive, Freud understood dissociation as a dynamic reaction to conflict. The pathogenic experience seems unbearable to the ego, which mobilizes the desire for defence and the wish to forget. The ego is viewed as possessing sufficient strength to actively repress traumatic memories and affects. Freud relinquished the term dissociation in favour of repression. At the same time, however, he quietly integrated the consciousness-splitting aspect of dissociation into his new concept of repression which always involves the operation of dissociative processes via amnesia (Hoffmann, Eckhardt-Henn, & Scheidt, 2004). Later, Freud would go on to refer to splits in the ego.

Freud's one-sided opposition to Janet oversimplified the problem (Berman, 1981), and, thereafter, the term dissociation disappeared from the vocabulary of psychoanalysis. Fairbairn (1952), however, represents an exception. His descriptions of "endopsychic ego structures" (libidinal ego, anti-libidinal ego, central ego) as dynamic agencies bear a striking resemblance to what would later be termed dissociated self-states. The clarification of the concept of splitting through Kleinian psychoanalysis and the exploration of narcissistic pathologies and borderline disorders brought dissociative phenomena back into discussion. They are now subsumed under the term splitting, with the concept of projective identification describing the splitting of the self. Kernberg (1975) speaks of ego states that are dissociated from one another: they are organized around affective polarities and find themselves in conflict. Kohut assumes a vertical split, enabling incompatible psychological attitudes—a grandiose self and a reality-orientated self—to exist side by side (1977). Grotstein (1981) proposes looking at the phenomenon of splitting from the standpoint of the dissociation of the personality. He speaks of subselves as an amalgam of I, self, and inner objects. In all of these discussions of splitting, however, the significance of trauma was never considered. Consequently, none of these psychodynamic definitions can do justice to the dissociative phenomena described. Neither splitting nor other psychoanalytic defence mechanisms adequately account for the altered states of consciousness that result from traumatic experiences.

In contrast to these earlier investigations, more recent trauma research considers dissociation to be a specific reaction of the ego to a severe external trauma. The aftermath of the Vietnam War and the increasing social awareness of the physical and sexual abuse of children in the 1980s led to the establishment of dissociative disorders in trauma research and in the psychiatric nomenclature of the *DSM III* and, to an even greater extent, the *DSM IV*. Its central characteristic was defined as the interruption of the integrative functions of consciousness, memory, identity, or the perception of one's environment. The disorder can appear suddenly, in stages, temporarily, or chronically. Alongside cases of combat trauma, dissociative disorders were primarily examined as consequences of sexual abuse, physical maltreatment, or severe emotional neglect suffered in childhood. However, dissociative phenomena do arise from other forms of severe traumatization as well.

In situations of extreme stress, the *mechanism of dissociation* functions as a shut-off mechanism which prevents the overstimulation or flooding of consciousness with unbearable anxiety and pain

(Loewenstein & Ross, 1992). The failure of the ego's capacity to affectively and mentally process states of the self results in the tearing of its psychic texture, which can then lead to the emergence of a *dissociative state*. The traumatic scene and its affects, which cannot be provided with symbolic verbal meaning, are split off. Metaphorically speaking, they remain psychically undigested and isolated from normal consciousness. In severe cases of dissociation, identity disorders can arise as distinct ego states develop in order to contain the traumatic experience. Such an identity disorder consists of complex identities that are kept separate through an amnestic autohypnotic mechanism. One example of this is "dissociative identity disorder" (DID).

The following are described as primarily clinical dissociative phenomena:

- amnesias relating to severely disturbing experiences;
- emerging transformations of consciousness and feelings of unreality;
- a feeling of estrangement in regard to one's own body or surroundings (depersonalizations and derealizations);
- a sensation of finding oneself outside of one's own body (out of body experiences).

Findings in attachment research have now begun to elaborate upon, or contradict, the explanation of dissociation as a specific reaction to a severe trauma. Longitudinal studies (Lyons-Ruth, 2003) examining forms of attachment in high-risk families have shown that traumatizing abuse or other relational traumas should not be viewed as the most likely cause of dissociative symptoms in late adolescence. In fact, the most predictive factor was located in maternal communication errors (contradictory affective signals) and maternal role confusion. These most frequently took the form of self-referential maternal behaviours, primarily in the child's first two years of life. The dissociative defence represents a structure of dialogue that was available to the child in infancy:

> The infant internalizes the intrinsic affect-imbued features of the two-person dialogue structure, scaffolded for the infant by early caregivers from the beginning of life, and makes those distortions

and deletions his own. That is, the child will develop unintegrated mental contents to the extent that the caregiver does not engage in an *integrated enough* affective, symbolic, and interactive dialogue with the child. [*ibid.*, p. 900]

Consequently, a dissociative lack of integration occurs.

The results of these studies do not necessarily contradict the supposition of a causal relationship between trauma and dissociative symptoms, since in the traumatic situation it is precisely this inner dialogue with reassuring object representations that is interrupted (see Chapter Four in this volume). In addition, these results confirm the clinical knowledge of the importance of providing a sense of safety in a therapeutic relationship in order for the patient to be able to articulate the kernel of his or her traumatic experiences.

Contemporary psychoanalytic studies of dissociation think of it, in keeping with Freudian tradition, as a dynamic but unsuccessful defence process. The dissociative defence initially allows for psychic survival, but the further course of its development ultimately entails a weakening of the ego functions. Dissociative consciousness disorders lead to a continual repetition of the injury to the feeling of self-coherence and self-continuity (Eckhardt-Henn, 2004). Likewise, Brenner (1994, 2001) refers to dissociation as a "two-step defense mechanism" which results in an enhanced separation of mental contents. While first serving as protection from overstimulation and pain, dissociation is also able to change its function and later be employed as a defence against the perceived internal danger posed by seemingly unbearable feelings or affective states of self. The essential difference between psychoanalytic approaches, as opposed to other research into dissociative traumatic disorders, lies in the inclusion of the psychic elaboration of traumatic experiences (Gullestad, 2005). In addition to the three contemporary authors already alluded to, Kluft (2000) should also be mentioned. Kluft has primarily dealt with dissociative identity disorders (DID).

The defence process does not exhaust itself in the overwhelming and disruptive aspects of the traumatic events; rather, conscious and unconscious fantasies and conflictive affects come into play and modify the dissociated traumatic memories. (This is described in more detail in Chapter Five.) Repression implies that mental contents are kept unconscious. Dissociation, however, does not make mental contents unconscious: they remain accessible to consciousness, even if only in specific states of consciousness. Dissociated experiences are at once "known" and "unknown". Patients sometimes describe them as follows: "It is there, yet also not there". During therapy, patients sometimes wonder why they never thought to talk about the experiences before.

The mechanism of dissociation has acquired a special status in relational psychoanalysis (Howell, 2005; Stern, 1997). The emphasis that relational psychoanalysis places upon the multiple meanings of experiences and the theoretical unfolding of the unified self into multiple selves brought dissociation to the forefront of the approach. This theory did not assume that unacceptable thoughts, feelings, and experiences are repressed into the unconscious, as in a vertically structured model; instead, it held that they are split off through dissociation and stored horizontally, in multiple and discontinuous self states. This theoretical shift came about largely through the treatment of patients who had suffered severe sexual abuse as children. The unbearable fear, stimulation, and confusion which these indivduals had experienced in the overwhelmingly traumatic situations they had undergone had caused them to dissociate and form split-off states in which the traumatic self and the corresponding object representations were encapsulated. This process left other parts of the self (that is, other self states) more or less unharmed and able to continue in their development. Here, dissociation has a protective and adaptive function.

Recently, Boulanger (2007) has begun distinguishing between dissociation triggered by the trauma of sexual abuse in childhood and trauma-induced dissociation in adults. Confusing them, she finds, is a serious mistake. The distinction Boulanger draws between the traumatization of children and of adults is anticipated in work of Krystal (1978). According to Krystal, a traumatic situation will cause a child to become overwhelmed by an intolerable affect, whereas an adult will recognize the overwhelming terror of the situation and automatically retreat from the sense of helplessness, thereby surrendering to the situation by numbing physical and psychic pain. Boulanger draws on this idea further, theorizing that traumatic dissociation has an adaptive function for a child. In reacting to the trauma, the traumatized self encapsulates itself as an entity that is "not me", giving rise to the formation of multiple discontinuous self-states. In an adult, however, a stable core self has already developed. For the adult, therefore, the trauma causes a collapse of the core self, resulting in a permanently altered sense of self: "the sense of a collapsed self, a mortal self first encountered during the catastrophe, permeates every aspect of the adult trauma survivor's conscious and unconscious life; it is manifest in each self state" (Boulanger, 2007, p. 69).

Boulanger's distinction between childhood and adult trauma strikes me as far too rigid and her understanding of childhood trauma appears overly optimistic. Indeed, apart from sexual abuse, here Boulanger does not consider any other form of childhood trauma. Children are not limited to multiple self states; they also have a core self at their disposal. As my own experience in treating patients with severe childhood traumas shows, individuals who have suffered childhood trauma have not simply dissociatively encapsulated the traumatic experience; the trauma has also left an enduring mark on their core self. This is manifest in a persistent narcissistic retreat from relationships bearing affect and a damaged capacity to trust. All of these patients have the feeling that they are not firmly anchored in the world.

Case studies

The following case study is an example of a psychogenic amnesia after severe traumatizations.

A thirty-five-year-old man, Mr M, comes for analytic treatment because of severe depressive states. He is afraid that he will no longer be able to practise his profession as a social worker and provide for his family. He fears that he might one day kill himself. Anamnesis reveals that his father killed himself by jumping off a high-rise building when the patient was nine. After his father's death, Mr M developed obsessive–compulsive behaviour and other symptoms. He describes how, growing up with one other sibling (a sister who is two years older), he became the mother's darling and obtained very good marks in school. His identity problem began to appear during adolescence: he did not really know who he was. During his university studies and in the first years of his professional life, he was an active and very friendly colleague during the day. His mood changed in the evenings, however, and he often sat at home alone, severely depressed, drinking a great deal of alcohol. When he was twenty-five, his sister killed herself. During treatment, a central memory came back to him with increasing clarity: the scene in which the family learns that the father has killed himself. A neighbour came into the house and the patient saw from a distance that the neighbour began talking to his mother and she suddenly burst into tears. He also started crying, without really understanding what had happened. The memory remains without affect, however. His life before the age of nine remains split off and the memories of that time are not accessible to consciousness. He has pictures and letters from that period, however, and has learnt, through his enquiries among his relatives, that his father tried to kill himself several times before.

In other patients I have treated, a severe retrograde amnesia also came about after the traumatic loss of a parent during childhood. One may question whether this extended retrograde amnesia is a dissociative symptom, or whether it is more likely that it is the consequence of a severe process of repression. Today, dissociative amnesia is seen as a leading symptom of post traumatic stress disorder (Hofmann, 2004; Carlson, Armstrong, Loewenstein, & Roth, 1998). Usually, however, this kind of amnesia is attributed only to traumatic experiences of abuse or combat experiences, and is generally seen as reversible. Dissociation is considered to be an intrapsychic mechanism that serves to keep experiences that are psychically overwhelming separated from consciousness, through unintentional autoregulation. As a shut-off mechanism, it thereby prevents the overstimulation and flooding of consciousness by unbearable pain and fear. In contrast, the defence mechanism of repression is intentionally motivated, as conflictual ideas or memories associated with particular wishes are expelled into the unconscious. In this respect, dissociation in the traumatic situation is not psychologically motivated by conflicting tendencies and more closely resembles a psycho-biological mechanism. Seen psychoanalytically, however, we cannot draw a strict distinction between these mechanisms and their psychic effects. It is relatively unlikely that dissociated material is simply split off and not further processed secondarily. Dissociation can also be employed secondarily against undesirable intrapsychic material. In the case of Mr M, it can be assumed that the traumatic situation of receiving the news of his father's death gave rise to a dissociation of experience with amnesia. Its extension was then shaped by the rapid onset of processes of repression, which could have been triggered by feelings of guilt due to the aggressive impulses directed towards his father. In this manner, dissociative processes can connect themselves to other defence mechanisms. I will return to the problem of psychic reworking of traumatic material later, but I would now like to turn to another clinical case study.

*   *   *

A thirty-year-old bookseller, a diabetic, sought treatment with me after experiencing an acute crisis. The internist who was treating her had proposed that she stay in the hospital to get her blood sugar under better control. She was then suddenly overwhelmed by feelings and images from when she was five years old and was first diagnosed with diabetes and had to be hospitalized. She had tried to fight this intrusion, using alcohol and tranquillizers in an attempt to restore her mental balance.

Now she complained that she could not feel herself and felt empty. She said she had been overcome by a numbing feeling inside ever since that first time she was hospitalized and diagnosed with diabetes (type I). Actually, she had been searching for herself ever since, she said, and that was when the dissociative states and severe depersonalizations began.

Whenever she lost her sense of identity or could not feel herself, she felt compelled to incessantly rearrange her books or even the whole room at home, taking everything in hand. She projected self-representations into certain books, identifying with them by giving them a prominent place on the bookshelf, for example. If she was unable to find her feeling of self this way, then she felt the need to injure herself by scratching herself with a needle or cutting herself. She did the same thing when she could no longer control her self-hatred. This scratching or cutting relieved her of an unbearable inner tension. The moment the blood began to drip down her arm, she was able to feel once again. When the dissociation became more intense, she experienced multiple personality states, albeit in a relatively integrated form. She described how she would fall apart in these episodes and receive "visitors" inside: other people who talked from within her, screamed at, or attacked her. Essentially, she said, she was always with someone else: not an "I" but a "we". The dissociation sometimes went so far that she had the feeling of leaving her body from the back of her head or shoulder.

The patient's father worked at a bank, and her mother stopped working when the patient was a child. She had a sister who was five years older. When the patient was six months old, she developed asthma following a smallpox vaccination. When she was 3½ years old she had an eye operation to correct eye-crossing. When she was 5½ years old, she began suffering from diabetes (type I) following a flu shot. After that, the asthma disappeared. The diabetes was discovered when she started wetting the bed. Her mother took her to the doctor, who immediately put her in the hospital. A central experience for her was the "betrayal" by her mother, who promised to return straight away but did not come back until the next day. States of dissociation already began to occur in the hospital. When she was discharged from the hospital, she said, the image had been "engraved" in her of going down the stairs and thinking, "now everything's different". She felt that she was standing next to her body. It was indeed like a "spirit leaving the body," she said of the way she experienced it later. Her childhood was punctuated by constant blood-sugar measurements and insulin shots. In addition, she also could not bear any separation from her mother and usually remained close by. Her mother seems to have had little empathy with her daughter, however. The patient could not recall any physical contact with her or any signs of affection. She portrayed her parents as helpless and overwhelmed by her illness. During her turbulent adolescence she began drinking and taking drugs, and, as a result, her blood sugar was often out of control. Because of her brooding compulsion, she eventually failed in school and had to drop out. Her inner states fluctuated between helplessness and omnipotence. She never accepted her diabetes and was hardly able to stabilize her blood sugar.

In the psychoanalytic treatment, at first with three, then four sessions per week, a good emotional contact was established with her relatively quickly, in spite of the severe psychopathological picture of her disturbance. In the starting phase, I focused my interpretations on her need for safety and the struggle for control over internal and external intrusions. In the therapy sessions, she frequently broke the flow of communication by dropping out of the thoughts that had developed between us. In interpreting this repetition compulsion, I tell her more or less the following: "The diabetes was an intrusion that you couldn't do anything about, and you were helpless in the face of it. If you feel good today, you can't stand it; you're afraid that something will intrude again. That's why you would rather break things off from the corresponding thoughts, because that way, you have everything under control." With this interpretation, the patient feels that a central domain of her inner world has been understood. It is as if completely new spaces were opening up for her, she says. Without being consciously aware of it at the time, I had already become a good, safety-giving object for her in the transference, which her fragmented self urgently needed. In the further course of therapy, which was largely an attunement process, it became possible to identify her inner states and feelings, to understand her breaks in the flow of communication between us, and to initiate an internalization of self-regulation as a result. She had no idea that words could have a calming effect.

The patient was striving for absolute autonomy, and for a relatively long time warded off all feelings of dependence of any kind that were activated by the transference. The intersubjective exchange and its internalization threatened to dissolve her or merge her with the object. Consequently, her grandiose and sarcastic self often dominated. She treated feelings concretely, like her diabetes. Whenever undesirable thoughts or feelings arose, she drowned them in alcohol or with pills, stood next to herself, and saw herself like a stranger. She made active use of the mechanism of dissociation and deployed it to ward off feelings. This went on frequently in therapy sessions over a period of several months and could soon be interpreted in its defensive character. The changes in her state of consciousness sometimes took place abruptly, but at other times they were nearly imperceptible. Often, it was only evident as a heightened sense of irony, or only recognizable from my affective perception of the therapeutic relationship, that she, as we metaphorically called it, "had disappeared behind the wall again".

The patient's traumatic feelings of being abandoned, and her anxieties about loss in the weekend separations and over the holidays increasingly came to the fore during analysis, as a result of the growing positive transference. The patient feared that I might desert her or not come back again. After nine months of treatment, the first severe crisis occurred when I was away for a week. Following my absence, she came to the therapy session in a severely dissociated and hypnoid state and reported that she was fantasizing about the sea. In her fantasy, there were no sounds there; a train was waiting on the white sand, and she boarded it and rode away. In the session, she experiences scarves coming out of her shoulder and flapping around, about to blow away. I told her, "You've run away so that you don't have to feel the pain of separation and the anxiety of losing me." She looked at me incredulously and I sensed that she came back into herself. Afterwards she seemed more animated and gradually pulled out of this severe crisis.

I would now like to outline a central reconstructive intervention that occurred after about eighteen months of treatment. Prior to an upcoming laser treatment on her retina, the patient experienced panic attacks and began to dissociate again, which was her typical response whenever she had to go to visit an opthalmologist. During the session, she described, for the first time, the details of the traumatic events surrounding the operation on her crossing eye when she was 3½ years old. After the operation, she was tied down because she had tried to tear off the bandage and get out of bed. She still remembered how she had hovered up at the ceiling and looked down upon herself. She was not in her body with her feelings. I then said spontaneously about this peritraumatic dissociation, "That was when you left your body and that was when the break in you occurred." She later recalled that it had felt as if a shock, or a charge of adrenalin, had gone through her the moment I said that.

The reconstruction of this trauma, which had now become possible, caused an affective restructuring and a stronger mental integration. Her internal agitation and chronic hyperarousal began to disappear. She no longer had to exert such strong control over herself. The "we" disappeared, and she now felt more or less like one person. A split had been eliminated deep inside of her, she said. Moreover, she could suddenly see things in sharper focus. The forthcoming laser operation then transpired without any major intrusion of anxiety, as well as all visits to the doctor thereafter. She was now better able to distinguish the past from the present. It was as if a clamp had been loosened, she said. She no longer felt all bound up with anxiety the way she had before. Since then, she continued to have dissociated states, but they were of a much milder sort. For the first time in her life, she experienced a lasting feeling of unity and continuity in herself. While she lost it from time to time, she at least now knew what she had to win back each time.

After this 2½-year segment of the therapy, which brought about a basic integration of the self, the transference relationship changed. It was my impression that she no longer needed the control imposed by the face-to-face arrangement of the treatment setting and that, in fact, this was impeding progress and inhibiting access to the patient's anxieties and desire for closeness. I offered her the couch, which she was then able to use. She no longer had to completely ward off her desire for dependence. She was extremely afraid of losing her inner relationship with me over the weekend. She felt that she had to keep hold of her inner connection to me and worried that, if she turned to others, she might be unable to find me again. Having long avoided any extended or intimate conversation with her mother, she began talking with her. She learned that her mother was given up to a children's home, where she spent her first three years of her life, before returning to her mother, and hearing about this helped to explain her mother's unempathetic reactions.

Despite these improvements, it became increasingly apparent to me that the patient was not really in inner contact with herself. The alternation of her states of consciousness had become very subtle, and frequently I could only perceive them through my own feelings of tensed bodily discomfort. Her vivid language was impressive, but it seemed isolated and was not associatively anchored to unconscious contents. It seemed as if her rebellious, sarcastic self continued to dominate and make accusations. Her thoughts and the transference fantasies that she talked about seemed cold and strangely disconnected. I slowly became aware that I was failing to reach her suffering, fearfully worried, depressive self.

Despite all defence, something like a subterranean storm was compelling this needy self to speak. On one occasion, the patient's car broke down and she had to take it to a mechanic, fearful that she might not be able to make it to her session on time. She was unable to endure this worry and fear. She broke off the inner contact, dissociated, departed from, and ultimately lost herself. Again she had to protect her weak self from a threatening, traumatically feared separation. This pattern begins to repeat itself frequently: she sensed that she had developed a relationship with me that was unlike any she had ever had, but then that feeling would give way to numbness and an altered state of consciousness. She was struggling to gain access to her weak self. As had been common with her, she was again painting mental pictures in order to use them as a crutch and as a mirror, because she was incapable of producing or sensing an inner affective connection to her self. In one of these pictures, she saw herself as two people. One of of the individuals was weak and was led into a house by the other, where she sat in one of the rooms, and was speechless. In constructing these images, the patient was in danger of losing herself and became extremely fearful of never returning from them. This fear was transferred on to me in this session, and I became afraid myself that she might indeed go mad and never return. She must have noticed my reaction, because she suddenly began to tell me about a female colleague whom she liked but who had withdrawn from her. She then thought about how, as a girl, she would sit and brood, wondering, "Why doesn't mother love me . . . Should I bring her flowers or should I clean the bath?" After she told me this, it suddenly became clear to me that this was the part of herself which had no language: the fearful child who looked to see what her mother's mood was like, to see if she should turn towards or away from her. Without giving it much thought, I addressed her with her first name: "That is the small, needy Lisa, who is fighting for her mother's love and has become mute." It immediately became clear to me that I had now found the point which I had been looking for more or less preconsciously: the point from which I could affectively reach this split-off, dissociated, muted, needy, fearful, and childish self. All she could say was, "That really goes deep." Greatly moved inside, she was silent until the session ended soon thereafter. It was painful for her to realize that her dissociative wandering from her self had functioned like a narcotic, which she had used as a defence against feelings that seemed unbearable. However, this realization enabled her to leave her inner prison and to live life with a sense of self again. These phases of the patient's finding of herself were followed by yet more, but I am unable able to go into them in any detail here.

Discussion

The unbearable flood of fear and pain which the three-year-old girl presumably suffered during and after the eye operation brought about a hypnoid state, resulting in a peritraumatic dissociation that led to a splitting of her consciousness: the observing ego detached itself from the experiencing body and could view its own trauma-tizing experience from above. In this way, the splitting of her con-sciousness was preconditioned. The loss of her intact body image at the age of five, the stay in the clinic, and the lethal danger of a lack of insulin, was a second trauma for the five-year-old, which was accompanied by increased dissociative processes. She still retains a detailed recollection of the altered state of consciousness in which she found herself. The mental integrational capacity of the infantile ego was overwhelmed, leading to a fixation of dissociative pro-cesses. The connection between her observing self and her experi-encing self was broken. It seemed as if she no longer had any inner access to her lively, vulnerable, traumatized self. This fixation of dissociative defence was also a consequence of insufficient affective dialogue between parents and child about these traumatic events.

In addition, the massive traumatization had also disrupted the patient's capacity to discern between interior and exterior. The fear for survival, the daily injections, and the massive increase in sepa-ration anxiety from the mother, led to a close orientation on the exterior world and its physical and emotional dangers, so that hardly any room remained for the patient to develop a separate inner world. She experienced feelings as something foreign that entered from the outside. Later, these evolved into alien, personi-fied voices, which settled themselves like visitors, or raged and romped about within her. As a result, the traumatized, suffering self remained emotionally imperceptible to the patient.

Once this dissociation had occurred, the patient was able to use it later as a defence against non-traumatic feelings. Her ego was too fragile to withstand the return of fear and painful feelings. She protected herself against this by departing from herself in a self-induced hypnotic state. In so doing, she entered into unbearable states of tension and was often able to leave them only by scratching or cutting herself open. The dissociative defence was also marked by characteristics of omnipotence, for she used it to fend off the integration of what she viewed as her flawed diabetic "sugar-ego" and clung to the hope that she could make her diabetes vanish. Her traumatic numbness and her refusal to accept and to integrate her diabetic self also led her to try to suppress any inner feeling of continuity in order to maintain the illusion that she could start everything over again. This offers us impressive evidence of the way in which the experience of time is pathologically altered through traumatization and the way in which dissociation, if used as a defence mechanism, can lead to a lasting compartmentalization and fragmentation of the psyche and a feeling of emptiness.

Reconstruction of traumatic memories and mental integration

As we have seen, current research assumes that in traumatic experiences the overwhelming excitation and unbearable pain and fear cause the integrative functions of memory to be shut off, resulting in dissociated states of consciousness and in an exclusion of traumatic experiences from consciousness. This process involves "raw data", so to speak, which are stored as a traumatic memory. Because they are dissociated and split off from normal consciousness, they do not undergo any further mental processing, as other memories do. On this point, van der Kolk's hypothesis goes the furthest. He theorizes that traumatic experiences are stored in memory as affect states and indelible sensory imprints – as visual images, bodily sensations, sounds, and smells – separated from other life experiences. They are not organized into a unified whole. Once people start talking about these sensations, they are then transcribed, and these narratives become as vulnerable to distortion as people's stories about anything else. In contrast, the traumatic experience itself remains an indelible imprint "etched onto the mind". As van der Kolk observes: "Traumatic memories are timeless and ego-alien" (van der Kolk, 1996, pp. 295–296).

This model of trauma memory is open to the objection that stressful, emotionally significant events can generally be retained and explicitly remembered in the long term, although psychogenic amnesia unquestionably does occur. (For more extensive discussion, see Chapter Five in this volume.) Indeed, it can be assumed that the integrative functions of memory are disengaged by the excessive excitation in the traumatic situation, giving rise to a dissociated self-state. Traumatic memories can intrude suddenly into consciousness, however, when this encapsulated self-state is activated. An important qualification here is that these intrusions or flashbacks are not photographically accurate replicas of the traumatic experiences. Often, they are mixtures of real memory images and visualized anxieties, in which the worst fears can express themselves (Schacter, 1996).

These facts support the psychoanalytically-based thesis that, even if traumatic experiences and their memories are subject to specific psychodynamic restrictions and operations, they are not completely excluded from the associative stream of psychic material or from any transformation by conscious and unconscious fantasies.

If we must now consider traumatic memories to be reworked in a specific and restricted sense, the question arises as to whether a therapeutic reconstruction of traumatic events is possible or necessary. Traumatic memories are often activated in treatment by enactments in the transference relationship. Discovering the reality of the trauma and its associated affects, namely its historicization, however fragmentary or approximate, is the prerequisite for elucidating and comprehending its secondary revision and transformation by unconscious fantasies and meanings that contain guilt feelings and punitive impulses. Fantasy and traumatic reality are thereby disentangled and the ego gains an alleviating context of understanding. Historicization also involves recognizing the traumatic fact and understanding the individual experience and the emergent long-term consequences. When such a reconstructive interpretation succeeds, astonishing improvements frequently occur in the condition of patients, who then speak of a sensation of psychic integration, which is a sign that the self-organization is restructuring itself. If an encapsulated traumatic part of the self becomes permeable again, it can also be better interconnected associatively. However, an inaccurate reconstruction remains ineffective, no matter how meaningful it may continue to appear.

What are the underlying reasons for this? A reconstruction must correspond with the reality of the patient's trauma and grasp the reality that caused the traumatization. It is necessary to recognize what has been suffered, to articulate screen memories and split-off convictions, and to understand and interpret them in connection with the traumatic events. The interpretation must account for the elements that were already set or inherent in the traumatic experience itself, along with their secondary development of meaning. However, this is does not mean that all aspects of experience can be verbalized. There are also varying levels of psychic representation upon which the dissociated contents are organized. Further, a number of gaps have to be bridged by constructions, or only various indications are suggested by somatic symptoms, repetitive dreams, or hints from others that are given externally. In a reconstructive, hence verbal, formulation of the traumatic event that overwhelmed the patient within the therapeutic relationship, the self state dissociated through the trauma can once again be connected to non-dissociated mental material. The narrative that emerges from this reconstruction simultaneously expresses and furthers an ongoing process of mental integration. When a dissociated state is reactivated, it also helps the patient to avoid becoming completely passive and overwhelmed; instead, it brings about or intensifies an active self-reflection necessary to escape from the situation. Central to this narrative is that it be tied to an awareness that something has in fact occurred, no matter how fragmentary its reconstruction was. This can provide patients with a sense of truth and security with which to understand their traumatic transformations of the self, their object relationships, and their affects, instead of processing them in terms of guilt. At stake here is the reconstruction of the historical truth of the traumatic experience. Therefore, it does not get to the heart of the matter if the only meaning constructed with a narrative seeks to integrate the dissociated mental material in the manner formulated by those practising relational psychoanalysis. Boulanger will serve here as an example. She characterizes therapeutic work with traumatized patients as follows:

> The importance lies not in the memory itself but in the power to gather all the disparate impressions into a coherent whole, and in

the rigorously intersubjective experience necessary to this process. . . . We do not believe that this process reveals the truth, *per se*, indeed, we do not believe that there is *a* truth to be discovered, but we do hope to help the patient construct a living narrative that does justice to her experience [2007, pp. 149–150, my emphasis]

Yet, it is entirely insufficient to analyse the transference and countertransference in therapy solely in the here-and-now of the analytic situation, as this can give rise to meaningful narratives that lack any reconstruction of the causative traumatic reality. Such narratives are in danger of failing to distinguish between fantasy and reality and, in the worst case scenario, of retraumatizing the patient.

Conclusion

The concept of dissociation was long banned from the body of psychoanalytic theory. Trauma research has brought about its gradual return, however. Indeed, dissociation has even assumed a key position within relational psychoanalysis. At the same time, however, this field has expanded the concept to such a point that it is at risk of once again losing whatever meaning it has gained. Dissociation has long been incorporated into psychiatric nomenclature, for example, that of the *DSM IV*. Dissociative disorders are, according to the state of present research, a specific consequence of severe traumatization in childhood and/or adulthood. Dissociation has a dual function: first, in the traumatic situation itself it serves as protection against an unbearable reality, and second, it represents a pathological attempt at self-regulation. As such, it can also serve as a defence against conflictual scenarios that are not conditioned by trauma.

As a whole, the phenomenon has yet to be sufficiently researched within psychoanalysis. Dissociative states range from subtle changes in awareness, as depicted at the outset, all the way to severe dissociative identity disorders. Here, I can only name a few of the questions that still need to be addressed. First, how narrowly or widely should we define dissociation? Is it a specific reaction to traumatic situations (peritraumatic dissociation) that not all people have? Or should we think of dissociation very generally as the altered state of the self in the catastrophic situation? This state would be defined as one in which the capacity for reflection is lost due to overwhelming mortal fear and pain, leading to cognitive and affective numbing and constriction, a reaction that persists after the event itself and culminates in a dissociative self state. Alternatively, should we understand dissociation as involving very general aspects of experiences or mental contents that have remained unintegrated or unformulated? Further, what affective–cognitive level of organization do these dissociated and unintegrated mental contents possess, and which form of mental registration? Clinically, we also have to ask how dissociated traumatic self parts can be further processed by the psyche. We also have yet to understand how the defensive function of dissociation is to be distinguished from other defence mechanisms such as repression, denial, and splitting. An important step in addressing these questions is for psychoanalysts to pay attention to, and record, dissociative phenomena in their clinical work. In this way, dissociation can be removed from its marginal position as a clinical phenomenon and once again be integrated into the body of psychoanalytic theory.

PART III
PSYCHOANALYSIS OF
IDEOLOGICAL DESTRUCTIVITY

CHAPTER SEVEN

Purity, unity, violence: unconscious determinants of anti-Semitism in Germany

Introduction and overview

Many of the better-known psychoanalytic studies on anti-Semitism were written in circumstances marked by involuntary emigration and first-hand experience of the persecution and extermination of Jews by the Nazi regime. Without exception, the authors were themselves Jewish. One response to the imminent dangers spawned by anti-Semitism was an attempt to fathom the specific characteristics of Jewish identity from a psychoanalytic vantage point (Beland, 1992). These studies investigated traditional and Christian hostility to Jews, as well as the racist variety that had developed into a barbaric, exterminatory anti-Semitism in Germany. The psychoanalysts who wrote them sought to comprehend the destructive hatred with which Jews were persecuted, a hatred that for all of them had turned into a trauma and a severe threat to their very lives. These studies date from the 1930s and 1940s. Sigmund Freud's monograph *Moses and Monotheism* first appeared in 1939. In 1938, Otto Fenichel had produced the first version of his essay on anti-Semitism, written in exile in Prague. Rudolf Loewenstein began his study on anti-Semitism and the cultural comparison between Christianity and Judaism in France in 1941. In 1944, Ernst Simmel presented his analysis of anti-Semitism as a form of mass psychopathology at a symposium he had organized in San Francisco. Other prominent speakers at this famous symposium on anti-Semitism were Max Horkheimer, Otto Fenichel, Bernhard Berliner, Else Frenkel-Brunswik, and Theodor Adorno (Simmel, 1946). 1950 saw the publication of *The Authoritarian Personality* by Adorno, Frenkel-Brunswik, Levinson and Sanford (1950b) that was based largely on psychoanalytic concepts. Another study that appeared at the time was *Anti-Semitism and Emotional Disorder* (1950), by Ackerman and Jahoda.

If we leave aside the more general sociological debate on the authoritarian personality, little else was published on anti-Semitism from a psychoanalytic perspective in the 1950s. In 1962, Alexander Mitscherlich organized a symposium on anti-Semitism at which Grunberger described the oedipal and narcissistic dynamic operative in anti-Semitic psychology (see also Grunberger, 1964, 1984), while Wangh (1962, 1964) sought to elucidate Nazi anti-Semitism by relating it to the social crisis in Germany following the First World War and the intergenerational dynamic prevailing between defeated fathers and their sons (Loewenberg [1969] takes a similar approach). Ostow (1986, 1996a,b) discussed the links between anti-Semitism and apocalyptic thinking, Beland (1991) and Loewenberg (1992) the continuity between religious and racist anti-Semitism, and Brainin, Ligeti, and Teicher (1993) anti-Semitism in the Nazi era. Chasseguet-Smirgel (1990) examined the racist ideology of National Socialism, and Vogt (1995), and Vogt and Vogt (1997) described the repercussions of Nazi introjects in present-day German society and anti-Semitism as a form of self-absolution from guilt. 1997 saw the appearance of the major study by Grunberger and Dessuant on Christianity and anti-Semitism.

In the early 1980s, German psychoanalysts had embarked on a painful process of considering the involvement of their own profession in the Nazi era. This produced a heightened awareness of the ongoing effects of the Nazi heritage on subsequent generations. Psychoanalytic treatment for children of members of the second generation was discussed at conferences and in publications. Research was done (a) on the effects that the silence of parents about their involvement in the Nazi regime and the denial of guilt and responsibility had on the psyche of their children, and (b) on mechanisms operative in transgenerational forms of identification. But little of this engendered any genuine insights into anti-Semitism. In psychoanalytic treatment, anti-Semitic ideas and sentiments frequently materialized in a larval form or remained largely latent, thus making them difficult to pinpoint in the framework of a dynamic and/or genetic approach. Also, analysts were often reluctant to address this problem directly for fear of imposing their own preferences on the patients.

An American psychoanalytic research group on anti-Semitism came up with similar observations (Ostow, 1996a,b). In the nineteen case reports on patients undergoing psychoanalysis or psycho-therapy, only three of those patients turned out to be anti-Semitic. The others periodically expressed anti-Semitic sentiments in the course of treatment, but many of these resulted from aggressive or negative transference *vis-à-vis* their (frequently Jewish) analysts and could not be assigned to any specific dynamic constellation, form of defence, or organizing fantasy. The only thing that could be said with any certainty was that the intensity and explicitness of anti-Semitic utterances were proportional to the degree of aggression with which the patient had to come to terms in treatment. Knafo (1999) arrived at similar conclusions, indicating that very different repressed or split-off parts of the self can be clothed in anti-Semitic ideology and expressions that can then manifest themselves in transference. She suggests that individual nuances should not be neglected, but nor should they be subsumed under general anti-Semitic stereotypes. On closer inspection, however, her cases indicate one thing very clearly: the anti-Semitic prejudices of the patients are related to sexuality, superiority *vs.* inferiority feelings, and envy occasioning massive destructive rage. Ostow identifies the same constellation in his sample of patients, concluding that, in the anti-Semitic sentiments expressed, the individual differences in personality traits and psychodynamic structure that the patients displayed were, in almost every instance, overridden by stereotypical myths. In the emergence of individual anti-Semitic prejudices, these myths thus acquire the function of an organizing fantasy.

These findings prepared the ground for the analysis of socially widespread anti-Semitic convictions and the attempt to rephrase the question: what is it that makes anti-Semitic notions attractive for individuals projectively fending off their own conflictual and prohibited desires and/or looking for an external culprit on whom they can foist the blame for their disappointments and personal distress?

The historian Langmuir (1990) distinguishes two varieties of anti-Semitism:

1. Xenophobic anti-Semitism deriving from social reality in which there are contacts or rivalry with Jews and in which at least to a minimal degree prejudice is related to social experience;
2. Chimerical anti-Semitism rearing its head for the first time in the twelfth century after the introduction of the Catholic doctrine of transubstantiation and centring around such things as desecration of the Host, ritual murders of Christian children, etc. The accusation that Jews intentionally contaminated the water in urban wells first made its appearance in the fourteenth century in the course of the Great Plague. Chimerical anti-Semitism is based purely on fantasies, wishful thinking, and the projection of interior conflicts. Chimerical assertions served to present these interior conflicts as a social problem and to provide explanations for disappointments and personal or social disasters. Once established, this form of anti-Semitism recurred regularly and with fateful effects at various points in Western history, all the way up to the exterminatory anti-Semitism of the Nazis.

In the early nineteenth century, anti-Semitism moved into a new context. Individuals and groups of a nationalist persuasion fell back on ancient anti-Semitic notions and stereotypes, took them out of the Christian context, revalued them, and inserted them into the emerging nationalist framework. In this way, a new stock of anti-Semitic ideas took shape that anti-Semites of later ages could draw upon. Research has revealed an astonishing continuity in anti-Semitic ideas and arguments, but this will hardly surprise a psychoanalyst in view of their roots in the unconscious.

Historians have identified an increasingly radical tendency in nineteenth century German anti-Semitism, aiming progressively at the elimination of the Jews from German society (Erb & Bergmann,

1989; Rose, 1990). Goldhagen (1996) sees the origins of the Holocaust in this eliminationist anti-Semitism, culminating in the exterminatory form preached and practised by National Socialism. Some historians have disputed this continuity, but this is not the place to enlarge on the resultant controversy. In psychoanalytic terms, such radicalization would not be surprising, as notions of idealism and purification invariably involve extremist tendencies. This can be found prototypically in the relationship between nationalism and anti-Semitism. Modern research on nationalism provides significant support for this argument, describing nations as collective constructions strongly marked by phantasmal elements (Anderson, 1983). The idea of the nation is a compound of fact and fiction, thus providing rich scope for unconscious collective fantasies to intermingle with rational notions. In Germany, the nation was defined as an ethnically homogeneous community, thus providing a specific symbolic and phantasmal matrix in which various unconscious fantasy systems could materialize and thrive. These unconscious fantasy systems determined the psychological interdependence between nationalism and anti-Semitism. The idealized image of the nation was a dynamic, all-encompassing force allotting to the Jews the role of a counter-image functioning as a container for negative projections. Before enlarging on this constellation in my attempt to give a psychoanalytic description and explanation of the connection between anti-Semitic phantasms and increasingly radical destructiveness, I should first like to give an indication of the positions of a number of historians and social scientists on this issue.

From thought to deed: radicalization
tendencies in anti-Semitism

Rose (1990) has shown how the thinking of various nineteenth century anti-Semitic authors displayed increasingly radical tendencies as time went on, culminating first in a recommendation to banish Jews from society and later in the proposal to exterminate them altogether. Historians disagree over the extent to which these utterances were meant metaphorically or literally. With Auschwitz in mind, we, of course, have a different perception of such statements than a contemporary of these authors would have had.

However, even if these were more or less nebulous fantasies, we still need to understand the radicalism and the dynamics of these notions, as well as the logic inherent in them.

Volkov (1990) has taken issue with the theory of continuity between nineteenth century anti-Semitism and the Nazi variety. She insists that the role of anti-Semitism can only be understood in terms of the needs and problems of a given age. In the Second Reich (1871–1919), she sees anti-Semitism as performing four functions: it functioned as an instrument of integration, as a means of channelling social and political dissatisfaction, as an ideology for winning over sections of the liberal camp to the right, and as a means of communication and a cultural code within the political culture of the time. But whatever role anti-Semitism played in Germany under Kaiser Wilhelm, it was invariably part of its written culture. None of the anti-Semitic authors displayed any talent at implementing their grandiose ideas in practical terms. Neither the politicians nor the ideologists associated with this movement had any concrete plans. Anti-Semitism in this period never advanced beyond verbal aggression. However, after 1918, and then again with the advent of Hitler, anti-Semitism took on a new significance. Nazism, Volkov asserts, was a culture in which verbal aggression was not a substitute for action but a preparation for it: "The old written matter was transformed into an entirely new material—explosive, dangerous, leading directly to disaster" (p. 74, translated for this edition).

However, in psychological terms, insistence on discontinuity and on the different functions performed by anti-Semitism under Kaiser Wilhelm and in the Nazi era poses a number of problems. This fundamental distinction between anti-Semitism in word and deed suggests a difference in the nature of these two forms that does not, in fact, exist. Volkov herself is forced to concede that, in Hitler's case, anti-Semitic speech was a preparation for action. In other words, the conceptual world that such speech inhabited was totalitarian and geared to extermination. It is impossible to make such a clear psychological distinction between the two manifestations, although, in psychoanalytic terms, we must never, of course, neglect the difference between word and deed.

However, the question arises of whether there is a common psychological structure detectable in nineteenth and twentieth century anti-Semitism that is marked by increasing radicalization.

Were violence and a pogrom mentality not inherent in the conceptual world anti-Semitism inhabited? Von Brentano (1965) has
pointed out that distinctions like those made by Volkov can
frequently lead us astray in our attempt to understand anti-
Semitism:

> What we need to make clear to ourselves is how and why ordinary
> anti-Semitism has always had a tendency to turn into a totalitarian
> world view and to spawn violence and bloodshed, not just in the
> case of the Nazis. Its extremist inclinations are in fact the normal
> case. It is essential to grasp how and why, unlike other features of
> pre-Fascist society, it was not only integrated into a totalitarian
> system of terror in the Nazi period but was in itself able to become
> a pivot and a breeding-ground for the switchover to totalitarian
> terror. [pp. 40–41, translated for this edition]

Rose (1990) argues that the question of whether anti-Semitic
utterances and proposals should be understood metaphorically or
literally is in itself fallacious. This, he says, is quite the wrong
approach to achieving an understanding of German anti-Semitism.
Volkov herself asserts that we must not underestimate the effect of
nineteenth century anti-Semitic metaphors: even when they were
"false"—as in the slogan: "The social issue is the Jewish issue"—
they were still extremely effective.

> The power of metaphor is the result of the collusion between the
> discordant meaning symbolically pressed into a unified conceptual
> framework and the degree to which this metaphoric brace is able to
> overcome the inner resistance that such semantic tension is bound
> to trigger in anyone capable of perceiving it. [Geertz, quoted in
> Volkov, 1990, p. 30 (translated for this edition)]

Generally, metaphors and similes have an inherent tendency to lose
the character of "figurative" speech. In the eyes of many people,
anti-Semitic slogans had triumphed over the perception of reality;
the links they suggested were accepted as something self-evident.

*   *   *

Erb and Bergmann (1989) have shown how, in the course of the
attempt to backtrack on the emancipation of the Jews, a supply of

anti-Semitic ideas developed as early as the beginning of the nine-teenth century upon which the anti-Semites of the German Empire were able to draw. The authors' detailed analysis of source material demonstrates the astounding continuity of anti-Semitic motifs, ideas, and argumentation, and their flexibility in adapting their content to the *zeitgeist* of the respective eras in which they materi-alized. In the course of their investigations, Erb and Bergmann were surprised by the frequency and radicalism of the notions of segre-gation emerging in this early period and already containing advo-cacy for banishment and extermination. What did these nineteenth century authors actually mean when they spoke of the "downfall", "extermination", "destruction", and "annihilation" of Judaism or the Jews? Rose (1990) insists that we must first comprehend the meaning that the concept of Judaism had in Germany at that time. Judaism had a wide range of meanings designating the religion, the Jews themselves, and the Jewish way of thinking and behaving. He suggests that this multiplicity of meanings was the reason why the concepts listed above were used in different ways and, hence, fluc-tuated between metaphorical and literal meaning. For example, "downfall" was used literally and metaphorically at one and the same time, representing "a fluctuating dynamic feeling and idea" (*ibid.*, p. 35) in people's minds. This dynamic fluctuation facilitated the radicalization of the anti-Semitic authors' ideas and proposals: "This phenomenon suggests an inherent lethal logic in the whole idea of the destruction of Judaism that, once begun, was compelled to work itself out" (*ibid.*, p. 37). What Rose describes here is fruitful in psychological terms because a metaphorical image activates an unconscious set of notions in the human mind that influences and threatens to overwhelm the perception of reality: for example, when vermin metaphors are associated with murder fantasies. More than simple metaphors, the mythic descriptions of the Jews tended to crowd out the perception of actual individuals. The Jews encountered in the social environment were more or less vaguely invested with supernatural demonic meanings:

> Thus, more and more, a dreamlike symbolic perception of the Jews was being applied without mediation of any sort to the real world, so that in the increasingly bizarre world of German anti-Semitism, practical politics assumed the nature of a phantasm. [1990, pp. 57–58]

Subsequently, National Socialism completely obliterated the frontier between mythic fantasy and social reality. Once metaphorical comparison is equated with reality, symbolic thinking comes to an end, and a paranoid mentality holds sway.

Methodological considerations on the psychoanalysis of collective phantasms

Anti-Semitism is a social phenomenon and, as such, requires an interdisciplinary approach for its investigation. Psychoanalysis must pay due heed to the autonomy of the social sphere and the abstract nature of social control mechanisms and systemically stabilized patterns of action. This, however, does not impair its ability to trace back the attraction exerted by ideologies and nationalist/ ethnic phantasms and the extraordinarily strong affects associated with them to unconscious factors and to provide psychological explanations for them. In terms of both method and content, I take my bearings in the following from the concept of "ubiquitous unconscious fantasies" (see Bendkower, 1991). These are "primal fantasies" (Freud, 1916–1917) shared to a greater or lesser degree by all human individuals. They stem from needs common to all of us. They are ubiquitous because they have to do with the fundamental givens of human life, the connection between bodily needs, psychological development, and fantasy formation, notably in connection with psychosexual maturation, dependence on the mother and the care she provides, separation from the mother, and sibling rivalry, the primal scene, and the Oedipus complex or the recognition of the reality of the father. These archaic fantasies are socialized in the course of development, but they remain present in the unconscious. They penetrate into consciousness as derivatives of the unconscious and hence materialize in reality and in social life. In striving to fulfill themselves, they develop a propensity for externalization. Thus, unconscious fantasies can attach themselves to the perception and formation of social events, institutions, and cultural valuation patterns, leaving their imprint on them accordingly. On the other hand, they are pressed into service in the external sphere by social agencies, being thus shaped and channeled by objective structures, institutions, communicative conventions, and linguistic traditions.

They figure most prominently in highly irrational and affectively charged social processes. This tendency for unconscious fantasies to externalize themselves makes it impossible for the psychoanalyst to make a clear-cut distinction between inside and outside. A similar position is taken up by Traub-Werner (1984), who accords psychoanalysis a specific place alongside historical and social studies in the development of a general theory of prejudice. The actual target of prejudice is part of the social dimension, it is culturally conditioned, and its manifestations are a subject for the social sciences. By contrast, the intrapsychic dimension is where prejudice forms, a process steered by projective mechanisms and for which the ego possesses a defence function. The connecting link between the social and the intrapsychic dimension is symbolization: via symbolic equation, the conscious "targets" of prejudice represent the covert expression of unconscious forces and inclinations in the human mind.

*   *   *

The propensity for unconscious desires to attach themselves with such ease to national and ethnic ideologies is notably facilitated by the following circumstances.

1. Many social phenomena are associated with the primary developmental process at an early stage. Ontogenetically, fundamental notions about home, state, and nation are communicated at a time when the contents and the meanings of love and hate and the notion of the self are first being established (Balibar, 1988; Volkan, 1988), Accordingly, collective and individual identity are not only metaphorically connected, but intrapsychically associated. They are experienced concomitantly. This means that external frontiers are conceived of as a projection and protection of an interior collective identity that we all carry within us and that enables us to experience the state both spatially and temporally as a place where we have always been, and where we will always be, at home. Accordingly, the categories and symbols figuring in universal conceptions of the nation are a mass phenomenon and an individuation factor at one and the same time.

2. Alongside familial representations ("fatherland", "mother country"), bodily metaphors are also drawn upon to establish the idea of the substantialist cohesion of ethnic or national communities at a profound level in the imagination. In her studies on rituals in different cultures, the ethnologist Douglas (1966) shows how the body provides a model for the notion of society. The individual projects the notion of the body on to society, while in rituals the dangers and forces existing in the social structure are expressed by the body. Rituals enact a form of social relations, and in giving these relations visible expression they enable individuals to know their society. Rituals have their effect on the body politic via the symbolic medium of the physical body. Given the concrete experiences of the individual, body symbols are emotionally highly charged. Thus, on account of the anthropogenetically manifold and stratified experiences of the individual that have become unconscious in the course of his/her socialization, body symbols can be used for a huge variety of purposes. Societies resort to different bodily experiences to symbolize specific social problems and hazards. Body, limbs, organism, fatherland, mother country, and so on form a symbolic conceptual system used by every society to address political and social identity problems, the relationship between inside and outside, between borders, purity, homogeneity, and ethnic mix, etc. An especially interesting issue in our context is the question of which aspects and sectors of this conceptual world are drawn upon to represent notions of national identity and the specific nature of a society's collective identity. How are anti-Semitic notions articulated via body phantasms and familial representations, and how do they express feelings of threat, anxieties, and aggressive and destructive strivings? In the following, I examine these questions in greater detail.

Unconscious fantasies in anti-Semitic and nationalist thinking

The increasingly racist nature of anti-Semitism in the nineteenth and early twentieth centuries placed the content of traditional anti-Judaism in a new context. The opposite pole was no longer

Christianity, but the German nation. The collective fantasy systems described in the following display both a generally xenophobic dynamic and specifically anti-Semitic features. This description also serves to analyse the imaginary substance of the national(ist) thought-world. To the present day, the "emotional impact" (Elias, 1989) that the idea of the nation exerts on individuals has been one of the challenging aspects of research on nationalism. Psychoanalysis can help us to understand the specific dynamics involved as rooted both in the idealization of an idea and in projective hatred.

Provision fantasies and anti-Semitism

Jacob Arlow (1992, 1994) has given us a psychoanalytic investigation of the accusations of ritual murder levelled at the Jews. Notably, in the Middle Ages, accusations that Jews would steal and kill Christian children to use their blood for the preparation of matzos for the Passover and for other rituals were extremely widespread. Despite attempts made by the church and by secular institutions to combat these accusations and prohibit them as slanderous, they could never be eliminated altogether. They were also used by the Nazis in the twentieth century and turned up again in Poland after 1945 (the pogrom of Kielce, 1946). Arlow argues that such a grotesque idea could only ensconce itself in the human mind because it appeals to a profoundly primitive and unconscious desire. Arlow locates this desire in primitive sibling hostility. A characteristic unconscious fantasy of older siblings is that of destroying the newborn baby by eating and ingesting it. Alongside infanticide and cannibalism, this fantasy also involves identification with the neonate on which the parents lavish their admiration. The accusation of ritual murder stems from a projection of unconscious desires of infanticide and cannibalism from Christians on to Jews. For long periods in Western history, the Jews, as unfamiliar and alien figures, aroused deep-lying, unresolved hostility originally and ontogenetically directed at sibling rivals or anyone suspected of trespassing on a sphere regarded as ours by right:

> The dynamic of the blood libel accusation against the Jews and antisemitic ideology in general have at least one universal root

common to all humans: unconscious fantasies triggered by primitive conflicts about the fact that food, security, and maternal love
have to be shared. [Arlow, 1992, p. 1132, translated for this edition]

This same unconscious dynamic, combining oral–sadistic drive
urges and sibling rivalries, is identifiable in the vast range of metaphors relating to the Jews as parasites and scroungers attaching
themselves like leeches to the "host people" (*Wirtsvolk*) or the
"ethnic body" (*Volkskörper*) (on the following, see Bein, 1965). In the
nineteenth century, the medieval idea of Jews as blood-suckers and
exploiters or usurers took a new form in the image of the parasite.
But it was only in connection with the idea of the state as an organism that this image attained its full potential as the expression of a
vital threat. Many different creatures (notably insects) classifiable
as vermin and characterized by enormous voracity were used as
comparisons. In the botanical sphere, parasitic plants and weeds
were also drawn upon as similes. The idea of Jews as parasites
was combined with mythic notions from earlier epochs deriving
from deeper strata of the unconscious: the image of the devil, of the
extortionate usurer, the vampire. In myth, fantasy and reality
merge, making it impossible for the uncritical mind to determine
where reality ends and fantasy based on subjective belief begins.
With the emergence of pseudo-scientific race theories, this biological imagery was given a new lease of life and found its way into the
everyday conceptual world of broad sectors of the population, all
the way up to the early twentieth century. Nazi propaganda
exploited this further, giving it a new brand of radicalism and
brutality. Jäckel (1972) has studied *Mein Kampf* to categorize the
extensive vocabulary deriving from these images that the book
contains. Hitler rails against the Jews as maggots in a decomposing
body, as a pestilence, as bacillus-carriers, as the eternal fission
fungus of humanity, as drones worming their way into the rest of
humanity, as spiders slowly sucking the blood out of the pores of
the people, as a horde of rats fighting each other to the death, as
typical parasites, scroungers, eternal leeches, and vampires feasting
on the life-blood of the nation.

Why did this terminology catch on to such an extent that it can
be found in stereotypic form in countless anti-Semitic descriptions?
Obviously, the scope afforded to aggressive fantasies was more or

less unlimited, with constant references to clinging and creeping, penetration, infestation, debilitation, corrosion, decay, suffocation, decomposition, etc. (Hortzitz, 1995). Oral–sadistic voracity, greed, and exploitative impulses were projected on to the Jews to justify the call to free the community of Germans from such influences. Via their dehumanization as repulsive, nauseating vermin, the Jews were also excluded from human society. They were pilloried as unproductive consumers battening on what others had created. The notion we see developing here is that of self-provision without personal effort. The Jews were made into sibling interlopers and rivals disrupting the narcissistically idealized union with the collective maternal imago. In a newspaper article appearing in 1865, we are told that, just as caterpillars and snails devour everything that is green,

> so the Reform Jews gnaw away at everything that is green in human life, everything that warms the soul, everything that is fine and beautiful, and if it were up to them alone, there would long since be nothing left but dead bones and wilted stalks. [quoted in Erb & Bergmann, 1989, p. 206, translated for this edition]

This equation of the Jews with parasitic insects and worms involves contradictory evaluations of their potency. On the one hand, they are small, unprepossessing, and feeble; on the other hand, extremely powerful, threatening, and equipped with indescribable strength. These contradictions can also be found in other ascriptions, with Jews perceived both as emasculated and as representatives of powerful paternal authority.

Even for those advocating complete equality for the Jews in the nineteenth century, the only conceivable course was for Judaism to wither to the point of disintegration and for the Jews themselves to adapt to German society. These ideas were couched in terms revolving around extermination, annihilation, and disappearance, aggressive vocabulary reflecting the violence with which the requisite assimilation was to be engineered. The term "assimilation" stems from biology, where it designates a process of transformation into a substance with a nature of its own, while leaving the assimilating body intact and constant. Translated into political terminology, this concept was eminently suitable for the establishment of a new social semantics developing in the course of emergent nationalism (Bauman, 1991).

Anzieu (1975) describes how, in group constellations, an unconscious oral notion of the group as both a providing and engulfing unit takes hold of its members. The dynamic within the group activates oral–sadistic fantasies and enables them to penetrate into the consciousness of the participants. Simmel (1946) attempted to explain anti-Semitic hatred with reference to his concept of an "instinct to devour" (*Verschlingungstrieb*). Simmel sees the desire to incorporate the object as bound up with the desire to withdraw that object from conscious perception via assimilation with the ego. Thus, the process of social assimilation is connected with unconscious notions of oral devouring and anal digestion, an oral–sadistic form of destruction depriving the Jews of their identity and transforming them into indistinguishable and homogeneous members of a nation. The language of the day reflects this by referring to Jew-haters as "Jew-eaters" (*Judenfresser*). Xenophobia is fuelled by many fantasy systems, but, in ethnic conflicts, group fantasies invariably activate the unconscious fantasy of a powerful collective mother, providing security and sustenance on the one hand, but also capable of devouring and expulsion on the other. Here, the social question of membership and inclusion–exclusion is experienced not only as a problem of actual economic or political engagement. On the unconscious plane, it also releases archaic aggression seeking to assert exclusive ownership of, and participatory fusion with, a maternal imago. The unproductive consumer is the sibling rival in the guise of an interloper that must be expelled or destroyed. On the one hand, anti-Semites project greed and oral–devouring aggression on to the Jews, by whom they then feel threatened, while, at the same time, identifying with a powerful, devouring oral–aggressive mother imago. The inhumanity and fantastic voracity ascribed to the Jews as insects and worms is projectively held apart from the ideal, harmonious community by seeing disease and voracity as coming from the outside. Conflicts and distribution problems are not regarded as requiring a solution within society itself. Instead, an ideal picture is generated of the Germans interacting peacefully and harmoniously with one another, and the threatening problem is seen as one posed by the aliens excluded from society.

Purity notions and anti-Semitism

Anti-Semites seek a pure and unified world that they attempt to safeguard by fending off aliens (Jews), projecting on to them everything that causes misery and distress. They charge the figure of the Jew with repressed drive strivings that have become alien and dirty. This is, however, not enough to explain anti-Semitic notions of purity fully. The massive destructiveness they can generate needs to be seen in terms of the psychodynamics of narcissism rather than drive conflicts.

Neubauer (1992) points to a disposition in human development that engenders susceptibility to prejudices, feelings, and ideas of the kind that crystallize in anti-Semitism. As the work done by Spitz (1965) and Mahler, Pine, and Bergmann (1975) indicates, the structure of the perception of the stranger is bipolar. The child's fear of strangers is not a consequence of the fact that an unfamiliar person is unknown and alien, it is a response to the perception that the person's face does not square with the memory traces of the image of the mother. The child makes a comparison, and the stranger is made to feel that he/she is not the familiar mother. The perception of the stranger makes the child turn back to the mother and, thus, reinforces the attachment. It is on this basis that the fear or shyness triggered by the stranger can be overcome. The anxiety, though, becomes more intense if the child's security in connection with its attachment to the mother is unstable, thus triggering a violent defence reaction to the stranger. In adulthood, strangers then remind the individual at an unconscious level that he/she has lost the narcissistic union with the mother. This basic structure of the response to strangers can also be transposed to groups. The more pathological the group and the more precarious the balance within it, the more violent the defence and aggression towards strangers will be, leading to a massive regression of individual capacities for decision-making and criticism within such groups. Narcissistic identification suppresses individual distinctions, thus enabling people to see those who are like them as mirrors of themselves and, thus, to assure themselves of allegiance and identity (Freud, 1921c). This species of narcissistic identification with the ideal of purity is unstable and can easily be disrupted by anything that does not square with it. The disruption is projected and leads to a highly charged and distorted image of the stranger or alien as posing a severe threat to cohesion. The National Socialist idea of racial purity and purity of the blood reinforced this all-encompassing internal identification process and brooked no compromise. Aliens-Jews—had to be eliminated from society.

At this psychic level, purity has close links with identity. Aliens figure as an impurity factor. Uncertainty, insecurity, and ambivalence cannot be tolerated. In anti-Semitic prejudice Jews are not only dirty and impure, they are also aliens representing ambiguity and ambivalence. In 1903, Weininger put it this way: "Inner ambivalence . . . is absolutely Jewish, straightforwardness is absolutely un-Jewish" (quoted in von Braun, 1994). In anti-Semitism, absoluteness is experienced as the liberation from doubt, ambiguity, and ambivalence and idealized as "purity". "Unity through purity" was one of the slogans of the anti-Semites. The destruction of the impure was designed to create one "symbolically consistent universe" (Lifton, 1986).

Purity is a utopian and extremely vague ideal that has to be defined negatively by reference to what is impure and alien. Purity can only be achieved by discrimination and is imagined as something that materializes through the expulsion of evil and impurity. This concatenation is the reason why new objects have to be constantly sought for purposes of exclusion or destruction. In its delusively concretistic conception of blood purity and the pure ethnic "body", racist anti-Semitism became the quintessence of such thinking.

Ostow (1996a) regards this violence aimed at the destruction of impurity as the fruit of a "pogrom mentality", a similar idea to Adorno's concept of "psychic totalitarianism":

> Nothing can be left untouched, everything has to be "aligned" with the ego ideal of the rigid, hypostasized "band of brothers". The alien group—the chosen enemy—represents an unremitting challenge. As long as there is anything deviant left of this enemy, the Fascist character feels threatened, however weak the other may be. [Adorno, 1950a, p. 143, translated for this edition]

A narcissistic ideal of uniformity and/or homogenization via purification is forcibly imposed, tolerating nothing that is alien or different. Paranoid ideas achieve supremacy and trigger massive persecutory aggression. Allegiance to an ideal object and persecutory violence exacerbate one another.

What is it, though, that makes participation in such an ideal group phantasm of purity so attractive and seductive? What unconscious communal fantasy is activated and addressed by this group ideology? Memmi (1982) proposes a simple answer:

> As this purity is not real, it can only be a wish, i.e. a longing or a hope. Racists worship the ideal of a perfect home country, but they would find it difficult to describe its actual features. They would be equally hard put to it to say what consummation it is that they so devoutly wish: reversion to an earlier condition or imposition of a new order, restoring a paradise lost or ushering in a messianic Golden Age . . . The future is seen as a projection of the past, and the past is reconstructed in terms of the future. [pp. 70–71, translated for this edition]

Racism is action. As a return to the happy world of childhood is impossible, the racist sets out to ensure that the future squares with that image. His aim is to restore homogeneity, eliminating anything that disturbs or befouls it.

Anti-Semitism and the phantasm of organic unity

The great promise held out by Nationalism was equality through unity. Both these *desiderata* rest on emotional identification with the superordinate idea of the nation. As we have seen, the holistic idea essential to the unity of the national community is formed analogously to the world of the individual and, hence, related above all to bodily processes and to the relational world of the primary family. It is thus that the nation as fatherland or mother country acquires its imaginative and emotional power.

Recent psychoanalytic research on group behaviour (Anzieu, 1975; Bion, 1961; Jaques, 1981; Kreeger, 1975, Money-Kyrle, 1951) has revealed that in a group or a mass movement regression goes back far beyond the oedipal level described by Freud to generate different and much more profound narcissistic identifications. The regressive fusion of the members turns the group into an illusory substitute for the first lost object, the mother in infancy. Group fantasy revolves not around a mass ideal embodied by a leader taking up and rehearsing the expectations of the masses, but around the fantasy of an ideal ego state in which the illusion of the restoration of a symbiotic relationship with the early mother is operative (Chasseguet-Smirgel, 1975). It is not the leader himself but the group fantasy that replaces the individual ideal ego by a collective ideal ego, thus generating manic elation.

This research is highly significant for extensive group fantasies about the nation. At the core of national identification lies spuriously omnipotent elation at being part of a greater whole. If this elation gains the upper hand and combines with fantasies of superiority, individual reality testing and the claims of personal conscience are set at naught, while the feeling of selfhood is enormously stimulated by fusion with the national self. The upshot is an inflation of narcissistic feelings. The realistic image of the nation is forfeited, and an idealizing mentality takes the place of private interests.

This symbolic world is, in itself, universal, but the definition of nationality as membership of an ethnically homogeneous group (in line with the *ius sanguinis*) in the German political tradition gives it a specific significance. Berlin (1990) speaks of an "ideology of organicism". Values, objectives, and purposes only gain legitimacy through their organic association with the nation. This integrates the individual into an indissoluble organic whole that defies analysis. In the individual, a collective world of ideas like this activates fantasies of, and longings for, organic unity and unification with the early mother: one no longer belongs to oneself but is part of a greater whole.

For anti-Semites, this notional world has a very special attraction. The question "Who am I?" is replaced by "Where do I belong?" Collective identification makes the other group members into mirror images of the self. Individuality and differences are suppressed. Nineteenth-century anti-Semitic literature is full of comparisons between the organic "earthing" of the German character and the infinitely different Jewish character. The ancient myth of Ahasver, the eternally homeless Jew bowed down with guilt, was transformed into that of the rootless modern Jew. From here on, Jewish redemption was synonymous with assimilation into the organic whole of the German nation and German culture. Grunberger (1964) demonstrates that, for the anti-Semite, the castration of Jews lies not only in circumcision but in segregation from the community and banishment to a position outside the system. He sees this perception as highly typical of anti-Semites because of their anally regressive character. For people like these, organic integration into a structured social system is the only way in which the individual can be narcissistically upgraded.

In line with these fantasies of an organic world, the influence of the Jews on political and intellectual life was designated as "corruptive" (*zersetzend*). When the concept of race made participation in political life a biological matter, National Socialism gave the idea of corruption a concrete destructive significance in connection with the organically conceived ethnic body. As the analysis of present-day right-wing radicals indicates, fear of commingling is a major anxiety displayed by all racist xenophobes. They are obsessed with the fear that a unified whole imagined as pure might disintegrate or be shattered or blown apart. It is the fear of encounter with "the other" as one who refuses to be assimilated by the organic whole.

Sartre has given us an accurate description of this anti-Semitic bugbear:

> The egalitarianism that the anti-Semite strives for with such zeal has nothing to do with the equality that democracies have elevated to programmatic status . . . The anti-Semite calls for the equality of all Aryans *against* the hierarchy of functions. Here equality is the fruit of the non-differentiation of functions. The social bond is anger; the community pursues no other aim than to impose a diffuse repressive sanction on certain individuals . . . Unable to understand the modern form in which society is organized, he (the anti-Semite) longs for periods of crisis in which primal communal forms suddenly resurface and reach fusion temperature. The anti-Semite wants to fuse with the group and be carried away by the collective current. [Sartre, 1954, pp. 21–22, translated for this edition]

Experience with patients who long for symbiotic states and who stand up for ideologies of uniformity indicates that these desires function as a defence against differences perceived in conjunction with castration anxiety and as a means of evading any engagement with the world of the oedipal father. These people divide reality into the world of universal symbiotic unity and—completely split off from it—the world of rivalry, competition, and plurality. Since the perception of differences is felt to entail a loss of sameness, the stranger/alien represents an attack on their own omnipotence, which need not be questioned as long as they continue to surround themselves with narcissistic ideas of sameness. Thus, idealization of unity and uniformity may result in extreme violence towards anything that is felt to threaten this ideal.

Discussion

Many traditional anti-Jewish ideas have found their way into the modern nexus between nationalism and anti-Semitism. For the consolidation of Christian identity, the Jews were indispensable as a negative concomitant and point of reference. Later, they came to represent the quintessential aliens and enemies that had to be aggressively excluded and marginalized to preserve national identity. There is a complex interactive relationship between societal/situational factors and collective mentality and the individual psyche that determines the extent to which collective and individual projections are centred on Jews, and a manic phantasmagoric image can dictate action. To this extent, we can say that anti-Semitism does not display a dynamic of its own that develops independently of concrete circumstances and social conditions. But, in Germany, there was a radicalization tendency inherent in the mental world of modern anti-Semitism, and psychoanalytic explanations for this fact can contribute to our understanding of this fateful development. Present-day historical and sociological research on Nazism proceeds on the assumption that it was an escalation in the history both of institutions and of mentality that led to the policy of mass murder.

I have described some unconscious fantasy systems that are not only activated and channelled by certain nationalist and anti-Semitic notions, but also play an active part in shaping them and determining people's sentiments, ideas, and actions. The unconscious fantasies I have derived from these nationalist and anti-Semitic notions revolve around ideal states (a) being the only one to receive maternal affection and care and eliminating rivals; (b) participating in an ideal, pure state undisturbed by any kind of otherness; (c) merging with and being assimilated into an organic whole, which is unconsciously imagined as restoration of the union with the maternal primary object and felt to be the overcoming of an individual, split-off, and alienated existence.

Psychodynamically, in anti-Semitism, aspiration to ideal–narcissistic states like these is bound up with violence directed at Jews, defined as interlopers and embodiments of a negative image. Enemies are indispensable in maintaining this ideality in individual and collective thinking. Once one enemy has been eliminated, another has to be created. The feeling of purity is a highly unstable condition with a tendency to radicalization. New dirt has to be constantly invented so that it can be done away with. Thus, there is a psychodynamic kinship between purity, homogeneity, harmony, paranoia, and violence.

I am not alone in my interpretation of modern anti-Semitism as a collusion between notions of ideality and massive destructiveness. With his concept of the "instinct to devour" (*Verschlingungstrieb*) Simmel (1946) was one of the first to describe the desire to eliminate the alien object from perception in order to produce internal and external uniformity. He explains it as a regression to primary narcissism.

For Ostow (1996a,b) irrational anti-Semitic hatred is the expression of a primary process form of thinking that creates a myth designed to explain all suffering and misery. Jews are perceived as malignant elements, and getting rid of them is equated with purification from all evil. Ostow sees this thinking as rooted in the notional world of the apocalypse revolving around dirt, purification, destruction, and rebirth. A new community is fantasized as a harmonious band of believers sustained by God's benevolence. According to Ostow, both Christian and post-Christian anti-Semitism is marked by an apocalyptic frame of mind. Inherent to both is massive violence transforming anti-Semitic prejudices into anti-Semitic persecution. Fundamentalist groups are particularly prone to devise deadly pogroms on the basis of this kind of thinking. Ostow suggests that, in clinical terms, apocalyptic thinking derives from suicidal thinking that is initially fended off and directed at others, but ultimately reverts to its self-destructive nature. He anchors this apocalyptic frame of mind in primary process thinking and deficient affect regulation that result in a dualist perception of the world in categories of good and evil. However, I doubt whether the massive degree of destructiveness can be appropriately explained in this theoretical framework. In the post-Christian era, the apocalypse only generates meaning in a secularized framework; it is no longer a powerful force based on belief and incentivizing action. Fantasies of destruction and rebirth and the violence resulting from them are better understood in the framework of a narcissistic dynamic in which the ideal notion of a community of the select spawns the destructive forces harnessed to the cause of purification.

Grunberger and Dessuant (1997) also see narcissism as the key to anti-Semitism. They distinguish between positive and negative narcissism. Positive narcissistic vitality is a maximalist form of self-expansion encountered in connection with perfection, aesthetics, morality, omnipotence, and autonomy. Engagement with oedipal conflicts restricts this narcissistic expansion and regulates narcissism and the drives via identification with the paternal principle and adjustment of the pleasure principle to the claims of reality. Grunberger and Dessuant describe psychic developments that attempt to evade the Oedipus complex. For them, the anti-Semite is the prototype of such a narcissistic solution and evasion of oedipal conflicts. As representatives of the law and the paternal principle, Jews are the fundamental signifier of a principle opposed to narcissism. Accordingly, they are predestined to be the objects of anti-Semitic hatred, as anti-Semitism derives from narcissistic disappointment. At the core of this narcissism is a one-sided ideology capable of generating enormous destructiveness in the name of narcissistic purity. Grunberger and Dessuant also see Christianity as determined by a psychological logic based on narcissism. Christ's divine nature is a function of his oneness with the Father and the Holy Ghost. As such, it is a version of pure narcissism incapable of tolerating the contradiction embodied in Christ's physical and organic humanity and thus ultimately expelling it as impure. In a 2,000-year-old purification process, Christians freed themselves from evil and narcissistic injuries by projecting them on to the Jews. This culminated in the apocalypse of the Holocaust.

I cannot go into any greater detail here on Grunberger and Dessuant's generalizing view of Christianity, but I believe their approach to the understanding of anti-Semitism as a product of narcissism to be correct. They see anti-Semitic violence as stemming from negative narcissism. The narcissistic drive turns negative when the development of positive narcissism is thwarted or traumatized, potentially resulting in extreme violence. Everything that does not accord with the positive narcissistic fantasy or ideology is destroyed in the name of purity. However, Grunberger and Dessuant see anti-Semitism as situated in personality structure and, accordingly, divide populations into narcissistic (and hence latently anti-Semitic) and non-narcissistic personalities. My approach, by contrast, is geared to collective fantasy systems whose narcissistic blandishments are most likely to gain power over people and their thinking in times of individual and collective crisis. The alarming thing is that Nazi racial ideology was able to achieve such a high degree of acceptance in the population. Here, psychopathological personality diagnoses are not really helpful. What we need to explain is the attractiveness of this totalitarian ideology as a large-scale group fantasy.

Chasseguet-Smirgel's investigation of racist Nazi ideology (1990) identifies a universal and unconscious fantasy underlying it. In structural terms, this fantasy is rooted in the organization of the human mind as the archaic matrix of the Oedipus complex. In it, we find the expression of an archaic desire to return to a world devoid of organization, to a universe marked by homogeneity and the continuum present before birth (*ibid.*, p. 186). Racist ideology is based on the fantasy of the symbiosis of the subject with Mother Nature, in this case Germany as the mother country. Accordingly, the "body" of the nation must be purified of all foreign elements responsible for the vitiation of its homogeneity. Only then can the German people become a "single body". Hatred of the Jews thus stems not only from their classification as elements defiling the national body, but also from the fact that they are perceived as representatives of the Law and the paternal principle of separation. This makes them into enemies who interfere with the need for homogeneity. Chasseguet-Smirgel regards this unconscious fantasy of the archaic matrix of the Oedipus complex, as implicit in all extremist ideologies. She interprets the fact that this fantasy found such blatant expression in German social and political thinking as the upshot of a specific historical situation, the tragic experiences of the Germans after their defeat in the First World War, and in the subsequent period of economic and social depression, as well as the result of the cultural tradition of Romantic thinking with its yearning for fusion with Mother Nature and its unconscious hatred of the paternal principle.

Thus, Chasseguet-Smirgel also traces the attractiveness of this unconscious fantasy back to a certain psychopathological constellation. Although she describes it as a potential universal in human thought and fantasy formation, in clinical terms it is, in fact, a highly specific narcissistic pathology serving to evade Oedipal structures.

My approach is situated on the plane of the dynamics of large groups and the power of collective phantasms, without recourse to specific individual psychopathological constellations. Societies construct or propagate the relationship between Self and Other in various ways. In this, social agencies may draw upon notions of ideal states revolving around care, unity, and purity. The reason why they have such a powerful impact on group members is that they tie up with unconscious fantasy systems common to all humans and, thus, are enabled to acquire an organizing influence on the world of conscious notions. Such narcissistic phantasms of ideal states are invariably bound up with the projection and banishment of otherness, both in the self and in society. Contradictory and ambiguous elements are equally reprehensible. Modern anti-Semitism and its fateful synthesis with the idea of the nation in Europe, and particularly in Germany, is an exemplary instance of the inner connection between ideological ideals and violence and the inherent inclination towards mutual exacerbation as a result of social circumstances.

CHAPTER EIGHT

Ideality and destructiveness: towards a psychodynamics of fundamentalist terrorist violence

September 11th, religious terrorism, and collective defence mechanisms

The September 11th terrorist attack has profoundly marked our collective consciousness. In this act of mass murder, aeroplanes full of passengers were crashed into skyscrapers as human bombs, causing massive destruction, with harrowing, deadly, and traumatic consequences for the victims. Prior to the attack, such an act was almost unthinkable. When it did occur, however, the entire world took part in the disaster as media spectators. Subsequent terrorist attacks have clearly demonstrated the global dimension of a form of terrorism that combines the most advanced technological know-how with the religious ideology of Islamic fundamentalism.

Even though we are conscious of these seemingly senseless acts of mass destruction, it is also evident that we subject them to a particular form of denial and regard them with partial blindness. Here, we might recall how earlier terrorist attacks seem to have slipped from memory, such as the attempt on the World Trade Center in 1993. If this attack had succeeded, it would have been even more devastating than the aeroplane attacks of 2001, yet it largely evaporated from memory, as questions of causes, blame, or further dangers were either overlooked or actively ignored. Investigations following the attacks have examined whether government agencies had properly evaluated the intelligence data they had gathered prior to the attacks. It was known, for instance, that Al-Qaeda had been establishing itself in Spanish cities since the mid-1990s. Fernando Reinares, an internationally respected terrorism expert, warned a year prior to the attacks in Madrid that intelligence analysis had indicated that Al-Qaeda had been using the city as a major European base and that it was probable "that Spain's citizens and government could become a target of global terrorism" (Reinares, 2005, p. 74). Despite his warning, Spain's security strategists were caught unprepared and responded by chaotically generating a mass of information and launching numerous investigations whose tangled details could only gradually be unravelled.

How might we understand the "blind eye" turned toward these events? Acts of such massively devastating and terrorizing destruction trigger powerful affects and fantasies in us, thereby activating unconscious layers. On the one hand, they spawn feelings of helplessness, impotence, and rage, along with an empathetic identification with those fellow human beings who have suddenly become victims; on the other, our own destructive–sadistic impulses and fantasies are also triggered and begin emerging from the unconscious. Yet, we are unable to continually subject our psyches to these two dimensions of senseless destruction. Studies of psychological defence mechanisms have shown that we react with disbelief to the perception of massive, horrific, and seemingly senseless destruction. We tend to distance ourselves from our fright and horror, to minimize or rationalize the violence, or even to implicate ourselves in assuming partial responsibility. Some have argued, for instance, that the Al-Qaeda attacks were the revenge of the oppressed Third World against the USA for its exploitation by American political or economic interests. Likewise, in discussions about September 11th and terrorism more generally, others quickly arrive at a kind of western-national self-critique or self-inculpation that is accompanied by a corresponding sense of guilt.

While self-criticism is important, in conjunction with terrorism it can also serve to rationalize an apparently senseless act in order to integrate it into one's own framework for generating meaning. Seen psychoanalytically, an act of violence of this magnitude undermines our most basic sense of security and trust in the reliability and predictability of human life, thereby eroding the criteria by which we differentiate between safety and danger. This reaction is similar to that resulting from a psychic trauma that breaks through the protection mechanisms of our inner world and cannot be integrated into our system of meaning. In response, we begin seeking reasons that might make the experience more understandable. This often involves creating false cognitive–affective associations in order to transform the traumatic event from an event that we experienced passively and helplessly to something that we actively invest with meaning. Another form of defence is the mystification of terrorist violence as radical evil. Here, the inverse danger exists that an attack is considered so inhuman and monstrous that we stop trying to analyse and comprehend the internal and external processes that might have led to such massively destructive acts.

In the past thirty years, the number of religious terrorist organizations has greatly increased, with almost all of the most serious terrorist attacks of the 1990s linked to religious motives (Hoffmann, 1998). Groups associated with Islamic fundamentalism have been the most significant in this respect, a fact that the September 11th attacks have thrown into particularly stark relief. It is no surprise, therefore, that religion has suddenly returned to the political and social stage, in particular its dark and destructive side. The controversy surrounding a critical confrontation with religion also forces us to consider what enlightened Western societies have lost or cast off on their way to modernity. Until recently, religion had largely been regarded as a remnant of pre-modern thinking, a marginal phenomenon no longer meriting much attention. Likewise, the growth and steady spread of religious fundamentalism throughout all regions of the world was long of little interest in Europe. Only in the wake of September 11th have we become more prepared to confront actively the political tactics and violence associated with fundamentalism. One particularly telling example is the cult of martyrdom surrounding suicide attackers. Seen psychoanalytically, it illustrates how the act of mass murder and suicidal killing is connected to the fantasy of an ensuing narcissistic harmonious condition in which the terrorist is welcomed into paradise. Here, we are again faced by the question of what psychological links exist between devout belief and hatred, and between the fantasy of an ideal narcissistic condition and murderous violence. In light of these ties, it is all the more astounding that some terrorism experts downplay fanatical religious belief as a motif and concrete component of destructive terrorist acts. As Sofsky (2002), for example, writes about the September 11th hijackers,

> Becoming a terrorist requires more than simply the belief in a few holy verses or slogans . . . Presumably, ritual prayers helped the attackers to overcome their fear of death by numbing themselves at the crucial moment. For hatred and the desire to murder, however, fanaticism is neither necessary nor sufficient . . . Experience has shown that profane facts are more powerful than all promises of salvation: the social pressure among the underground fighters to remain loyal . . . the conspiratorial climate of the social control in the isolated microcosm of the plotters; furthermore, the fixation on the authority of a charismatic leader. [p. 177, translated for this edition]

As relevant as these factors may be, they also seem thin and unconvincing, primarily because they apply to all attacks, no matter what their origin, and fail to illuminate the specifics of fundamentalist–religious terror. In the wake of the vast atrocities of the twentieth century, psychoanalysis has arrived at important insights in past decades into the links between unconscious phantasms, destructive ideology, and malignant narcissism. Using these findings as a guide, the task facing us today is to seek a psychoanalytic explanation for the way in which terrorism takes root in the mental world of religious fundamentalism. Above all, this means focusing on fundamentalism's appeal and function within the psychodynamics of personality, to which my examination now turns.

Key characteristics of fundamentalist thought and the fundamentalist personality

To begin, a few general characteristics: fundamentalist movements have arisen not only in the world's three monotheistic religions, but in every major religion as a reaction to a variety of threats posed by modernity and secularization. In addition, some fundamentalist movements have aligned themselves with a nationalist ideology, thereby assuming the form of nationalist–religious variants. In social science research, it is generally held that all religious fundamentalist groups share particular characteristics and structures (Marty & Appleby, 1991, 1995; Riesebrodt, 1990). Almond, Appleby, and Sivan (2003) define fundamentalism as referring to

> a discernible pattern of religious militance by which self-styled "true believers" attempt to arrest the erosion of religious identity, fortify the borders of the religious community, and create viable alternatives to secular institutions and behaviors. [p. 17]

The most important characteristics can be summarized as follows.

1. Fundamentalist movements constitute themselves as defenders against the processes and consequences of secularization, modernization, and liberalization that have pervaded the larger religious communities and are seen as signs of decline. Fundamentalism is a militant attempt to undo these developments. At the same time, however, these movements are themselves not conservatively and traditionally orientated: they exploit modernity in that they accept the Western premise of instrumental rationality and use technology, the mass media in particular, to achieve their goals.

2. Religious traditions are selectively adopted and then functionalized to serve an explicitly political purpose. Fundamentalists oppose any form of historical consciousness that threatens to contextualize or relativize sacred texts. Likewise, they oppose all forms of hermeneutics. Sacred texts are seen as God-given, and therefore infallible. The religious identity that this engenders is nearly ontological, not to be shaken by historical and social change.

3. Fundamentalists draw a clear line separating believers from non-believers. This boundary protects the group from pollution and mixing in order to ensure its purity. Likewise, worldly contradictions and the ambivalence of all psychic reality are summarily rescinded. The outside world is deemed sinful, damned, and impure, whereas the inner world is blessed and

pure. Conversion rituals deepen this dividing line. Strict social and moral codes of conduct and the designation of holy shrines have a pronounced, affectively egalitarian effect, whereas enemies are mystified. Within Islamist fundamentalism, the West is considered the great Satan. Yet, the main enemies are found within the religious community itself – those fellow believers who have been corrupted by Western liberals and modernist ideas.

4. The desire to obtain an unshakably secure personal and social identity assumes an urgency through a heightened perception of imminent danger. Fundamentalism blossoms in times of crisis, be it real or imagined. Turmoil is not evaluated socially or politically, however, but is, instead, experienced as a crisis of identity, in which religion is in danger of being abolished or subsumed by a syncretic culture. Crises are structured as part of a story of salvation, a narrative that grants meaning to loss and demise and signals both the end of an era and hope for the future.

5. Fundamentalists seek to replace existing social and political structures with a comprehensive, religiously based system regulating all aspects of daily life: law, politics, society, economics, and culture. The guiding principle that all institutions are to be subordinate to the law of God lends fundamentalism a totalitarian impetus.

Based on these general observations, I would now like to discuss some additional characteristics of personality development among fundamentalists. I will base my remarks on, among other things, research conducted by Strozier (2002), who carried out psychoanalytically orientated biographical interviews with Protestant fundamentalists in the USA in the 1990s. The most striking feature of these biographies is their broken narratives. A decisive moment of conversion is depicted, which usually took place in late adolescence or as a young adult, and led to the depiction of a before–after division in one's life and the image of a divided self. Often, this is preceded by a serious long-term personal crisis or a traumatization, which is described as a psychic death that leads to a rebirth through faith. Here, conversion becomes an overpowering authentic experience and rebirth a dramatic act of self-creation. In this biographical reconstruction, fundamentalist structures for generating religious meaning become a framework that shapes individual experiences. The convert submerges himself and his personal history in a redemption drama of destruction and salvation. In rejecting one's previous life, a strong break is made with the past. This desire for transformation takes on its own dynamic and gives rise to an apocalyptic drama of the end of time. Indeed, it is believed that this moment will soon be upon us, bringing with it the obliteration of infidels, a purification of the Earth from filth and sin, and the salvation of the believer, who, in a final paradisiacal state, will join Jesus in heaven, where he reins over a peaceful and harmonious world. The coldness and mercilessness with which the destruction of non-believers is described is striking in these apocalyptic fundamentalist narratives. The infidels embody one's own previous sinful and vile self, which has been expelled by projecting it on to others. Now they are to be annihilated. Hence, this apocalyptic world view serves as a vehicle for one's own destructiveness and is linked to an ideal harmonious final state into which the believer will someday enter.

Drawn from notions of the self and the world within Christian fundamentalism, variations of these deep psychological structures are likewise found in the world of fundamentalist Islam, to which I now turn my attention.

The mental world of fundamentalist Islam

Researchers involved in the sweeping study of fundamentalism led by the American Academy of Art and Sciences (Marty & Appleby, 1991, 1995) consider the fundamentalist movements of the twentieth century to be the third major attempt to abolish the consequences of the modernization, secularization, and liberalization set in motion by the Enlightenment. In opposing these developments, fundamentalist movements bear a resemblance to fascism and Bolshevism, the other two totalitarian movements of the twentieth century. Most recently, Berman (2003) has highlighted its similarity to various strands of totalitarianism. As Berman observes, all of these movements arose in the wake of the First World War and the attendant collapse of a European idealistic and liberal belief in progress. In making this argument, he points to an often overlooked segment of a video made by Bin Laden following the September 11th attacks. In it, Bin Laden talks about how America was stricken with horror following the attacks, adding: "For over 80 years our Islamic nation has felt the same way—humiliation and shame—it has had to see its sons killed, blood flow, and its shrines dese-crated." By turning to the years around 1920, Bin Laden is making reference to the reforms of Kemal Atatürk, which represented a leap into Western modernity and culminated in the abolition of the Caliphate in 1924. He considers this development to be part of a Western and Jewish conspiracy to destroy Islam and the great Islamic nation.

Following the failure of social and political reform efforts in the Arab states after the fall of the Ottoman Empire, the fundamentalist movement grew increasingly in strength, thanks in small measure to the founding of the Muslim brotherhood in Egypt around 1920 (see Armstrong, 2007; Lewis, 1994, 2003; Qutb, 1964; Serauky, 2000). It thought of itself as a "third path", an alternative to Western capital-ism and Eastern communism, receiving its impetus, above all, from the Iranian Revolution in 1979. This Islamist-fundamentalist move-ment is one of the main strands in the Muslim world today. Its followers castigate the adoption of Western lifestyles and ways of thinking, branding such changes a serious crisis for Islam, a new barbarism, and a relapse to a pre-Islamic age. Their goal is to rejoin religion and politics, do away with secular regimes, and return to a unified religious–political world view. They seek to bring about a return to their own model of society and idealize a return to the supposedly idyllic and unspoiled era of the original Muslim community in seventh-century Medina. In keeping with this vision, the modern nation state is to be replaced by an Islamic theocracy governed by Islamic law, the Sharia. Persecution is a means to this end, which fundamentalists primarily direct against dissenters or non-conformists within their own country in addition to targeting the most progressive forms of Islam and, above all, secular Western thought. For them, no culture can exist outside the Islamic religion. Roy (2004), regarded as a leading expert on Islamism, considers its strategy of reuniting religion and politics in an Islamic state and a truly Islamic society as having failed, due both to their own authoritarian regimes in Muslim countries and the undeniable westernization and modernization of Muslim societies. Islam, he believes, has begun moving beyond territorial boundaries and drifting away from its moorings in specific cultures. He traces this, for one, to globalization, which has led to the formation of Islamic minorities in Western countries and has resulted in an increasingly deterritorialized and globalized Islamism.

Roy sees post-Islamism and neo-fundamentalism on the rise that draws heavily from Salafism and Saudi Arabian Wahhabism. Although mistakenly viewed as the reaction of a traditional culture that feels threatened, he argues that these movements are actually the clearest signal of a process of deculturation and uprooting of the individual by the forces of modernity. The emphasis now no longer lies on a social religious order that should be reinstated, but, rather, on the individual and his or her belief. It is no longer the way in which a religion is embedded within a particular culture that is at stake, but the religious beliefs of the individual. Therefore, religion and politics are seen as separate spheres. The goal is the creation of a pure Islamic religion that has freed itself of all profane and secular elements. The purification of the self and the sacralization of everyday life through strict observation of religious rules and codes of conduct take centre stage, whereby their adaptation to modern life is only allowed when absolutely necessary. As a community of belief, the Ummah is also deterritorialized and is no longer tied to geographic areas. It becomes, instead, a homogenous community of equals without a connection to a natural environment that is dedicated solely to the goal of practising an authentic Islam. The Ummah becomes an abstract, virtual community of belief and is, therefore, shaped to an even greater extent by imaginary elements than in the traditional version. The radicals among the neo-fundamentalists who have committed themselves to jihad no longer seek the creation of an Islamic nation; for them, terrorism is to be practised on a global scale. They see themselves as part of a worldwide revolution, and dream that the West and its civilization will one day be conquered and all people will be united under the rule of Islam.

*   *   *

Now let us more closely examine some of the important psychological elements of this mental world. The main goal of fundamentalism is to subordinate all aspects of life to religion. The socio-political realm is also to be completely subjected to the divine. Indeed, as seen from a fundamentalist standpoint, the state is to be discarded and every material civilization and culture rejected. Likewise, Sharia law is to be strictly applied and enforced, thereby cleansing Islam of all cultural influences. Man's only choice is to completely submit himself to the will of God, whose omnipotence governs all aspects of life. The system is a totality that provides no room for others. For such fundamentalists, all that matters is one God, one book (the Koran, the text of which came directly from God by way of his messengers), and one sacred language, Arabic.

Such religious idealization represents a highly ambivalent psychological process. The idealization of the religious object necessitates the believer's self-humiliation or degradation, even to the point of self-dissolution. Often, projection is the only means available to deal with the painful feelings that result: hence, others are dismissed as non-believers and become the target of aggression or destruction (Jones, 2002). Reik (1923) was one of the first to study the connection between religion and aggression. For him, all religions hinge on the fact that they can never rid themselves of the power of the ambivalence of emotional impulses. Therefore, an unconscious animosity towards God must be seen as a constitutive element of religion. The recurring impulse to rebel and revolt against one's own God, and the unconscious feelings of guilt in which they result, are satisfied in the persecution of non-believers. Reik's thesis would still seem to apply in many ways to the religious system of Islamic fundamentalism. Seen psychoanalytically, its demands ask a great deal of the individual and require an enormous degree of subordination and self-sacrifice. Rebellious impulses against the absolute power of God must be completely repressed and are therefore projected on to non-believers and enemies, who are to be bitterly persecuted and destroyed. Likewise, independent human thought is considered extraneous and must be eliminated, for only the word of God in the Koran is afforded any validity. Meddeb (2002) characterizes the views of Sayyid Qutb, one of the founding fathers and most-read authors of fundamentalist Islam, as follows:

> In the history of humanity, as in the present, everything is unnecessary, every thought, every representation is so inadequate that

they all deserve to simply be cast off together. Everything should disappear except for the word of God, as it is written in the Koran. The word will bring "human liberation" to the world, or rather, humanity's "true birth". After man has assumed the subservience required by God's sovereignty . . . he will be freed from all other forms of slavery in our time. [*ibid.*, p. 137, translated for this edition]

Such a religious system extensively mobilizes this apocalyptic aspect in seeking to bring about a sweeping process of purification, and, therefore, salvation, necessary for harmony and unity to return to the world under the reign of Islam. Here, evil is externalized through projection, as demonstrated most clearly in fundamentalism's xenophobia and anti-Semitism: the failure of one's own group and of Muslim societies as a whole is blamed on a plot of subversive foreigners, usually consisting of Westerners and Jews.

Meddeb (*ibid.*) describes fundamentalism as an illness within Islam that promises salvation while only causing misery. Alongside fundamentalists' totalitarian demands, Meddeb also includes the hatred of sensuality, desire, and pleasure among the main symptoms of this malady. Islamic society has abandoned and repressed a tradition of taking pleasure in life. In past centuries, the sensuous culture of Islam fascinated the Christian occident and gave rise to a phantasm of the "Orient". Today, however, Meddeb argues that we are experiencing

a strange change in the way the body is seen and treated. Islam is becoming a centre of modesty, whose inhabitants are made to suffer from nihilism and resentment. In the meantime, the body has liberated itself in the West from inherited coercions and constraints. As noticeable as this change may be, the Islamic subject is not conscious of it, for he or she is proud of the fact that the virtue of his or her society is providing a counter-example to the West, thought of as a centre of vice. . . . They never become conscious of the way in which they derive their pride directly from the signs of their sickness. [*ibid.*, p. 158, translated for this edition]

It is primarily those who have gone to study in the West who have had to struggle with the inner conflicts arising from repression and resentment in an Islamic society. Most notoriously, this group includes the leading members of the Hamburg cell of

Al-Qaeda, who had come to Germany in order to study science or engineering. At some point, all of them broke with their traditional religious past, and probably also with their families. Instrumental in this departure was their attendance at mosques led by radical hate mongers: they experienced an individual Islamic rebirth in a small circle of similarly uprooted like-minded people and adopted their own form of Islam (Roy, 2004). A brief sketch of their biographies demonstrates more similarities (see also McDermott, 2005): Mohammed Atta, born in 1968, received a religious upbringing from his father. He was an obedient son and excellent student, receiving a scholarship to study in Hamburg at the age of twenty-four. He stood out because of his devout belief and his attempt to adhere to a strictly Muslim lifestyle to help him resist the temptations of Western civilization. His landlord's family reported that he would, for example, close his eyes when certain scenes appeared on television. Atta was uncomfortable in the mixed company of men and women, keeping his distance from women, with whom he was, apparently, never even able to shake hands. Throughout the course of his studies, Atta often travelled between his Arabic homeland and Germany. In Aleppo, he fell in love with a city planner, but ended the relationship because she refused to wear a headscarf, and he found her mode of dress too revealing.

Atta's fundamentalist world view appears to have become increasingly radical as a result of his defensive posture against Western culture and civilization. He attacked the Americanization of Egyptian culture, for instance, and witness testimony in the first trials against Al-Qaeda members in Hamburg have shed light on his anti-Semitic views. He was convinced that Jews sought world domination, that they were "the rich puppetmasters of the media, the financial world, and politics" and that New York was the centre of world Judaism (*Der Spiegel*, 36/2002). Other members, such as Ziad al Jarrah, who piloted the aeroplane that crashed into the second tower, had been rather cheerful and active until they broke with their previous convictions and world view. Jarrah is described as a playboy, who, at age twenty-one, suddenly became a devout fundamentalist and demanded that his Turkish girlfriend wear a headscarf and cover her hands. Accounts of Said Bahai's biography are similar. Born in Germany, he emigrated as a nine-year-old with his parents to Morocco, but then returned to Germany to study at the age of twenty. Following a severe romantic disappointment when he was twenty-one, he became religious and assumed a radically different attitude towards women. He became devout, began adhering to Islamist ideals, and asserted that Islam needed to achieve world domination and destroy the Jews.

This radicalization during their late adolescent identity formation, especially in their ideological and religious views, appears to have directly sown the seeds for their turn to terrorism. Kippenberg (2008) has described the way in which a transformed warrior ethos, prefigured by the Shiites in the Iranian revolution, emerged from neo-fundamentalism and its radicalization by Bin Laden. The struggle now became a means of gaining personal salvation, and it was no longer subject to the approval of Islamic authorities. A fighter can only become a martyr if his intention was truly pure, not sullied by expectations of material reward or heightened religious prestige. Salvation is solely dependent on one's way of thinking. This corresponds with the redefinition of the Ummah, which was freed from geographic bounds and instead became a community that was based on a pure, religious way of life. This aim of assuring personal salvation was also that of the spiritual guide followed by the hijackers in their suicide attack on September 11th.

We cannot speculate about these individuals' specific psychological conflicts, but it is safe to say that fundamentalist political ideology and a new ethos of martyrdom led to modes of thought and action that apparently offered a solution to serious intercultural conflicts and other problems. At the same time, however, this also halted their late adolescent processes of development. Fundamentalist religion is radical, harsh, and can serve as a defence against passive and libidinal needs. It provides external objects upon which fears and affects, as well as weak and despised parts of one's self, can be projected, and where they can then be persecuted and destroyed. For Atta and others who found their destiny in the battle against Western infidels and vice, the repressed in their own cultural history returns in this fight, which they then seek to destroy in the war against the West and its notions of culture.

Such a dynamic gives rise to a megalomaniacal and militant self. Atta and others thought of themselves as the *avant-garde* in a global holy war that promised the victory of Islam. At the same time, the fearlessness in the face of death, and, indeed, its idealization, are prized as a miracle weapon against effeminate Westerners. As an Al-Qaeda manifesto formulates it: "We are the nation that loves death more than life" (Fielding & Fouda, 2003, p. 238). Despised are those who cling to their lives and value it more than death. In a 1998 interview, Bin Laden made the following revealing remark about the weakness of American soldiers:

> That was proven in Beirut when the Marines fled after two explosions. The incident also shows that they can run in less than 24 hours, something also repeated in Somalia . . . [Our] young people were surprised by the poor morale of American soldiers . . . after just a few attacks, they ran away defeated . . . They completely forgot that they were the leading world power and the head of the new world order. [They] retreated with their corpses and their shameful defeat in tow. [cited in Lewis, 2003, pp. 172–173, translated for this edition]

The deep structure of the Islamic fundamentalist mentality

Roy (2004) asks how the narrow and spiritually unsophisticated world view of fundamentalism and neo-fundamentalism could become so deeply rooted among modern and educated Muslims. He finds an answer in the explicit process of deculturation that Islam goes through and that neo-fundamentalism seeks to channel in its own way by bringing believers to identify with an abstract, deterritorialized, and homogeneously egalitarian community of belief. Neo-fundamentalism gives believers an alternative group identity that does not collide with their individual lives, precisely because it involves an imaginary community without any real basis. This speaks to a level of collective phantasms, whose attraction can be further examined in terms of psychoanalysis. Therefore, we have to ask how religious–political fundamentalism can become so psychologically appealing for individuals or groups at certain times and in certain societal constellations. My aim is to discern which unconscious fantasies come into play here. In doing so, I am not only concerned with making the magnetism of fundamentalist ideologies more transparent, but also with illuminating their inherent tendency towards radicalization.

In order to clarify, I would like to make a few general observations about the psychoanalysis of collective phenomena and
social ideologies: psychoanalysis must take account of the independence of the social and the abstraction of social control mechanisms
and systemically stabilized actions within the social system. This
does not, however, diminish its capacity to trace the appeal of
ideologies and collective phantasms and the extraordinarily strong
affects associated with them back to unconscious factors or to
explain them psychologically. Methodologically and conceptually, I
am drawing here on the concept of ubiquitous unconscious
fantasies (see Bendkower, 1991). These are fantasies that all people
share to some degree. They are ubiquitous in that they involve
the fundamental facts of life, that is, the connection of bodily
needs to mental and psychic development, especially psychosexual
maturity, care-taking by, and dependence on, the mother, sibling
rivalry, the primal scene, and the Oedipus complex. As derivatives
of the unconscious, these infantile fantasies press themselves into
consciousness and emerge in reality and social life. They possess
a tendency towards externalization in clinging to and shaping the
perception and formation of societal events, institutions, and
cultural value systems. At the same time, however, they are also
activated from the outside, that is, by societal agents, who shape
and channel these fantasies through objective structures such as
institutions, social conventions, and linguistic traditions.

In an earlier work (1997a, see Chapter Seven in this volume),
I used the example of German nationalism and anti-Semitism to
examine the emotions, affects, and associated unconscious phantasms activated in the mind when imagining the nation. Especially
during times of social crisis, they can bring about a strong sense
of fascination and trigger massive violence and aggression. A comparison of the ideational worlds of radical German nationalism
after 1918 with Islamist fundamentalism reveals amazing similarities. One could challenge this comparison by arguing that Western-
style nationalism did not unfold with the same degree of phantasmatic potential in Islamic nations, in which older and more
deeply rooted religious loyalties held sway. Kakar (1996) points out,
for example, that, compared to ethnic nationalism, religion im-
bues group conflicts with a greater emotional intensity and a

deeper motivational force. In making this argument, however, Kakar loses sight of the fact that nationalism has often been the heir of religion and, especially in its extreme and totalitarian forms, has taken on the character of a political or secular religion (Bärsch, 1998). With all due caution in light of the differences, it still seems worthwhile to look to the level of deep psychic structures to compare the ideational worlds of nationalism and politico–religious Islam, which considers the Ummah to be a community of all Muslims and the sole Islamic nation. Such a comparison is supported by the work of Anderson (1983), who posits the existence of a subterranean connection in defining the nation as an "imagined community" based on cultural systems of "kinship" and "religion".

The following unconscious ideational complexes proved significant in the analysis of radical nationalism and will serve as a heuristic basis from which to examine the deep dimension of political visions in Islamist fundamentalism:

- care-taking fantasies and sibling rivalry;
- purity and the ideational conception of the other;
- visions of group unity and fantasies of fusion.

In the first fantasy system, involving unconscious care-taking fantasies and sibling rivalry, the foreigner is perceived as an intruder, who enters a sphere thought to be one's own rightful property, thereby displacing the native inhabitant, robbing him of his possessions (in the unconscious this means the possession of the primary object) and taking up residence as a parasite and freeloader. Unconsciously, this foreigner is the sibling rival, who destroys the narcissistically idealized union with the collective mother figure. In Islamism, however, this seems to be the least apparent fantasy system. The available evidence shows that they do not possess the same phantasmatic power as one finds in German anti-Semitism, in which Jews were seen as gluttonous vermin. To point to one example: in Bin Laden's declaration calling for jihad against the Americans and their allies, he says that the Arabian Peninsula is being infested by crusaders, who are devouring their riches like locusts (cited in Kippenberg, 2008, p. 164).

Purity and the vision of the Other

Compared to the projection of forbidden instinctual impulses on to the other, the connection between visions of purity and group identity are more complex. As Freud demonstrated (1921c), members of the group let individual differences fade away in a narcissistic identification with each other. They assure themselves of their ties and identity in that they are like all other group members. Difference and otherness thereby emerge as the impure. As Douglas has determined (1966), dirt has long been defined in a cultural–historical sense as that which is in the wrong place; therefore, it cannot be accepted if a model or symbolic system is to continue to exist. Uncertainty, insecurity, and ambivalence cannot be tolerated and, as an impurity, must be abolished in order to create a homogenous, symbolically consistent universe.

Ritual purity plays a significant role in Islam, and, therefore, it is not surprising that fantasies of purity have extraordinary significance for self-identity in Islamism. To take one example, a major Islamist political newspaper describes the invasion of Western ideas and ways of life as follows:

The likeness of Islam and of the unbelievers are like fresh clear spring water and water brought up from the bottom of a suburban sewer. If even a drop of the filthy water enters the clear water, the clarity diminishes. Likewise, it takes only a drop of the filth of disbelief to contaminate Islam in the West. [cited by Raban, 2002, p. 32]

Sayyid Qutb attributes this destruction of purity to the Jews: "The Jews free sensual desires from their boundaries and they destroy the moral basis upon which belief is based. They do this so that belief is sullied by the same filth they so freely spread around the world" (Nettler, 1986, p. 104). (I would like to thank Matthias Küntzel for calling my attention to this by giving me access to the partial English documentation of Qutb's essay in Nettler's work.) Examples of such beliefs abound. Alongside pollution, images of poisoning are also quite prevalent. The feminine body is charged with a particularly strong power to pollute, seduce, and destroy. It also serves as a metaphor for a society that sees itself threatened by seductive, evil powers (Riesebrodt, 2000, p. 121).

At this point, I would like to expand upon one further point: the perception of the other, or the stranger, reciprocally connected to the perception of oneself. As Spitz has outlined it (1965), the child's stranger anxiety is not a consequence of the strangeness of this person, but a reaction to the perception that the face of the stranger is not the same as the memory of the mother's face. In this way, the perception of the stranger leads the child back to the mother and heightens the attachment to her, assuming that the child feels secure in the relationship to her. Thereafter, the child can resume contact without anxiety and can then get to know the stranger.

In contrast, the pathological form of this relation seeks to exclude the stranger and to reassure oneself through a narcissistic mirroring in the mother. If a fantasy of homogeneity dominates at the level of the group, mirroring and self-reassurance take place in those group members who are like oneself. Ambivalence is unavoidable, however, and gives an aggressive charge to differences within the group, which must then be erased and projected outward. Such a world of narcissistic mirroring and purity results in massive persecutory aggression against those who are different and, thereby, threaten internal cohesion. This narcissism cannot tolerate the coexistence of anything different or deviant and has the tendency to become progressively more radical. Purity is only to be obtained through exclusion. In this way, belonging to an idealized, pure community and persecutory violence are closely connected and mutually dependent. In order keep the ideal of purity present, ever new impurities have to be found. This process never ends, instead becoming increasingly radical. Ostow speaks in this context of a "pogrom mentality" (1996a), and Adorno refers to a "psychic totalitarianism" (1950a).

Visions of unity and fantasies of fusion

Current psychoanalytic research into groups has shown that the regression in a group or mass goes well beyond the Oedipal level Freud described, extending to other active, deeper-seated narcissistic identifications. In so far as members regressively fuse into a group, it becomes an illusory substitute for the lost object, the mother of infancy. The group fantasy substitutes a communal ego-ideal for that of the individual and results in manic elation. If it comes to power and merges with individual fantasies of superiority, the reality testing of the individuals involved and the demands of their own conscience are nullified, while their sense of self is enormously stimulated by the fusion with the national or group sense of self. The question "Who am I?" is replaced by "To whom do I belong?" For these people there exists, on the one hand, a world of great symbiotic unity, and, on the other, split off from the first, a world of rivalry, competition, and plurality.

The Islamist conception of the Ummah as a community of all Muslims is one of the most vivid examples of this fusionary thinking in terms of unities. In the eyes of Muslims, humanity consists of collectivities. Islam does acknowledge individuation, but only partially. The designation of man as a free individual, as in the Western tradition (Tibi, 1993) is largely absent in Islam, even if transformations might now be under way because of Muslim migration to Western countries. A Muslim belongs to the Ummah as the community of all Muslims, a membership that defines him and, similar to an irrevocable tribal origin, from which he can never depart. Thus, the Ummah figures as a homogeneous society without division and social stratifications. It follows that the Ummah idealizes the pilgrimage to Mecca, in which the self-centredness of the individual is to be overcome. The charismatic Iranian philosopher, Schari'ati, offers the following description of the seven times that one walks in a circle around the Ka'ba:

> You are carried by the cradle of the enthusiasm and magnetism of the community; this is no longer a you. There is only the community . . . Now you have become part of creation. You find yourself within the orbit of this solar system; you revolve around God and eventually you no longer feel. [cited in Armstrong, 2007, p. 360, translated for this edition]

Levy (1995) describes the Ummah with another metaphor: "It is a mass, an ocean, that lives in fear of mixing, but also of differentiation" (p. 102). The community of the Ummah is, however, by no means homogenous and is, instead, marked by division, argument, and discord. Unity is a fantasy vision, which becomes more powerful in people's minds the more destructive tendencies and hostile impulses can be projected upon ethnic and religious minorities in the world of Islam or upon the unbelievers who have conspired against them. This gives birth to a phantasm of a pure and unified Muslim community. In forming such a collective, one cannot see the threatening, foreign other as an independent individual, but solely as an agent of the enemy seeking to destroy one's own homogeneity. Relations with the outside world are perceived in a Manichaean way. The imaginary Ummah stands on one side, and the demonized world of the enemies on the other. Discord, problems, and mistakes are not one's own doing, but, rather, are seen as resulting from the evil and satanic machinations of the West and from the perceived victimization at the hands of the Jews. A Muslim who thinks otherwise can be easily branded a traitor.

Such conspiratorial thinking is widespread in the Arab world. This plot is considered part of a longstanding plan that began with the crusades, then brought about the dissolution of the Caliphate and the separation of religion and state, and now seeks the destruction of Islamic religion and culture. As Tibi has demonstrated, these conspiracy theories employ a radical rhetoric that "no longer serves to communicate or share knowledge; its sole function is to psychologically and rhetorically bolster one's own unrealistic perception against an outside world that stands in contradiction to it" (Tibi, 1993, p. 43, translated for this edition). In this way, Islamic fundamentalism becomes a closed, religiously totalitarian system, governed by imaginary conceptions that feed on unconscious phantasms. An imaginary community is idealized in order to shield itself against any reality. Harmony and peace, the final state one longs for, require the abolition and destruction of a spoiled and rotting Western civilization. As we have seen here, ideality and terror are indeed interrelated.

The terrorist transformation of the personality

I have tried to show how the inherent connection between narcissistic notions of purity, unity, and equality uses massive violence to call upon the fantasy of a pre-ambivalent, narcissistic, ideal condition. The other, or outsider, therefore becomes the non-believer, an intruder and troublemaker, necessary both for projection and persecution in order to phantasmatically maintain the ideal condition.

Such ideological notions and fantasies activate a capacity for aggression with an enormously destructive potential. Yet, such a radical ideology is not enough to make someone a terrorist, a development that would require the transformation of one's personality. At the same time, however, the conversion to a radical fundamentalist ideology does represent the first stage of just such a transformation evident in late adolescence or young adulthood among many suicide attackers. In addition to military training, a violent indoctrination and re-education is necessary, which usually takes place in training camps or in isolated totalitarian group settings. Here, the connection to one's previous relationships is ruptured. This results in a submersion in a "parallel world" that is prepared, in part, by a series of initiation rites. The practices employed by various terrorist groups have similarities as well as important differences.

Lifton (1999) has described and analysed these processes of violent mental conditioning in totalitarian group settings through an examination of the Japanese AUM sect that launched a Sarin attack on the Tokyo subway. Such groups are dominated by an absolute sense of control, in which all forms of communication are monitored and the psyche of group members is governed by an ethos of self-disclosure and self-flagellation. These personal confessions represent the path to purity and fusion with the group. Reality, and the perception thereof, become the property of the group and are manipulated and legitimized by the group's ideals. Among them, absolute purity is the highest and is contrasted with the outside world of pure evil. In order to create this separation between purity and impurity, these groups employ massive violence, which is then justified as a process of purification. Such a change requires the catharsis brought about by the destruction of the person one had previously been. In the course of this transformation, the distinction between education and punishment is often blurred, especially in procedures such as submerging group members in extremely cold or hot water, hanging them up by their feet, or locking them up alone in a cell for several days.

Such violent tests of strength are also used in the training of Palestinian suicide bombers, alongside psychological and religious indoctrination. Croitoru (2003) has reported that those wishing to take part in suicide operations were taken to cemeteries and briefly buried alive. In addition, they were read the most horrific passages from the Koran about the Islamic angel of the grave in order to demonstrate what they would be spared by entering directly into paradise. Another test of strength reportedly takes place in Iranian training camps for martyrs of the jihad (*ibid.*). Prisoners sentenced to death are selected to be brain-washed, then placed in cars loaded with explosives, and made to crash into a wall or each other while the recruits look on.

How can we explain such practices and their effects psychoanalytically? Through such traumatizing treatment, the function of internal good objects to give one a sense of safety collapses and is replaced by what becomes the only available object: the leader, the guru, or the group as a whole, and the identification with group ideals. In order not to break down, and not to be killed immediately, the incipient terrorist must identify with the religious leader's intentions even more as the only accessible object and the only one capable of granting safety from the fear of a life-threatening situation. He is also served by the professed vision of an eternal life in paradise.

Little is known about the terrorist training of the September 11th hijackers. However, from a text found in Atta's baggage, referred to as a "spiritual guide", we do know the instructions for their final preparations and the execution of the attack. In the intervening years, this document has been exhaustively analysed (see Kippenberg, 2008). Psychologically, they found themselves in a religious drama. Already, sometime prior, they had been given battle names from the early age of Islam that had belonged to the followers of the prophet Mohammed. The guide describes each individual step in great detail, beginning with a pledge of allegiance, the renewal of a religious motivation for the act, as well as purification rituals and prayers for overcoming the fear of death. The attack in the aeroplane itself is also carefully detailed. The attackers all recited to themselves the same holy verses from the Koran, invoking those seventh-century battles in which Mohammed and a small army of believers fought and conquered the infidels. Indeed, the word used to characterize the killing of the passengers was a verb found in the Koran for the "butchering" of an animal sacrifice. Yet, they also recited verses dealing with the paradise they dreamt of entering soon, which helped them to ward off the fear of death. This ideological, religious, and psychological manipulation assured the synchrony of the four separate groups, which operated independently yet in tune, so that no one made a mistake due to a fear of death.

All of these practices help to bring about a "shared state of aggressive numbing" (Lifton, 1999), that is, an orientation towards the attack ahead, an erasure of all prior scruples, and an eradication of all doubts and any sense of empathy with the victims. This represents the submersion in a parallel world, from which there is no "point of return", especially after the first murder has already been committed, either of a group member penalized for weakness or of an outsider. Such acts kill one's own weaknesses, doubts, and conscience, projecting them upon the other.

Conclusion

As the past century has made apparent, idealization and terror are quite frequently interrelated. The terrorism we are now confronting at the start of our century represents a new form of this coupling. I have attempted here to illuminate a few areas of Islamist fundamentalism and terrorism, a world that psychoanalysis has only now begun to explore. Indeed, many of my own considerations have had to remain provisional, leaving us with an urgent need to explore the issues introduced here in much greater detail.

REFERENCES

Abraham, K. (1907a). Über die Bedeutung sexueller Jugendtraumen für die Symptomatologie der Dementia praecox. In: K. Abraham, *Psychoanalytische Studien, Vol. II* (pp. 125–131). Frankfurt: Fischer, 1971. English edition: H. Abraham (Ed.), *Clinical Papers and Essays on Psycho-Analysis*. London: Hogarth Press, 1955.

Abraham, K. (1907b). Das Erleiden sexueller Traumen als Form der Sexualbetätigung. In: K. Abraham, *Psychoanalytische Studien, Vol.II* (pp. 167–181). Frankfurt: Fischer, 1971. English edition: H. Abraham (Ed.), *Clinical Papers and Essays on Psycho-Analysis*. London: Hogarth Press, 1955.

Abraham, N. (1987). Notes on the phantom: a complement to Freud's metapsychology. *Critical Inquiry, 13*: 287–292 [(1991). Aufzeichnungen über das Phantom. Ergänzungen zu Freuds Metapsychologie. *Psyche, Zeitschrift für Psychoanalyse und ihre Anwendungen, 45*: 691–698].

Abraham, N., & Torok, M. (1976). *Cryptomanie. Le verbier de l'homme aux loups*. Paris: Editions Aubier Flammarion.

Ackerman, N., & Jahoda, M. (1950). *Antisemitism and Emotional Disorder: A Psychoanalytic Interpretation*. New York: Harper.

Adorno, T. W. (1950a). *Studien zum autoritären Charakter*. Frankfurt: Suhrkamp, 1973.

Adorno, T. W., Frenkel-Brunswik, E., Levinson, D., & Sanford, N. (1950b). *The Authoritarian Personality*. New York: Harper Bros.

Akhtar, S. (1999). *Immigration and Identity. Turmoil, Treatment, and Transformation*. Lanham, MD: Jason Aronson.

Alford, F. C. (2002). *Levinas, the Frankfurt School and Psychoanalysis*. London: Continuum.

Allen, J., & Land, D. (1999). Attachment in adolescence. In: J. Cassidy & P. Shaver (Eds.), *Handbook of Attachment. Theory, Research, and Clinical Applications* (pp. 319–335). New York: Guilford Press.

Almond, G., Appleby, S., & Sivan, E. (2003). *Strong Religion. The Rise of Fundamentalism Around The World*. Chicago. IL: Universities of Chicago Press.

Amati, S. (1990). Die Rückgewinnung des Schamgefühls. *Psyche, Zeitschrift für Psychoanalyse und ihre Anwendungen*, 44: 724–740.

Ammaniti, M., & Sergi, G. (2003). Clinical dynamics during adolescence: psychoanalytic and attachment perspectives. *Psychoanalytic Inquiry*, 23: 54–80.

Anderson, B. (1983). *Imagined Communities: Reflections on the Origin and Spread of Nationalism*. London: Verso.

Anzieu, D. (1975). *The Group and the Unconscious*. London: Routledge & Kegan Paul, 1984.

Argelander, H. (1968). Der psychoanalytische Dialog. *Psyche, Zeitschrift für Psychoanalyse und ihre Anwendungen*, 22: 325–339.

Argelander, H. (1970). Die szenische Funktion des Ichs und ihr Anteil an der Symptom- und Charakterbildung. *Psyche, Zeitschrift für Psychoanalyse und ihre Anwendungen*, 24: 325–345.

Arlow, J. (1979). Metaphor and the psychoanalytic situation. *Psychoanalytic Quarterly*, 48: 363–385.

Arlow, J. (1991). Methodology and reconstruction. *Psychoanalytic Quarterly*, 60: 539–563.

Arlow, J. (1992). Aggression und Vorurteil: Psychoanalytische Betrachtungen zur Ritualmordbeschuldigung gegen die Juden. *Psyche, Zeitschrift für Psychoanalyse und ihre Anwendungen*, 46: 1122–1132.

Arlow, J. (1994). Aggression and prejudice: some psychoanalytic observations on the blood libel accusations against the Jews. In: A. K. Richards & A. D. Richards (Eds.), *The Spectrum of Psychoanalysis*. Madison, NJ: International Universities Press.

Armstrong, K. (2007). *Im Kampf für Gott*. München: Goldmann.

Aron, L. (1996). *A Meeting of Minds. Mutuality in Psychoanalysis*. Hillsdale, NJ: Analytic Press.

Assmann, A. (1998). Stabilisatoren der Erinnerung-Affekt, Symbol, Trauma [Stabilizers of the memory-Affect, symbol, trauma]. In: J. Rüsen & J. Straub (Eds.), *Die dunkle Spur der Vergangenheit. Psychoanalytische Zugänge zum Geschichtsbewusstsein. Erinnerung, Geschichte, Identität* [The dark trace of the past. Psychoanalytical accesses to historical consciousness. Memory, history, identity], *Vol.* 2 (pp. 131–152). Frankfurt: Suhrkamp.

Balibar, E. (1988). Die Nation-Form: Geschichte und Ideologie. In: E. Balibar & I. Wallerstein (Eds.), *Rasse – Klasse – Nation: Ambivalente Identitäten* (pp. 107–130). Hamburg: Argument-Verlag, 1990.

Balint, M. (1965). *Primary Love and Psycho-analytic Technique.* London: Tavistock.

Balint, M. (1969). Trauma and object relationship. *International Journal of Psychoanalysis, 50:* 429–436.

Baranger, M. (2005). Field theory. In: S. Lewkowicz & S. Flechner (Eds.), *Truth, Reality, and the Psychoanalyst. Latin American Contributions to Psychoanalysis* (pp. 49–71). London: International Psychoanalytical Association.

Baranger, M., Baranger, W., & Mom, J. (1988). The infantile trauma from us to Freud. Pure trauma, retroactivity and reconstruction. *International Journal of Psychoanalysis, 69:* 113–128.

Bärsch, C. E. (1998). *Die politische Religion des Nationalsozialismus.* Munich: Fink.

Bauman, Z. (1991). *Modernity and Ambivalence.* London: Polity Press.

Bauman, Z. (1997). *Postmodernity and its Discontents.* London: Polity Press.

Bedorf, T. (2003). *Dimensionen des Dritten. Sozialphilosophische Modelle zwischen Ethischem und Politischem.* Munich: Fink.

Beebe, B., & Lachmann, F. (2002). *Infant Research and Adult Treatment. Co-Constructing Interactions.* Hillsdale, NJ: Analytic Press.

Bein, A. (1965). "Der jüdische Parasit". Bemerkungen zur Semantik der Judenfrage. *Vierteljahreshefte für Zeitgeschichte, 13:* 121–149.

Beland, H. (1991). Religiöse Wurzeln des Antisemitismus. *Psyche, Zeitschrift für Psychoanalyse und ihre Anwendungen, 45:* 448–470.

Beland, H. (1992). Psychoanalytische Antisemitismustheorien im Vergleich. In: W. Bohleber & J.S. Kafka (Eds.), *Antisemitismus* (pp. 93–121). Bielefeld: Aisthesis.

Bendkower, J. (1991). *Psychoanalyse zwischen Politik und Religion.* Frankfurt: Campus.

Benjamin, J. (1998). *The Shadow of the Other. Intersubjectivity and Gender in Psychoanalysis*. New York: Routledge.

Berenstein, I. (2001). The link and the other. *International Journal of Psychoanalysis, 82*: 141–149.

Berg, N. (2003). *Der Holocaust und die westdeutschen Historiker. Erforschung und Erinnerung* [The Holocaust and West German historians. Research and remembrance]. Göttingen: Wallstein.

Bergmann, M. (1996). Fünf Stadien in der Entwicklung der psychoanalytischen Trauma-Konzeption. *Mittelweg 36, Zeitschrift des Hamburger Instituts für Sozialforschung, 5*(2): 12–22.

Bergmann, M., & Jucovy, M. (1982). Introduction. In: M. Bergmann & M. Jucovy (Eds.), *Generations of the Holocaust*. New York: Columbia Universities Press, 1990.

Berlin, I. (1990). *Der Nationalismus*. Frankfurt: Hain.

Berman, E. (1981). Multiple personality: psychoanalytic perspectives. *International Journal of Psychoanalysis, 62*: 283–300.

Berman, P. (2003). *Terror and Liberalism*. New York: Norton.

Bernfeld, S. (1923). Über eine typische Form der männlichen Pubertät. In: S. Bernfeld (Ed.), *Antiautoritäre Erziehung und Psychoanalyse. Ausgewählte Schriften, Vol. III* (pp. 64–81). Frankfurt: Ullstein.

Binswanger, L. (1942). *Grundformen und Erkenntnis menschlichen Daseins* (2nd ed.). Zürich: Max Niehans, 1953.

Bion, W. R. (1961). *Experiences in Groups and other Papers*. London: Tavistock Publications.

Birksted-Breen, D. (2003). Time and the après-coup. *International Journal of Psychoanalysis, 84*: 1501–1515.

Blass, R., & Simon, B. (1994). The value of the historical perspective to contemporary psychoanalysis: Freud's "Seduction hypothesis". *International Journal of Psychoanalysis, 75*: 677–694.

Blatt, S., & Levy, K. (2003). Attachment theory, psychoanalysis, personality development, an psychopathology. *Psychoanalytic Inquiry, 23*: 102–150.

Blos, P. (1979). *The Adolescent Passage. Developmental Issues*. New York: International Universities Press.

Blum, H. (1994). *Reconstruction in Psychoanalysis: Childhood Revisited and Recreated*. Madison, WI: International Universities Press.

Bohleber, W. (1987). Die verlängerte Adoleszenz. Identitätsbildung und Identitätsstörungen im jungen Erwachsenenalter. *Jahrbuch der Psychoanalyse, 21*: 58–84.

Bohleber, W. (1992). Identity and the self—interactional and intrapsychic paradigm. Significance of infant research for psychoanalytic theory. In: M. Leuzinger-Bohleber, H. Schneider & R. Pfeiffer (Eds.), *"Two Butterflies on my Head"—Psychoanalysis in the Interdisciplinary Scientific Dialogue* (pp. 107–132). Berlin: Springer.

Bohleber, W. (1997a). Die Konstruktion imaginärer Gemeinschaften und das Bild von den Juden – unbewußte Determinanten des Antisemitismus in Deutschland. *Psyche, Zeitschrift für Psychoanalyse und ihre Anwendungen, 51*: 570–605.

Bohleber, W. (1997b). Trauma, Identifizierung und historischer Kontext. Über die Notwendigkeit, die NS-Vergangenheit in den psychoanalytischen Deutungsprozess einzubeziehen. *Psyche, Zeitschrift für Psychoanalyse und ihre Anwendungen, 51*: 958–995.

Bohleber, W. (2001). Trauma, Trauer und Geschichte. In: J. Rüsen & B. Liebsch (Eds.), *Trauer und Geschichte* (pp. 131–145). Köln: Böhlau.

Bohleber, W. (2003). Between hermeneutics and natural science: some focal points in the development of psychoanalytic clinical theory in Germany after 1945. In: M. Leuzinger-Bohleber, A. U. Dreher, & J. Canestri (Eds.), *Pluralism and Unity? Methods of Research in Psychoanalysis* (pp. 63–80). London: International Psychoanalytical Association.

Boll, F. (2001). *Sprechen als Last und Befreiung. Holocaust-Überlebende und politisch Verfolgte zweier Diktaturen. Ein Beitrag zur deutsch-deutschen Erinnerungskultur* [Speech as burden and release. Holocaust survivors and the politically persecuted of two dictatorships. A contribution to the German–German culture of remembrance]. Bonn: Dietz.

Bollas, C. (1987). *The Shadow of the Object: Psychoanalysis of the Unthought Known.* London: Free Association Books.

Bollas, C. (1992). *Being a Character. Psychoanalysis and Self Experience.* London: Routledge, 1993.

Bollas, C. (1995). *Cracking up. The Work of the Unconscious.* New York: Hill and Wang.

Boulanger, G. (2007). *Wounded by Reality. Understanding and Treating Adult Onset Trauma.* Mahwah, NJ: Analytic Press.

Bowlby, J. (1973). *Separation, Anxiety and Anger.* London: Hogarth Press.

Brainin, E., Ligeti, V., & Teicher, S. (1993). *Vom Gedanken zur Tat. Zur Psychoanalyse des Antisemitismus.* Frankfurt: Brandes & Apsel.

Brenneis, C. B. (1997). *Recovered Memories of Trauma: Transferring the Present to the Past.* Madison, WI: International Universities Press.

Brenneis, C. B. (1999). The analytic present in psychoanalytic reconstructions of the historical past. *Journal of the American Psychoanalytic Association, 47*: 187–201.

Brenner, I. (1994). The dissociative character: a reconsideration of "multiple personality". *Journal of the American Psychoanalytic Association*, 42: 819–846.

Brenner, I. (2001). *Dissociation of Trauma: Theory, Phenomenology, and Technique*. Madison, WI: International Universities Press.

Breuer, J., & Freud, S. (1893a). On the psychical mechanism of hysterical phenomena: preliminary communication. *S.E.*, 2: 3–17. London: Hogarth Press.

Breuer, J., & Freud, S. (1895d). *Studies on Hysteria. S.E.*, 2. London: Hogarth Press.

Bruner, J. (1990). *Acts of Meaning*. Cambridge, MA: Harvard University Press.

Buber, M. (1954). *Das dialogische Prinzip* (7th ed.). Gerlingen: Lambert Schneider, 1994.

Buchholz, M. (Ed.) (1993). *Metaphernanalyse*. Göttingen: Vandenhoeck & Ruprecht.

Buchholz, M. (1998). Die Metapher im psychoanalytischen Dialog. *Psyche, Zeitschrift für Psychoanalyse und ihre Anwendungen*, 52: 545–571.

Buchholz, M. (2003). *Metaphern der Kur*. Giessen: Psychosozial.

Carlson, E., Armstrong, J., Loewenstein, R., & Roth, D. (1998). Relationships between traumatic experiences and symptoms of posttraumatic experiences and symptoms of posttraumatic stress, dissociation, and amnesia. In: D. Bremner & C. Marmar (Eds.), *Trauma, Memory, and Dissociation* (pp. 205–228). Washington, DC: American Psychiatric Press.

Caruth, C. (1995). Trauma als historische Erfahrung: Die Vergangenheit einholen. In: U. Baer (Ed.), *"Niemand zeugt für den Zeugen". Erinnerungskultur nach der Shoa* (pp. 84–98). Frankfurt: Suhrkamp, 2000.

Carveth, D. (1984). The analyst's metaphors. A deconstructivist perspective. *Psychoanalysis and Contemporary Thought*, 7: 491–560.

Cavell, M. (1998). In response to Owen Renik's "The analyst's subjectivity and the analyst's objectivity". *International Journal of Psychoanalysis*, 79: 1195–1202.

Chasseguet-Smirgel, J. (1975). *The Ego-Ideal*. London: Free Association, 1985.

Chasseguet-Smirgel, J. (1990). Reflections of a psychoanalyst upon the Nazi biocracy and genocide. *International Review of Psychoanalysis*, 17: 167–176.

Cohen, J. (1985). Trauma and repression. *Psychoanalytic Inquiry, 5*: 163–189.

Cooper, A. (1986). Toward a limited definition of psychic trauma. In: A. Rothstein (Ed.), *The Reconstruction of Trauma. Its Significance in Clinical Work* (pp. 41–56). Madison, WI: International Universities Press.

Croitoru, J. (2003). *Der Märtyrer als Waffe. Die historischen Wurzeln des Selbstmordattentats*. Munich: Hanser.

Davies, J., & Frawley, M. (1994). *Treating the Adult Survivor of Childhood Sexual Abuse: A Psychoanalytic Perspective*. New York: Basic Books.

Domansky, E. (1993). Die gespaltene Erinnerung [Split memory]. In: M. Koeppen, G. Bauer & R. Steinlein (Eds.), *Kunst und Literatur nach Auschwitz* [Art and literature after Auschwitz] (pp. 178–196). Berlin: Schmidt.

Dornes, M. (1998). Bindungstheorie und Psychoanalyse. *Psyche, Zeitschrift für Psychoanalyse und ihre Anwendungen, 52*: 299–348.

Douglas, M. (1966). *Purity and Danger: An Analysis of Concept of Pollution and Taboo*. London: Routledge.

Dupont, J. (Ed.) (1988). *The Clinical Diary of Sándor Ferenczi*. Cambridge, MA: Harvard University Press. [Ohne Sympathie keine Heilung [Without sympathy no healing]. Das klinische Tagebuch von 1932. Frankfurt am Main: Fischer.]

Eagle, M., Wolitzky, D., & Wakefield, J. (2001). The analyst's knowledge and authority: a critique of the "new view" in psychoanalysis. *Journal of the American Psychoanalytic Association, 49*: 457–489.

Eckhardt-Henn, A. (2004). Dissoziation als spezifische Abwehrfunktion schwerer traumatischer Erlebnisse – eine psychoanalytische Perspektive. In: A. Eckhardt-Henn & S. O. Hoffmann (Eds.), *Dissoziative Bewusstseinsstörungen. Theorie, Symptomatik, Therapie* (pp. 276–294). Stuttgart: Schattauer.

Ehlert, M., & Lorke, B. (1988). Zur Psychodynamik der traumatischen Reaktion. *Psyche, Zeitschrift für Psychoanalyse und ihre Anwendungen, 42*: 502–532.

Ehlert-Balzer, M. (1996). Das Trauma als Objektbeziehung. *Forum der Psychoanalyse, 12*: 291–314.

Ehrenberg, A. (1998). *La Fatigue d'Etre Soi*. Paris: Editions Odile Jacob. [Das erschöpfte Selbst. Depression und Gesellschaft in der Gegenwart. Frankfurt: Campus, 2004].

Eissler, K. R. (1968). Weitere Bemerkungen zum Problem der KZ-Psychologie. *Psyche, Zeitschrift für Psychoanalyse und ihre Anwendungen, 22*: 452–463.

Elias, N. (1989). *Studien über die Deutschen: Machtkämpfe und Habitusentwicklung im 19. und 20. Jahrhundert.* Frankfurt: Suhrkamp. [*The Germans. Power Struggles and the Development of Habitus in the Nineteenth and Twentieth Centuries.* Cambridge: Polity Press, 1996].

Emde, R. (1983). The prerepresentational self and its affective core. *Psychoanalytic Study of the Child, 38:* 165–192.

Erb, R., & Bergmann, W. (1989). *Die Nachtseite der Judenemanzipation. Der Widerstand gegen die Integration der Juden in Deutschland 1780–1860.* Berlin: Metropol.

Erikson, E. (1959). *Identity and the Life Cycle. Selected Papers.* New York: International Universities Press.

Fairbairn, W. (1952). *Psychoanalytic Studies of the Personality.* London: Routledge & Kegan Paul.

Fenichel, O. (1937). Der Begriff "Trauma" in der heutigen psychoanalytischen Neurosenlehre. In: *Aufsätze, Vol. II* (pp.58–79). Olten: Walter, 1981.

Fenichel, O. (1945). *Psychoanalytic Theory of Neurosis, Vol. I.* New York: Norton.

Ferenczi, S. (1949). Confusion of tongues between adults and the child [1933]. *International Journal of Psychoanalysis, 30:* 225–230. [(1982). Sprachverwirrung zwischen den Erwachsenen und dem Kind. In: S. Ferenczi, *Schriften zur Psychoanalyse, Vol. 2* (pp. 303–313). Frankfurt: Fischer.]

Ferro, A. (1999). *The Bi-personal Field. Experiences in Child Analysis.* London: Routledge.

Ferro, A. (2005). Commentary. In: S. Lewkowicz & S. Flechner (Eds.), *Truth, Reality, and the Psychoanalyst. Latin American Contributions to Psychoanalysis* (pp. 87–96). London: International Psychoanalytical Association.

Fielding, N., & Fouda, Y. (2003). *Masterminds of Terror. The Truth Behind the Most Devastating Terrorist Attack the World has Ever Seen.* Edinburgh: Mainstream.

Fischer, G., & Riedesser, P. (1998). *Lehrbuch der Psychotraumatologie.* Munich: Reinhardt.

Fonagy, P. (1996). The significance of the development of metacognitive control over mental representations in parenting and infant development. *Journal of Clinical Psychoanalysis, 5:* 67–86.

Fonagy, P. (1999). Memory and therapeutic action. *International Journal of Psychoanalysis, 80:* 215–223.

Fonagy, P. (2003). Repression, transference and reconstruction: rejoinder to Harold Blum [Psychoanalytic controversies]. *International Journal of Psychoanalysis, 84*: 503–509.

Fonagy, P., & Target, M. (1997). Perspectives on the recovered memory debate. In: J. Sandler & P. Fonagy (Eds.), *Recovered Memories of Abuse: True or False?* (pp. 183–216). London: Karnac.

Fonagy, P., Gergely, G., Jurist, E., & Target, M. (2002). *Affect Regulation, Mentalization, and the Development of the Self.* New York: Other Press.

Fonagy, P., Target, M., & Allison, L. (2003). Gedächtnis und therapeutische Wirkung. *Psyche, Zeitschrift für Psychoanalyse und ihre Anwendungen, 57*: 841–856.

Freeman, M. (1985). Psychoanalytic narration and the problem of historical knowledge. *Psychoanalysis and Contemporary Thought, 8*: 133–82.

Freud, S. (1899a). Screen memories. *S.E., 3*: 303–322. London: Hogarth Press.

Freud, S. (1900a). *The Interpretation of Dreams. S.E., 4–5.* London: Hogarth Press.

Freud, S. (1905d). *Three Essays on the Theory of Sexuality. S.E., 7*: 135–243. London: Hogarth Press.

Freud, S. (1909d). *Notes upon a Case of Obsessional Neurosis. S.E., 10*: 155–318. London: Hogarth Press.

Freud, S. (1912b). The dynamics of transference. *S.E., 12*: 99–108. London: Hogarth Press

Freud, S. (1912e). Recommendations to physicians practising psychoanalysis. *S.E., 12*: 111–120. London: Hogarth Press.

Freud, S. (1914g). Remembering, repeating and working through. *S.E., 12*: 145–156. London: Hogarth Press.

Freud, S. (1916–1917). *Introductory Lectures on Psycho-Analysis (Part III). S.E., 16.* London: Hogarth Press.

Freud, S. (1919a). Lines of advance in psycho-analytic therapy. *S.E., 17*: 159–168. London: Hogarth Press.

Freud, S. (1919d). Introduction to *Psychoanalysis and the War Neuroses. S.E., 17*: 207–210). London: Hogarth Press.

Freud, S. (1920g). *Beyond the Pleasure Principle. S.E., 18*: 7–64. London: Hogarth Press.

Freud, S. (1921c). *Group Psychology and the Analysis of the Ego. S.E., 18*: 69–143. London: Hogarth Press.

Freud, S. (1923b). *The Ego and the Id. S.E., 19*: 3–66. London: Hogarth Press.

Freud, S. (1926d). *Inhibitions, Symptoms and Anxiety. S.E.*, 20: 87–172. London: Hogarth Press.

Freud, S. (1926e). The question of lay analysis. *S.E.*, 20: 183–250. London: Hogarth Press.

Freud. S. (1930a). *Civilization and its Discontents. S.E.*, 21: 64–145. London: Hogarth Press.

Freud, S. (1937b). Constructions in analysis. *S.E.*, 23: 255–269. London: Hogarth Press.

Freud, S. (1939a). *Moses and Monotheism. S.E.*, 23: 7–137.

Freud, S. (1985). *The Complete Letters of Sigmund Freud to Wilhelm Fliess 1887–1904*, J. M. Masson (Ed. & Trans.). Cambridge, MA: Harvard Universities Press.

Friedländer, S. (1997). *Nazi Germany and the Jews, Vol. 1: The Years of Persecution, 1933–1939*. New York: Harper Collins.

Friedman, L. (1996). Overview: knowledge and authority in the psychoanalytic relationship. *Psychoanalytic Quarterly*, 65: 254–265.

Friedman, P. (1949). Some aspects of concentration camp psychology. *American Journal of Psychiatry*, 105: 601–605.

Frosh, S. (1991). *Identity Crisis. Modernity, Psychoanalysis and the Self*. Basingstoke: Macmillan Press.

Furst, S. (1967). Psychic trauma. A survey. In: S. Furst (Ed.), *Psychic Trauma* (pp. 3–50). New York: Basic Books.

Gabbard, G. O., & Westen, D. (2003). Rethinking therapeutic action. *International Journal of Psychoanalysis*, 84: 823–841.

Gadamer, H. G. (1960). Wahrheit und Methode. In: H. G. Gadamer, *Gesammelte Werke I*. Tübingen: Mohr & Siebeck, 1990 [*Truth and Method* (2nd edn). New York: Continuum, 2004].

Gaensbauer, T. J. (1995). Trauma in the preverbal period: symptoms, memories, and developmental impact. *Psychoanalytic Study of the Child*, 50: 122–149.

Galatzer-Levy, R., & Cohler, B. (1993). *The Essential Other. A Developmental Psychology of the Self*. New York: Basic Books.

Garland, C. (1998). Thinking about trauma. In: C. Garland (Ed.), *Understanding Trauma. A Psychoanalytic Approach*. London: Karnac.

Garza-Guerrero, A. C. (1974). Culture shock: its mourning and the vicissitudes of identity. *Journal of the American Psychoanalytic Association*, 22: 408–429.

Gedo, J. E. (1986). *Conceptual Issues in Psychoanalysis. Essays in History and Method*. Hillsdale, NJ: Analytic Press.

Giddens, A. (1999). *Runaway World. How Globalization is Reshaping our Lives*. New York: Routledge.

Gilligan, C. (1982). *In a Different Voice*. Cambridge, MA: Harvard University Press.

Gilligan, C. (1988). Exit-voice dilemmas in adolescent development. In: D. L. Browning (Ed.), *Adolescent Identities. A Collection of Readings* (pp. 141–156). New York: Analytic Press, 2008.

Goldhagen, D. (1996). *Hitler's Willing Executioners. Ordinary Germans and the Holocaust*. London: Little, Brown.

Good, M. (1994). The reconstruction of early childhood trauma: fantasy, reality, and verification. *Journal of the American Psychoanalytic Association, 42*: 79–101.

Good, M. (1995). Karl Abraham, Sigmund Freud and the fate of the seduction theory. *Journal of the American Psychoanalytic Association, 43*: 1137–1167.

Good, M. (1998). Screen reconstructions: traumatic memory, conviction, and the problem of verification. *Journal of the American Psychoanalytic Association, 46*: 149–183.

Grand, S. (2000). *The Reproduction of Evil: A Clinical and Cultural Perspective*. Hillsdale, NJ: Analytic Press.

Granzow, S. (1994). *Das autobiographische Gedächtnis. Kognitionspsychologische und psychoanalytische Perspektiven* [Autobiographical memory. Cognitive psychology and psychoanalytical perspectives]. Munich: Quintessenz.

Green, A. (1975). The analyst, symbolization and absence in the analytic setting (on changes in analytic practice and analytic experience). *International Journal of Psychoanalysis, 56*: 1–22.

Green, A. (1999). *The Work of the Negative*. London: Free Association.

Green, A. (2000). The intrapsychic and the intersubjective in psychoanalysis. *Psychoanalytic Quarterly, 69*: 1–39.

Green, A. (2001). *Time in Psychoanalysis. Some Contradictory Aspects*. London: Free Association Books.

Grotstein, J. (1981). *Splitting and Projective Identification*. New York: Jason Aronson.

Grubrich-Simitis, I. (1979). Extreme traumatization as cumulative trauma: study of survivors. *Psychoanalytic Study of the Child, 36*: 1981, 415–450.

Grubrich-Simitis, I. (1984). From concretism to metaphor: thoughts on some theoretical and technical aspects of the psychoanalytic work with children of Holocaust survivors. *Psychoanalytic Study of the Child, 39*: 301–319.

Grubrich-Simitis, I. (1987). Trauma oder Trieb – Trieb und Trauma. Lektionen aus Sigmund Freuds phylogenetischer Phantasie von 1915. *Psyche, Zeitschrift für Psychoanalyse und ihre Anwendungen, 41*: 992–1023.

Grunberger, B. (1964). The anti-semite and the oedipal conflict. *International Journal of Psychoanalysis, 45*: 380–385.

Grunberger, B. (1984). Kurzer Beitrag über Narzissmus, Aggressivität und Antisemitismus. In: *Narziss und Anubis: die Psychoanalyse jenseits der Triebtheorie, Vol. 2* (pp. 132–138). Munich: Internationale Psychoanalyse, 1988.

Grunberger, B., & Dessuant, P. (1997). *Narcissisme, Christianisme, Antisémitisme. Étude Psychanalytique.* Arles: Actes Sud.

Gullestad, S. (2005). Who is "who" in dissociation? A plea for psychodynamics in a time of trauma. *International Journal of Psychoanalysis, 86*: 639–656.

Hanly, C., & Hanly, M. F. (2001). Critical realism: distinguishing the psychological subjectivity of the analyst from epistemological subjectivism. *Journal of the American Psychoanalytic Association, 49*: 515–533.

Haverkamp. A. (1983). *Theorie der Metapher* (2nd edn). Darmstadt: Wissenschaftliche Buchgesellschaft, 1996.

Herman, J. L. (1992). *Trauma and Recovery.* New York: Basic Books.

Hirsch, M. (1987). Realer Inzest. Psychodynamik des sexuellen Missbrauchs in der Familie (3rd edn). Berlin: Springer, 1994.

Hock, U. (2003). Die Zeit des Erinnerns [Time to remember]. *Psyche, Zeitschrift für Psychoanalyse und ihre Anwendungen, 57*: 812–40.

Hoffer, W. (1952). The mutual influences in the development of ego and id: earliest stages. *Psychoanalytic Study of the Child, 7*: 31–41.

Hoffman, I. Z. (1998). *Ritual and Spontaneity in the Psychoanalytic Process. A Dialectical-Constructivist View.* Hillsdale, NJ: Analytic Press.

Hoffmann, B. (1998). *Inside Terrorism.* New York: Columbia Universities Press.

Hoffmann, S. O., Eckhardt-Henn, A., & Scheidt, C. (2004). Konversion, Dissoziation und Somatisierung: historische Aspekte und Entwurf eines integrativen Modells. In: A. Eckhardt-Henn & S. O. Hoffmann (Eds.), *Dissoziative Bewusstseinsstörungen – Theorie, Symptomatik, Therapie* (pp. 114–130). Stuttgart: Schattauer.

Hofmann, A. (2004). Dissoziation und Posttraumatische Belastungsstörung. In: A. Eckhardt-Henn & S. O. Hoffmann (Eds.), *Dissoziative Bewusstseinsstörungen – Theorie, Symptomatik, Therapie* (pp. 295–303). Stuttgart: Schattauer.

Holmes, J. (2006). Mentalizing from a psychoanalytic perspective: what's new? In: J. Allen & P. Fonagy (Eds.), *Handbook of Mentalization-Based Treatment* (pp. 31–49). Chichester: Wiley.

Honneth, A. (2001). Facetten des vorsozialen Selbst. Eine Erwiderung auf Joel Whitebook. *Psyche, Zeitschrift für Psychoanalyse und ihre Anwendungen, 55*: 790–802.

Honneth, A. (2002). Organisierte Selbstverwirklichung. Paradoxien der Individualisierung. In: A. Honneth (Ed.), *Befreiung aus der Mündigkeit. Paradoxien des gegenwärtigen Kapitalismus* (pp. 141–158). Frankfurt: Campus.

Hoppe, K. D. (1962). Verfolgung, Aggression und Depression. *Psyche, Zeitschrift für Psychoanalyse und ihre Anwendungen, 16*: 521–537.

Hoppe, K. D. (1965). Psychotherapie bei Konzentrationslageropfern. *Psyche, Zeitschrift für Psychoanalyse und ihre Anwendungen, 19*: 290–319.

Hoppe, K. D. (1968). Psychosomatische Reaktionen und Erkrankungen bei überlebenden schwerer Verfolgung. *Psyche, Zeitschrift für Psychoanalyse und ihre Anwendungen, 22*: 465– 477.

Hortzitz, N. (1995). Die Sprache der Judenfeindschaft. In: J. Schoeps & J. Schlör (Eds.), *Antisemitismus. Vorurteile und Mythen* (pp. 19–40). Munich: Piper.

Howell, E. (2005). *The Dissociative Mind.* Hillsdale, NJ: Analytic Press.

Illouz, E. (2006). *Gefühle in Zeiten des Kapitalismus.* Frankfurt: Suhrkamp.

Jacobson, E. (1964). *The Self and the Object World.* New York: International Universities Press.

Jäckel, E. (1972). *Hitler's Weltanschauung: A Blueprint for Power.* Cambridge, MA: Harvard University Press.

Jaques, E. (1981). Social systems as a defense against persecutory and depressive anxiety. In: G. Gibbard, J. Hartmann & R. Mann (Eds.), *Analysis of Groups* (pp. 277–299). San Francisco: Jossey Bass.

Jones, J. W. (2002). *Terror and Transformation. The Ambiguity of Religion in Psychoanalytic Perspective.* Hove: Brunner-Routledge.

Joseph, B. (1985). Transference: The total situation. *International Journal of Psychoanalysis, 66*: 447–454.

Jureit, U., & Wildt, M. (2005). *Generationen. Zur Relevanz eines wissenschaftlichen Grundbegriffs* [Generations. On the relevance of a fundamental scientific idea]. Hamburg: Hamburger Edition.

Kakar, S. (1996). *The Colors of Violence. Cultural Identities, Religion, and Conflicts.* Chicago, IL: University of Chicago Press.

Kardiner, A. (1941). *The Traumatic Neuroses of War.* New York: Hoeber.

Keilson, H. (1979). *Sequentielle Traumatisierung bei Kindern.* Stuttgart: Enke. *Sequential Traumatization in Children: a Clinical and Statistical Follow-up Study on the Fate of the Jewish War Orphans in the Netherlands.* Jerusalem: Magnes Press, 1992.

Kennedy, R. (2002). *Psychoanalysis, History, and Subjectivity: Now of the Past.* Hove: Brunner-Routledge.

Kernberg, O. (1975). *Borderline Conditions and Pathological Narcissism.* New York: Jason Aronson.

Keupp, H., Ahbe, T., Gmür, W., Höfer, R., Mitzscherlich, B., Kraus, W., & Straus, F. (Eds.) (1999). *Identitätskonstruktionen. Das Patchwork der Identitäten in der Spätmoderne.* Reinbek: Rowohlt.

Khan, M. (1963). The concept of cumulative trauma. *Psychoanalytic Study of the Child, 18*: 286–306.

Kihlstrom, J. (2006). Trauma and memory revisited. In: B. Uttl, N. Ohta, & A. L. Siegenthaler (Eds.), *Memory and Emotion: Interdisciplinary Perspectives* (pp. 259–291). Oxford: Blackwell.

Kinston, W., & Cohen, J. (1986). Primal repression: clinical and theoretical aspects. *International Journal Psychoanalysis, 67*: 337–355.

Kippenberg, H. (2008). *Gewalt als Gottesdienst. Religionskriege im Zeitalter der Globalisierung.* Munich: Beck.

Kirshner, L. (1994). Trauma, the good object and the symbolic: a theoretical integration. *International Journal Psychoanalysis, 75*: 235–242.

Kluft, R. (1990). *Incest-related Syndromes of Adult Psychopathology.* Washington, DC: American Psychiatric Press.

Kluft, R. (1999). Memory (book reviews). *Journal of the American Psychoanalytic Association, 47*: 227–237.

Kluft, R. (2000). The psychoanalytic psychotherapy of dissociative identity disorder in the context of trauma therapy. *Psychoanalytic Inquiry, 20*: 259–286.

Knafo, D. (1999). Anti-Semitism in the clinical setting: transference and countertransference dimensions. *Journal of the American Psychoanalytic Association, 47*: 35–63.

Knigge, V., & Frei, N. (2002). *Verbrechen erinnern. Die Auseinandersetzung mit Holocaust und Völkermord* [Remembering crimes. Dealing with holocaust and genocide]. Munich: Beck.

Kohut, H. (1971). *The Analysis of the Self. A Systematic Approach to the Psychoanalytic Treatment of Narcissistic Personality Disorders.* New York: International Universities Press.

Kohut, H. (1977). *The Restoration of the Self.* New York: International Universities Press.

Kramer, S., & Akhtar, S. (1991). *The Trauma of Transgression: Psychotherapy of Incest Victims*. Northvale, NJ: Jason Aronson.

Kraus, W., & Mitzscherlich, B. (1998). Abschied vom Grossprojekt. Normative Grundlagen der empirischen Identitätsforschung in der Tradition von James E. Marcia und die Notwendigkeit ihrer Reformulierung. In: H. Keupp & R. Höfer (Eds.), *Identitätsarbeit heute. Klassische und aktuelle Perspektiven der Identitätsforschung* (pp. 149–173). Frankfurt: Suhrkamp.

Kreeger, L. (Ed.) (1975). *The Large Group: Dynamics and Therapy*. London: Constable.

Kris, E. (1956). The recovery of childhood memories in psychoanalysis. *Psychoanalytic Study of the Child, 11*: 54–88.

Krystal, H. (Ed.) (1968). *Massive Psychic Trauma*. New York: International Universities Press.

Krystal, H. (1978). Trauma and affects. *The Psychoanalytic Study of the Child, 33*: 81–116.

Krystal, H. (1988). *Integration and Self-Healing. Affect, Trauma, Alexithymia*. Hillsdale, NJ: Analytic Press.

Küchenhoff, J. (2004). Verlust des Selbst, Verlust des Anderen – die doppelte Zerstörung von Nähe und Ferne im Trauma. *Psyche, Zeitschrift für Psychoanalyse und ihre Anwendungen, 58*: 811–835.

Lacan, J. (1949). The mirror stage as formative of the function of the I as revealed in psychoanalytic experience. In: J. Lacan, *Ecrits*. New York: Norton, 2006.

Lakoff, G., & Johnson, M. (1980). *Metaphors We Live By*. Chicago, IL: The University of Chicago Press.

Langer, L. (1995). Memory's time: chronology and duration in Holocaust testimonies. In: *Admitting the Holocaust: Collected Papers* (pp. 13–23). New York: Oxford University Press.

Langmuir, G. (1990). *Towards a Definition of Antisemitism*. Berkeley, CA: University of California Press.

Lansky, M., & Bley, C. (1995). *Posttraumatic Nightmares: Psychodynamic Explorations*. Hillsdale, NJ: Analytic Press.

Laplanche, J. (1976). *Life and Death in Psychoanalysis*. Baltimore, MD: Johns Hopkins University Press.

Laplanche, J. (1988). *Die allgemeine Verführungstheorie und andere Aufsätze*. Tübingen: Edition Diskord.

Laplanche, J. (1992). *La révolution copernicienne inachevée: Travaux 1965–1992* [The unfinished Copernican revolution: Works 1965–1992]. Paris: Aubier.

Laplanche, J., & Pontalis, J.-B. (1988). *The Language of Psychoanalysis, Vol. 1 & 2*. London: Karnac.

Laub, D. (1992). Zeugnis ablegen oder Die Schwierigkeit des Zuhörens. In: U. Baer (Ed.), *"Niemand zeugt für den Zeugen"*. *Erinnerungskultur nach der Shoa* (pp. 68–83). Frankfurt: Suhrkamp, 2000.

Laub, D. (1998). The empty circle: children of survivors and the limits of reconstruction. *Journal of the American Psychoanalytic Association*, 46: 507–529.

Laub, D., & Auerhahn, C. (1991). Zentrale Erfahrung des Überlebenden: Die Versagung von Mitmenschlichkeit. In: H. Stoffels (Ed.), *Schicksale der Verfolgten. Psychische und somatische Auswirkungen von Terrorherrschaft* (pp. 254–276). Berlin: Springer.

Laub, D., & Auerhahn, N. (1993). Knowing and not knowing massive psychic trauma: forms of traumatic memory. *International Journal of Psychoanalysis, 74*: 287–302.

Laub, D., & Podell, D. (1995). Art and trauma. *International Journal of Psychoanalysis, 76*: 991–1005.

Leuzinger-Bohleber, M., & Pfeifer, R. (2002). Remembering a depressive primary object: Memory in the dialogue between psychoanalysis and cognitive science. *International Journal of Psychoanalysis, 83*: 3–33.

Lévinas, E. (1968). *Totalité et infini. Essay sur l'exteriorité*. La Haye: Nijhoff. *Totality and infinity: an Essay on exteriority*. Boston: Kluwe, 1979.

Lévinas, E. (1978). *Autrement qu'être ou au-delà de l'essence*. La Haye: Nijhoff.

Levine, H. (1990). *Adult Analysis and Childhood Sexual Abuse*. Hillsdale, NJ: Analytic Press.

Levy, B.-H. (1995). *Gefährliche Reinheit*. Wien: Passagen-Verlag.

Lewis, B. (1994). *The Shaping of the Modern Middle East*. Oxford: Oxford University Press.

Lewis, B. (2003). *Die Wut der arabischen Welt. Warum der jahrhundertelange Konflikt zwischen dem Islam und dem Westen weiter eskaliert*. Frankfurt: Campus.

Leys, R. (2000). *Trauma: A Genealogy*. Chicago IL: University of Chicago Press.

Lichtenstein, H. (1977). *The Dilemma of Human Identity*. New York: Jason Aronson.

Lifton, R. J. (1986). *The Nazi Doctors. Medical Killing and the Psychology of Genozid*. New York: Basic Books.

Lifton, R. J. (1999). *Destroying the World To Save It. Aum Shinrikyo, Apocalyptic Violence, and the New Global Terrorism*. New York: Holt.

Loch, W. (1965). *Voraussetzungen, Mechanismen und Grenzen des psychoanalytischen Prozesses*. Berne: Huber.

Loch, W. (1974). Der Analytiker als Gesetzgeber und Lehrer. *Psyche, Zeitschrift für Psychoanalyse und ihre Anwendungen, 28*: 431–460.

Loewald, H. (1960). On the therapeutic action of psycho-analysis. *International Journal of Psychoanalysis, 41*: 16–33.

Loewenberg, P. (1969). *Decoding the Past. The Psychohistorical Approach*. Berkeley, CA: University of California Press.

Loewenberg, P. (1992). Die Psychodynamik des Antijudaismus in historischer Perspektive. *Psyche, Zeitschrift für Psychoanalyse und ihre Anwendungen, 46*: 1095–1121.

Loewenstein, R., & Ross, D. (1992). Multiple personality and psychoanalysis: an introduction. *Psychoanalytic Inquiry, 12*: 3–48.

Loftus, E., & Ketcham, K. (1994). *The Myth of Repressed Memory: False Memories and Allegations of Sexual Abuse*. New York: St Martin's Press.

Lorenzer, A. (1965). Ein Abwehrsyndrom bei traumatischen Verläufen. *Psyche, Zeitschrift für Psychoanalyse und ihre Anwendungen, 18*: 685–700.

Lorenzer, A. (1966). Zum Begriff der "traumatischen Neurose". *Psyche, Zeitschrift für Psychoanalyse und ihre Anwendungen, 20*: 481–492.

Lorenzer, A. (1968a). Methodologische Probleme der Untersuchung traumatischer Neurosen. *Psyche, Zeitschrift für Psychoanalyse und ihre Anwendungen, 22*: 861–874.

Lorenzer, A. (1968b). Some observations on the latency of symptoms in patients suffering from persecution sequelae. *International Journal of Psychoanalysis, 49*: 316–318.

Lorenzer, A. (1983). Sprache, Lebenspraxis und szenisches Verstehen in der psychoanalytischen Therapie. *Psyche, Zeitschrift für Psychoanalyse und ihre Anwendungen, 37*: 97–115.

Lorenzer, A. (2002). *Die Sprache, der Sinn, das Unbewusste. Psychoanalytisches Grundverständnis und Neurowissenschaften*, U. Prokop (Ed.). Stuttgart: Klett-Cotta.

Lorenzer, A., & Thomä, H. (1965). Über die zweiphasige Symptomentwicklung bei traumatischen Neurosen. *Psyche, Zeitschrift für Psychoanalyse und ihre Anwendungen, 18*: 674–684.

Lyons-Ruth, K. (2003). Dissociation and the parent–infant dialogue: a longitudinal perspective from attachment research. *Journal of the American Psychoanalytic Association, 51*: 883–911.

Mahler, M., Pine, F., & Bergmann, A. (1975). *The Psychological Birth of the Human Infant: Symbiosis and Individuation*. London: Hutchinson.

Marcia, J. (1994). Ego identity and object relations. In: J. Masling & R. Bornstein (Eds.), *Empirical Perspectives on Object Relations Theory* (pp. 59–103). Washington, DC: American Psychological Association.

Marcia, J., Waterman, A., & Matteson, D. (1993). *Ego Identity: A Handbook for Psychosocial Research*. Berlin: Springer.

Marty, M., & Appleby, S. (Eds.) (1991). *Fundamentalisms Observed*. Chicago, IL: University of Chicago Press.

Marty, M., & Appleby, S. (Eds.) (1995). *Fundamentalisms Comprehended*. Chicago, IL: University of Chicago Press.

Marty, P., & de M'Uzan, M. (1963). La pensée opératoire. *Revue Française de Psychanalyse, 27*(Suppl.): 345–356.

Marzi, A., Hautmann, G., & Maestro, S. (2005). Critical reflections on intersubjectivity in psychoanalysis. *International Journal of Psychoanalysis, 87*: 1297–1314.

McDermott, J. (2005). *Perfect Soldiers. The Hijackers: Who They Were, Why They Did It*. New York: HarperCollins.

McNally, R. (2003). *Remembering Trauma*. Cambridge, MA: Belknap.

McNally, R. (2005). Debunking myths about trauma and memory. *Canadian Journal of Psychiatry, 50*: 817–22.

Meddeb, A. (2002). *Die Krankheit des Islam*. Heidelberg: Wunderhorn.

Memmi, A. (1982). *Rassismus*. Frankfurt: Hain, 1992.

Merridale, C. (2000). *Night of Stone—Death and Memory in Russia*. London: Granta.

Mitchell, S. (1991). Contemporary perspectives on the self: towards an integration. *Psychoanalytic Dialogues, 1*: 121–147.

Mitchell, S. (1997). *Influence and Autonomy in Psychoanalysis*. Hillsdale, NJ: Analytic Press.

Mitchell, S. (1998). The analyst's knowledge and authority. *Psychoanalytic Quarterly, 67*: 1–31.

Mitchell, S. (2000). *Relationality. From Attachment to Intersubjectivity*. Hillsdale, NJ: Analytic Press.

Mitscherlich, A., & Mitscherlich, M. (1967). *The Inability to Mourn. Principles of Collective Behavior*. B. R. Placzek (Trans.). New York: Grove Press, 1975.

Money-Kyrle, R. (1951). *Psychoanalysis and Politics*. New York: Norton.

Moore, R. (1999). *The Creation of Reality in Psychoanalysis. A View of the Contributions of Donald Spence, Roy Schafer, Robert Stolorow, Irwin Z. Hoffman, and Beyond*. Hillsdale, NJ: Analytic Press.

Moses, R. (1978). Adult psychic trauma: the question of early predisposition and some detailed mechanisms. *International Journal of Psychoanalysis, 59*: 353–363.

Nemiah, J. (1998). Early concepts of trauma, dissociation, and the unconscious: their history and current implications. In: D. Bremner & C. Marmar (Eds.), *Trauma, Memory, and Dissociation* (pp. 1–26). Washington, DC: American Psychiatric Press.

Neubauer, P. (1992). Die Reaktion auf Fremde und deren Beziehung zur Schuld. In: W. Bohleber & J. S. Kafka (Eds.), *Antisemitismus* (pp. 126–137). Bielefeld: Aisthesis.

Nettler, R. L. (1986). Past trials and present tribulations: a Muslim fundamentalist speaks on the Jews. In: M. Curtis (Ed.), *Antisemitism in the Contemporary World* (pp. 102ff). Boulder, CO: Westview Press.

Niederland, W. (1968). Clinical observations on the "Survivor Syndrome". *International Journal of Psychoanalysis, 49*: 313–315.

Niederland, W. (1981). The survivor syndrome: further observations and dimensions. *Journal of the American Psychoanalytic Association, 29*: 413–425.

Ogden, T. (1997). Reverie and metaphor. Some thought on how I work as a psychoanalyst. *International Journal of Psychoanalysis, 78*: 719–732.

Oliner, M. (1996). External reality: the elusive dimension of psychoanalysis. *Psychoanalytic Quarterly, 65*: 267–300.

Orange, D., Atwood, G., & Stolorow, R. (1997). *Working Intersubjectively. Contextualism in Psychoanalytic Practice*. Hillsdale, NJ: Analytic Press.

Ostow, M. (1986). The psychodynamics of apocalyptic: discussion of papers on identification and the Nazi phenomenon. *International Journal of Psychoanalysis, 67*: 277–285.

Ostow, M. (1996a). Myth and madness: a report of a psychoanalytic study of antisemitism. *International Journal of Psychoanalysis, 77*: 15–31.

Ostow, M. (1996b). *Myth and Madness. The Psychodynamics of Antisemitism*. New Brunswick, Canada: Transaction.

Person, E. S., & Klar, H. (1994). Establishing trauma: the difficulty distinguishing between memories and fantasies. *Journal of the American Psychoanalytic Association, 42*: 1055–1081.

Polkinghore, D. E. (1998). Narrative Psychologie und Geschichtsbewusstsein. In: J. Straub (Ed.), *Erzählung, Identität und historisches Bewusstsein* (pp. 12–45). Frankfurt: Suhrkamp.

Process of Change Study Group (PCSG) (1998). Non-interpretive mechanisms in psychoanalytic therapy: the "something more" than interpretation. *International Journal of Psychoanalysis, 79*: 903–921.

Puget, J. (2004). Intersubjektivität. Krise der Repräsentation. *Psyche, Zeitschrift für Psychoanalyse und ihre Anwendungen, 58*: 914–934.

Pugh, G. (2002). Freud's "problem": cognitive neuroscience and psychoanalysis working together on memory. *International Journal of Psychoanalysis, 83*: 1375–1394.

Quindeau, I. (2004). *Spur und Umschrift. Die konstitutive Bedeutung von Erinnerung in der Psychoanalyse* [Trace and transcription. The constitutive meaning of remembrance in psychoanalysis]. Munich: Fink.

Qutb, M. (1964). *Islam. The Misunderstood Religion.* Kuwait: Darul Bayan.

Raban, J. (2002). My holy war. *The New Yorker,* 4 February, 28–36.

Rangell, L. (1954). Similarities and differences between psychoanalysis and dynamic psychotherapy. *Journal of the American Psychoanalytic Association, 2*: 734–744.

Reik, T. (1923). *Der eigene und der fremde Gott. Zur Psychoanalyse der religiösen Entwicklung.* Frankfurt: Suhrkamp, 1972.

Reinares, F. (2003). *Terrorismus global. Aktionsfeld Europa.* Hamburg: Europäische Verlagsanstalt, 2005.

Renik, O. (1993). Analytic interaction: conceptualizing technique in light of the analyst's irreducible subjectivity. *Psychoanalytic Quarterly, 62*: 553–571.

Renik, O. (1999). Playing one's cards face up in analysis: an approach to the problem of self-disclosure. *Psychoanalytic Quarterly, 68*: 521–539.

Renik, O. (2004). Intersubjectivity in psychoanalysis. *International Journal of Psychoanalysis, 85*: 1053–1064.

Riesebrodt, M. (1990). *Fundamentalismus als patriarchalische Protestbewegung. Amerikanische Protestanten (1910–28) und iranische Schiiten im Vergleich.* Tübingen: Mohr.

Riesebrodt, M. (2000). *Die Rückkehr der Religionen. Fundamentalismus und der "Kampf der Kulturen".* Munich: Beck.

Riesenberg-Malcolm, R. (1986). Interpretation: The past in the present. *International Review of Psychoanalysis, 13*: 433–43. [(1991). Deutung: Die Vergangenheit in der Gegenwart. In: E. Bott Spillius (Ed.), *Melanie Klein heute* [Melanie Klein today], Vol. 2: Anwendungen [Applications] (pp. 101–122). Munich: Internationale Psychoanalyse.

Rosa, H. (2005). *Beschleunigung. Die Veränderung der Zeitstruktur in der Moderne.* Frankfurt: Suhrkamp.

Rose, P. (1990). *Revolutionary Antisemitism in Germany from Kant to Wagner.* Princeton: Princeton Universities Press.

Rosenkötter, L. (1979). Schatten der Zeitgeschichte auf psychoanalytischen Behandlungen. *Psyche, Zeitschrift für Psychoanalyse und ihre Anwendungen, 33*: 1024–1038.

Rosenkötter, L. (1981). Die Idealbildung in der Generationenfolge. *Psyche, Zeitschrift für Psychoanalyse und ihre Anwendungen, 35*: 593–599.

Roy, O. (2004). *Globalized Islam. The Search for a New Ummah*. London: C. Hurst.

Rüsen, J. (2001). *Zerbrechende Zeit. Über den Sinn der Geschichte*. [Shattering time. Concerning the sense of history]. Cologne: Böhlau.

Sander, L. (1995). Identity and the experience of specifity in a process of recognition. *Psychoanalytic Dialogues, 5*: 579–593.

Sandler, J. (1967). Trauma, strain, and development. In: S. Furst (Ed.), *Psychic Trauma* (pp. 154–174). New York: Basic Books.

Sandler, J., & Sandler, A.-M. (1998). *Internal Objects Revisited*. London: Karnac.

Sandler, J., Dreher, A. U., & Drews, S. (1991). An approach to conceptual research in psychoanalysis illustrated by a consideration of psychic trauma. *International Review of Psycho-Analysis, 18*: 133–142.

Sartre, J.-P. (1954). *Überlegungen zur Judenfrage*. Reinbek: Rowohlt, 1994.

Schacter, D. (1996). *Searching for Memory. The Brain, the Mind, and the Past*. New York: Basic Books.

Schacter, D. (2001). *The Seven Sins of Memory: How the Mind Forgets and Remembers*. Boston, MA: Houghton Mifflin.

Schafer, R. (1976). *A New Language for Psychoanalysis*. New Haven, CT: Yale Universities Press.

Schafer, R. (1982). The relevance of the "here and now" transference interpretation to the reconstruction of early development. *International Journal of Psychoanalysis, 63*: 77–82.

Schafer, R. (1992). *Retelling a Life*. New York: Basic Books.

Scheunert, G. (1959). Zum Problem der Gegenübertragung. *Psyche, Zeitschrift für Psychoanalyse und ihre Anwendungen, 13*: 574–593.

Schottlaender, F. (1952). Das Problem der Begegnung in der Psychotherapie. *Psyche, Zeitschrift für Psychoanalyse und ihre Anwendungen, 6*: 494–507.

Sennett, R. (1998). *The Corrosion of Character. The Personal Consequences of Work in the New Capitalism*. New York: Norton.

Serauky, E. (2000). *Im Namen Allahs. Der Terrorismus im Nahen Osten*. Berlin: Dietz.

Shell-Jugendstudie (1982). *Jugend '81. Lebensentwürfe, Alltagskulturen, Zukunftsbilder*. Opladen: Leske & Budrich.

Shengold, L. (1989). *Soul Murder: The Effects of Childhood Abuse and Deprivation*. New Haven, CT: Yale University Press.

Shevrin, H. (2002). A psychoanalytic view of memory in the light of recent cognitive and neuroscience research. *Neuro-Psychoanalysis, 4*: 131–139.

Simenauer, E. (1978). A double helix: some determinants of the self-perpetuation of Naziism. *Psychoanalytic Study of the Child, 33*: 411–425.

Simmel, E. (1944). Kriegsneurosen. In: *Psychoanalyse und ihre Anwendungen. Ausgewählte Schriften* (pp. 204–226). Frankfurt: Fischer.

Simmel, E. (1946). Anti-Semitism and mass psychopathology. In: E. Simmel, *Anti-Semitism: A Social Disease*. New York: International Universities Press.

Simon, B. (1992). "Incest—see under Oedipus complex": the history of an error in psychoanalysis. *Journal of the American Psychoanalytic Association, 40*: 955–988.

Sofsky, W. (2002). *Zeiten des Schreckens. Amok, Terror, Krieg*. Frankfurt: Fischer.

Solojed, K. (2006). Psychische Traumatisierung in den Familien von Opfern des Stalinismus [Psychic traumatization in the families of victims of Stalinism]. *Psyche, Zeitschrift für Psychoanalyse und ihre Anwendungen, 60*: 587–624.

Spence, D. (1982). *Narrative Truth and Historical Truth: Meaning and Interpretation in Psychoanalysis*. New York: Norton.

Spezzano, C. (1998). The triangle of clinical judgement. *Journal of the American Psychoanalytic Association, 46*: 365–388.

Spitz, R. (1965). *The First Year of Life: A Psychoanalytic Study of Normal and Deviant Development of Object Relations*. New York: International Universities Press.

Steele, B. F. (1994). Psychoanalysis and the maltreatment of children. *Journal of the American Psychoanalytic Association, 42*: 1001–1025.

Stern, D. B. (1997). *Unformulated Experience: From Dissociation to Imagination in Psychoanalysis*. Hillsdale, NJ: Analytic Press.

Stern, D. N. (1985). *The Interpersonal World of the Infant. A View from Psychoanalysis and Developmental Psychology*. New York: Basic Books.

Stern, D. N. (1995). *The Motherhood Constellation: A Unified View of Parent–Infant Psychotherapy*. New York: Basic Books.

Stern, D. N. (2004). *The Present Moment in Psychotherapy and Everyday Life*. New York: Norton.

Stolorow, R., & Atwood, G. (1992). *Contexts of Being: The Intersubjective Foundations of Psychological Life*. Hillsdale, NJ: Analytic Press.

Strenger, C. (1997). Psychoanalysis as art and discipline of the Self: a late modern perspective. *Psychoanalysis and Contemporary Thought, 20*: 69–110.

Strenger, C. (2002). *The Quest for Voice in Contemporary Psychoanalysis*. Madison, CT: International Universities Press.

Strozier, C. (2002). *Apocalypse. On the Psychology of Fundamentalism in America*. Eugene, OR: Wipf and Stock.

Sugarman, A. (Ed.) (1994). *Victims of Abuse. The Emotional Impact of Child and Adult Trauma*. Madison, CT: International Universities Press.

Theunissen, M. (1977). *The Other: Studies in the Social Ontology of Husserl, Heidegger, Sartre, and Buber*. Cambridge, MA: MIT Press, 1984.

Tibi, B. (1993). *Die Verschwörung. Das Trauma arabischer Politik*. Hamburg: Hoffmann & Campe, 1994.

Traub-Werner, D. (1984). Towards a theory of prejudice. *International Review of Psycho-Analysis, 11*: 407–412.

Van der Kolk, B. (1996). Trauma and memory. In: B. Van der Kolk, A. McFarlane, & L. Weisaeth (Eds.), *Traumatic Stress. The Effects of Overwhelming Experience On Mind, Body and Society* (pp. 279–302). New York: Guilford Press.

Van der Kolk, B., McFarlane, A., & Weisaeth, L. (Eds.) (1996). *Traumatic Stress. The Effects of Overwhelming Experience on Mind, Body and Society*. New York: Guilford Press.

Vogt, R. (1995). Rainer Werner Fassbinders "Der Müll, die Stadt und der Tod" – eine deutsche Seelenlandschaft. In: *Psyche, Zeitschrift für Psychoanalyse und ihre Anwendungen, 49*: 309–372.

Vogt, R., & Vogt, B. (1997). Goldhagen und die Deutschen. Psychoanalytische Reflexionen über die Resonanz auf ein Buch und seinen Autor in der deutschen Öffentlichkeit. *Psyche, Zeitschrift für Psychoanalyse und ihre Anwendungen, 51*: 494–569.

Volbert, R. (2004). *Beurteilung von Aussagen über Traumata. Erinnerungen und ihre psychologische Bewertung* [Evaluation of statements about traumata. Memories and their psychological evaluation]. Berne: Huber.

Volkan, V. (1988). *The Need to Have Enemies and Allies. From Clinical Practice to International Relationships*. Northvale, NJ: Jason Aronson.

Volkov, S. (1990). *Jüdisches Leben und Antisemitismus im 19. und 20. Jahrhundert*. Munich: Beck.

von Braun, C. (1994). Zur Bedeutung der Sexualbilder im Antisemitismus. Unpublished manuscript.

von Brentano, M. (1965). Die Endlösung – Ihre Funktion in Theorie und Praxis des Faschismus. In: H. Huss & A. Schröder (Eds.), *Antisemitismus. Zur Pathologie der bürgerlichen Gesellschaft* (pp. 35–76). Frankfurt: Europäische Verlagsanstalt.

Wallerstein, R. (1998). Erikson's concept of ego identity reconsidered. *Journal of the American Psychoanalytical Association,* 46: 229–247.

Wangh, M. (1962). Psychoanalytische Betrachtungen zu Dynamik und Genese des Vorurteils, des Antisemitismus und des Nazismus. *Psyche, Zeitschrift für Psychoanalyse und ihre Anwendungen,* 16: 273–284 (shortened version). *Psyche, Zeitschrift für Psychoanalyse und ihre Anwendungen,* 46, 1992: 1152–1176 (long version).

Wangh, M. (1964). National Socialism and the genocide of the Jews: a psychoanalytic study of a history event. *International Journal of Psychoanalysis,* 45: 386–395.

Warsitz, R.-P. (2004). Der Andere im Ich. Antlitz – Antwort – Verantwortung. *Psyche, Zeitschrift für Psychoanalyse und ihre Anwendungen,* 58: 783–810.

Welzer, H. (2002). *Das kommunikative Gedächtnis. Eine Theorie der Erinnerung* [The communicative memory. A theory of remembrance]. Munich: Beck.

Whitebook, J. (2001). Wechselseitige Anerkennung und die Arbeit des Negativen. *Psyche, Zeitschrift für Psychoanalyse und ihre Anwendungen,* 55: 755–789.

Whitebook, J. (2003). Die Grenzen des 'intersubjective turn'. Eine Erwiderung auf Axel Honneth. *Psyche, Zeitschrift für Psychoanalyse und ihre Anwendungen,* 57: 250–261.

Winnicott, D. (1971). *Playing and Reality.* London: Tavistock.

Wurmser, L. (1983). Plädoyer für die Verwendung von Metaphern in der psychoanalytischen Theoriebildung. *Psyche, Zeitschrift für Psychoanalyse und ihre Anwendungen,* 37: 673–700.

Zima, P. (2000). *Theorie des Subjekts. Subjektivität und Identität zwischen Moderne und Postmoderne.* Tübingen: Francke.